Ten Cultures, Twenty Lives

ten cultures, twenty lives

refugee life stories

daina jurika-owen

AMAYA BOOKS · ABILENE, TEXAS · 2018

Ten Cultures, Twenty Lives: Refugee Life Stories
by Daina Jurika-Owen

Published by
Amaya Books
1290 South Willis Street, Suite 91
Abilene, Texas 79605
www.amayabooks.com

For information about bulk purchases, contact sales@amayabooks.com.

Contact the author at daina@tencultures.com.

Nepali flag drawing and watercolor maps by Arta Suksta. Used by permission.

ISBN: 978-0-9993981-0-4 trade paperback
978-0-9993981-1-1 electronic book

LCCN: 2017956601

First printing

MANUFACTURED IN THE UNITED STATES OF AMERICA

Contents

Author's Note

As international migration soars, our neighbors become more diverse and more difficult to understand. Who are the people two houses down from us, dressed in those strange outfits? And why have they put artificial flowers under the live oak tree in their front yard? Where have they come from and what do they do?

Scholars of various disciplines—anthropology, sociology, philosophy, and folklore, to name a few—have studied personal experience stories and oral histories. But even we "average people" love to hear a good story. Otherwise, why would we ask each other in the evening, "How was your day?" We expect a good story, something we will enjoy hearing. Not only do we take to stories for their factual information, but we also view them as instances of performance, appreciating the storyteller's creative way of reconstructing the events and his or her role in what happened.

This book is a reflection on refugees and a collection of refugee personal experience stories about their life events, past losses and victories, magical survival, and "coming to America."

—Daina Jurika-Owen, October 2017

Preface

THE NUMBER OF REFUGEES and internally displaced people in the world has reached a staggering sixty-five million, but only a fraction of 1 percent of them ever get an opportunity to start a new life in a different country. The majority of refugees stay behind in one of the neighboring or so-called asylum or host countries, where they have fled for safety and live in refugee camps or on their own. At first, the flight seems temporary—"things will calm down soon" and "we'll go home." Refugees put life on hold for a while. But time ticks on, even in refugee camps, just not in the same way. Young people meet and marry, babies are born, children become teenagers, and parents try to make a living and take care of their kids. While asylum countries and refugee camps provide the bare minimum for existence, the disturbing events in home countries usually go on for many years. Civil wars never seem to stop; ethnic conflicts calm down a little, but then flare up again; coups d'état bring dictators to power who govern happily ever after. As the years pass but conditions at home do not get better, refugee hopes for peace and return fade.

For the lucky ones, the option to apply for resettlement to another country comes up. This chance is especially appealing to younger refugees who have grown up in the camp or in the asylum country and do not feel the same emotional attachment to their homeland as do their parents. To them, "the old country" lives on in their parents' stories and memories but is not a real place for which they yearn in the same way as their elders.

Many refugees hope to resettle to the US. "As long as I can remember myself in the camp," said one refugee storyteller, "I always dreamed about living in America and serving in the US military. I even bought a used US Air Force shirt and wore it every day. The happiest day in my life was the day when I found out that our family was approved for resettlement. I felt like I could fly!"

As of the summer of 2017, the Trump administration's indefinite ban on refugees without close family ties has slashed the annual refugee arrival numbers to an inadequate 50,000, and thousands of refugees' hopes for a fresh start in a new country have been shattered. Even in the most generous days of the resettlement program, the number of those lucky ones approved for resettlement was quite small, but now, it has been cut by half.

When all the processing is complete and the waiting time for actual travel is over, the lucky refugees are on their way to new countries and hometowns. Resettlement agency staff in the US pick up where the overseas workers left off, but in the end, everything is in the hands of refugees themselves. Are they going to make good use of this chance of a lifetime?

This book is a collection of personal experience stories from refugees of many cultures and countries presented in the context of my own personal reflections on work with refugees as a staff member of a resettlement agency in Abilene, Texas. My personal memories are interspersed with musings about refugee relations with the agency and with their new hometown of Abilene. Short "resettlement worker's notes" give an insight into the constantly changing life at the agency and contributes the agency staff member's perspective to refugee stories.

Besides inspirational value, refugees' stories offer fascinating insights into their cultures and the history of their countries. These are personal accounts of events that actually happened as they were experienced by the storytellers. Refugee stories and my "country introductions" are not intended to replace history books that usually offer one truth and one dominant interpretation of historic facts. Instead, refugee voices present a multitude of truths and interpretations of the same history from a refugee's own experiential perspective, and their stories may even contradict one another and challenge the official history. Readers will rediscover historic events and cultures through these stories.

Also, this book will reaffirm that refugees are just like all of us, despite cultural differences—people with their pasts, presents, and futures and their unique cultural traditions. They are our coworkers, fellow students, clerks who serve us, or our neighbors we see every day. Their story worlds offer a deeper understanding of humanitarian causes, cultural diversity, and the complex issues faced in a variety of ways.

Each chapter contains a hand-drawn map of the respective country that is to serve as the entry point to each culture and life story, along with one or two refugee photos as representations of each ethnic group. Some of the photos are of the storytellers and will be described in captions as such, but the majority of portraits depict other refugees from the same culture who agreed to be "the faces of their ethnic group" for the purpose of this book.

Acknowledgments

I KNOW THERE MUST be people out there who take dramatic changes in stride and even enjoy them. For me, quitting my job with refugees and starting a book-writing project was quite a challenge. But I had met so many refugees from all over the world whose life stories were so inspiring that they just *had* to be shared with others. Now that the project is completed three years later, I can look up to the eternally blue skies and breathe with relief. It is time to say, "Thank you." I feel a bit like the Oscar winner when called to the stage. A little crumpled piece of notepaper with all the names comes out of the pocket—the list I prepared "just in case."

My biggest thanks go to all my refugee storytellers who shared their personal life stories, volunteered their time, and opened their homes to me. Your stories expanded my understanding of your cultures, lives, and aspirations. You all know who you are—I cannot list all your names because many of you chose to be known by pseudonyms. Likewise, I want to recognize and thank all the people whose portraits grace my book. My gratitude goes to my children and my husband, who have had to read and reread my writings for these last few years. You did it so graciously and patiently—thank you.

Thanks to my editors: to Inta Gale-Carpenter, who swiftly weeded out repetitions and wrong words in my stories like an experienced gardener cleaning up a flower patch, and to Callie Revell and Nikki Busch, who cheerfully read and edited all the manuscript in the minutest details. I could not have done this without you. Both of you acknowledged the uniqueness of the stories and encouraged me to go on.

I am grateful to all my friends, both in the US and Latvia, and to former coworkers for their support. And kudos to the International Rescue Committee, the refugee resettlement agency that hired me thirteen years ago and gave me the chance to discover refugees. My life would have been different without it, and my refugee storybook would not have been written.

PART ONE

Refugees, Case Workers, and Texas

"Discovering" Refugees

M Y FIRST JOB IN the United States was with a refugee resettle-ment agency. Before that, I was not even aware that refugees still existed. I had recently moved to Abilene in West Texas from Latvia, a small country in Eastern Europe that had quietly regained independence from the Soviet Union in 1991. It was the fall of 2003, and I was somewhat new to American culture myself, although I had lived for one year in Bloomington, Indiana as a visiting folk-lore scholar. Now, it was eight years later, and things were quite different: this time, I had moved to the US to live, not just to visit, and I was in West Texas. And Texas is so big and Texans are so independent in spirit that it makes one wonder if Texas ever joined the Union at all.

During my first days in refugee work, I realized how little I knew about the groups that we were about to meet and get resettled. In Latvia, I lived in a society that had only two major cultural groups: Latvians and Russian-speakers. Most of the time, each group led one's own separate life. Here in the US—and in the agency in par-ticular—everything was different and fascinating: the diversity of people from different cultures, a multitude of languages and accents...I felt I was in the right place.

Besides my coworkers, my best educators were the arriving ref-ugees themselves, bringing their cultures and customs right to our agency and to Abilene. Before my job at the agency, I had only a vague idea about countries in Africa and their histories, languages, and cultures. In my mind, they were all one big "Africa." It was not that I hadn't done well in geography in high school, but why would you need to keep in mind any details about a continent from which you had never met anyone and probably never would? Of course, I knew about genocide in Rwanda and famine in Ethiopia from daily papers and TV news, but those sad events seemed so far away and so much out of my control that I had just "tuned them out." I never expected to have daily interactions with genocide survivors from Rwanda or with people who had lived through the famine in Ethiopia I had seen on TV. Refugees were here, and they told me their stories as I was driving them around town in search of a job or we were discussing their career plans in our office.

The first refugees we resettled in our Abilene office were Liberians who had fled the first Liberian Civil War. Then, a few Congolese from Congo-Brazzaville came, after years in exile in Ivory Coast. After them, some refugees from "the Big Congo" arrived. This was in the winter and spring of 2004. When the summer came, it brought a dozen Rwandese, three or four more families of Colombians, and more Congolese. These new people motivated me to explore their countries with different interest. What had happened there? Why did these people have to flee? And where did they go? Why there, and not somewhere else? How was life in these new countries? To my surprise, I soon became quite an expert on refugee cultures. The refugees did not even have to tell their stories; just the fact that they arrived and we worked with them created motivation for me.

Our resettlement office felt like the very center of the American "salad bowl" culture. On some days, we would attend to refugees from a dozen different ethnic groups and would juggle multiple languages. Where else, if not in the United States, could all cultural groups and ethnicities meet, interact, and gradually become "American society" while at the same time changing the actual perception of what it meant to be an "American"? And where else in the world would you have a French-speaking refugee from Congo-Brazzaville who happened to know a little Russian and a resettlement worker from Latvia who spoke English, Latvian, and some Russian meet and communicate in Russian—in the middle of West Texas, no less?[1]

I don't know why, but initially I had thought that "refugees" would be different from everybody else in some special way. Maybe it came from the way we talked about them in the office. Refugees were not all alike—that was lesson number one for me. They came from different countries, cities, and villages, from different walks of life, and they were as different as all other people around me. At first, people in our town also seemed to think that refugees would all be alike, as if the name "refugee" meant that they were mass produced, or the name "refugee" was like a badge to pin up on their lapels. Such a response was quite natural; after all, they did not know what to expect since "refugee" was a new concept to many. I remember how I once did a presentation about the refugee program for local business owners, hoping to get some jobs for refugees. One woman in the audience asked, "Are they good cooks?"

And I said, "You know, they are just like we all are. You may be a good cook, but the person sitting next to you may even not know how to use a can opener. I am sure I could find one or two who are really great with food if you can offer a job for them."

A couple of years later, I learned lesson number two, which was associated with a popular saying in refugee resettlement work: "never assume [things about refugees]." Don't assume that refugees who are fluent in English know all about the American way of life and culture. Don't assume that those refugees who do not speak English are deaf or somehow mentally handicapped.

I had a professional relationship with refugees in quite a few capacities: I helped them find their first jobs in the US, advised them on the best career steps, answered thousands of questions about "how things are done in the US" and "why this way," and helped get them reunited with their families. I spent more than nine years of my life in refugee resettlement work—or in agency jargon, "working in the field"—and that's why refugees and their stories are close to my heart.

CHAPTER 1

Who Are Refugees, After All?

A S I WRITE THIS IN September of 2016, refugees are receiving more press coverage than ever before due to the migrant crisis in the Middle East and Europe. Who are they?[2]

The United Nations High Commissioner for Refugees defines a refugee as "someone who is unable or unwilling to return to their country of origin owing to a well-founded fear of being persecuted for reasons of race, religion, nationality, membership of a particular social group, or political opinion. War and ethnic, tribal, and religious violence are leading causes of refugees fleeing their countries."[3]

This legal definition governs the US refugee resettlement program and related immigration processes. It is most often used in professional circles of refugee resettlement, such as nonprofit organizations and other providers of social services that work with refugees, as the general public is often unaware of this legal definition, and the word "refugee" is widely used to denote any person either "uprooted from home"—the victims of floods from Hurricane Katrina or Harvey were often referred to as "refugees" in various media sources—or somebody who simply "has left their home country." Thus, the definition is also essential when educating the US public about the refugee resettlement program and its recipients. Likewise, it helps counter the opponents of relief work by highlighting the core reasons why people become "refugees" and why they cannot go back home.

In fact, all refugees start out as "asylum seekers" when they cross the border and enter a neighboring country. Most often, the first country refugees enter is not affluent enough to offer much support. The majority of newcomers hope to either go home or be resettled elsewhere. Asylum seekers apply for refugee resettlement if a chance comes up for their ethnic, religious, or political group, but that does not happen very often, and usually, if it does, it's only after long years in exile.

For example, Bhutanese refugees in Nepal were confined to refugee camps for more than a decade, while Sudanese "lost boys" in Kenya refugee camps reached their adulthood by the time their resettlement chances came up. Asylum countries are usually quite hostile to the newcomers, and at best, refugees there are tolerated but not welcomed. Burmese refugees in Thailand and Malaysia used to live "in the shadows" trying not to attract the attention of police and government clerks, and Congolese refugees in Gabon were often harassed by local police. While some countries mandate that all refugees live in camps and leaving the camp is restricted, other countries allow a choice between living privately and staying in the camp.

One way or another, being registered with the UNHCR as asylum seeker allows refugees to stay in a country legally, although without official rights to work. Those employers that do choose to hire refugees without work permits often discriminate against them by paying much lower wages than to anyone else. The majority of storytellers admit that it was essential for their survival to have income from work, although the chances to obtain a job officially were close to zero. Several younger generation Burundian refugees from quite restrictive Tanzania camps remark that their parents, usually fathers, worked outside the camp, but if they got caught, their wages were taken away by the camp security guards. Still, it was essential that at least one family member was employed to provide for children's school fees and for some food to supplement their scarce daily meals.

Several Bhutanese-Nepali storytellers state that one of the hardest things in the refugee camp for them as law-abiding people was the moral dilemma whether to violate the camp rules and go to the nearby town to work, thus being able to provide for the family, or comply with the regulations and stay in the camp, but give up the chances to provide for the family's meals and pay for their children's education. I am mentioning this because we often hear and read about generic "hard conditions in refugee camps," but the moral dilemmas refugees had to face are rarely mentioned.

Refugees number in the millions, although different sources provide quite different statistics. Exact numbers are impossible to cite since people flee from warzones, move, and cross international borders daily. Estimates range from twenty-two and a half million to sixty-five million.[4] The higher number includes internally displaced persons and asylum seekers who may not yet be registered with UNHCR, while the lower number represents those who are officially registered.

Whatever the numbers, only a small fraction of 1 percent of all refugees get an opportunity to resettle to the third country. Generally, UNHCR first reviews the opportunities for refugee groups to repatriate after the war or conflict in their country is over. Unfortunately, many countries remain in limbo for decades, with localized war and ethnic clashes breaking out sporadically, which makes return dangerous. For example, the Democratic Republic of Congo has had on-and-off wars and localized military actions since the mid-1990s, and the fighting has not completely stopped until now, especially in the eastern part of the Congo where the Banyamulenge Tutsis ethnic group used to live.

Recent media reports portray the areas in the eastern part of Congo close to Kivu lake as devastated by constant wars and currently governed by militant or rebel troops that terrorize local villagers. The official army responsible for guarding peace and order has deserted this part of Congo, and the rebels themselves have forgotten what they are fighting for. These conflicts are usually rooted in previous slights and disappointments and lead to retaliation, so it is difficult to predict when peace could come to this part of Congo.[5]

The second common option that is always considered for refugees is to become residents or citizens of the asylum country. Very few countries have accepted their "refugee neighbors" permanently, and the majority is unable or unwilling to do so because of a weak economy and inability to provide shelter and jobs.

The third option is the lifesaver for many: resettlement in a third country, such as the US. Because of the number of refugees and the limited opportunities, the UNHCR and national governments involved in resettlement meet and jointly determine which of the many vulnerable cultural groups have the most pressing need to be resettled.

After overseas preparation work is completed, the US agency that has contracted with the US government to accept refugees and provide them with appropriate services "assures" the Department of State that staff members are ready for refugee reception. The agency accepting refugees is called a VOLAG, which means a "voluntary agency." Most sources quote nine main agencies that do this kind of work in the US.[6]

The International Rescue Committee, the agency where I worked, is one of the VOLAGs. The IRC works in many locations in the US and overseas. As their own website states, "The International Rescue Committee responds to the world's worst humanitarian crises, helping to restore health, safety, education, economic wellbeing, and power to people devastated by conflict and disaster. Founded in 1933 at the call of Albert Einstein, the IRC is at work in over 40 countries and 28 offices across the U.S. helping people to survive, reclaim control of their future, and strengthen their communities."[7]

Usually, VOLAGs receive government funding through grants to provide the newcomers with financial assistance and other services. Services may vary depending on other available grants, donations and resources, but every VOLAG signs a cooperative agreement with the US government to provide initial resettlement services to incoming refugees within the framework of a "resettlement and placement" program, known by the abbreviation R&P. According to this agreement, certain things have to be accomplished on behalf of refugees with their cooperation and within certain deadlines.[8]

In the life of a refugee, at least two agencies play a major role: the one in the country of asylum, which interviews refugees to determine their eligibility for resettlement to the US, and the resettlement agency in the US, which helps refugees after they arrive in their new homeland—America.

A View from the Office

"They Are Coming!"

January 2004

I remember the excitement in our resettlement office when we finally received a fax notice from headquarters in New York that our "first arrivals" were coming. It was the very beginning of 2004, about one month after I had started my new job. The notice meant that we finally had refugees assigned to our Abilene office. They would come to our town to live, and we would work with them to provide all resettlement services.

Since our office was newly opened, that was definitely a big step forward for us. We could now consider us a "real" resettlement office. The arrival date was set for January 15, 2004, and if I remember correctly, we received that notice a couple of weeks in advance. At that time, there was no refugee resettlement database like there is now, so there was no way to look anything up "in the database system" in advance. Our information came to us in the old-fashioned way: by fax from the agency's processing unit in New York. Thus, it was very important not to miss any documents from the fax machine which was also our copier and printer.

The official fax was called an "Arrival Notice," and it gave all relevant information about the person arriving, including name, date of birth, and country of origin. Most importantly, it gave us dates and flight numbers, from departure until arrival time at the Abilene airport. If things changed, if a flight got rescheduled or cancelled or arrival time changed, we would find out about it only from another fax (or an occasional emergency call from New York). We now came to regard that fax machine in the office corner with quite different respect.

Our first Arrival Notice said that we should expect two men from Liberia, traveling from Ivory Coast. They were both married but were coming by themselves, having been separated from their families during the Liberian Civil War.

"Yeah! Finally! They are coming!"

That was the general sentiment among the three of us: the site manager, Jennie; our assistant case manager, Peter; and me, the employment coordinator. We were all tired of just working in the office. My job was to find employers willing to hire newly arrived refugees, and I had already started looking for companies. We did not have a "case manager" yet because there were no refugee cases to manage.

Peter, a Burundian asylee, was hired soon after me, and he brought on board all the African languages (well, maybe not all, but five) and cultures as well as his outgoing, friendly personality. Nobody else in our office could greet people with such a genuine smile and welcoming embrace. Peter and I became good buddies in the office, as he had studied in Belarus (imagine, sent by the Burundian government). He had learned Russian in the process, so we could talk in Russian now and then if we did not have anyone else around, and it created a sense of camaraderie. He had lots of funny stories about how he was the only African in the small town in Belarus where his university was and the reactions people had to his dark skin.

"One little boy, he ran up to me and rubbed my skin with his little fingers and then turned back to his parents, screaming his head off: 'Mama, Pa, come see that man, he must be a drunk or something—his skin has turned all black!'" Peter remembered. "The parents were very embarrassed and tried to call the boy off, but I told them, 'Don't worry, it is okay. Let him touch me.' And I told the boy, 'I am from Africa, and the sun is very strong there, so it tanned me black like this.' I could imagine myself in that little boy's shoes, as little kids from remote villages in Africa often are shocked when they see white people for the first time. They run to touch them, too. It was the same here, just with black color."

The Arrival Notices gave a different urgency to all preparations. Household supplies and food needed to be purchased a day before the arrival date and delivered to their soon-to-be home. Furniture had to be ordered and delivered. Utilities switched on! And a ready-to-eat meal had to be in the apartment waiting for the new people. Peter was rushing to do all this, with planning help from Jennie.

The most challenging task was finding apartment complexes that would accommodate refugees and fit their needs. Refugees would arrive without social security numbers and no jobs, and usually people like that would not be allowed to rent an apartment. Also, many refugees would not speak any English, so it would be harder for apartment managers to talk to them. To make it more complicated, not every apartment complex would be acceptable. The guidelines stated that housing had to be in a safe area, within walking distance of a grocery store and a bus stop, and be reasonably priced.

This task was not easy, and Stevo, the site manager from the IRC Dallas office, came out to help with the apartment search. Both site managers went around for a couple of weeks, talking to several apartment complex managers and owners in town. Some days, they came back upset and quiet, which meant that some meetings did not go well. But sometimes they returned happier, which meant they were more successful and had hope that things would work out. All apartment managers had to talk to their owners to get approval since accommodating refugees would entail not doing things by the book, so it was hard to get an immediate answer. Eventually, with Stevo's winning sales skills paired up with our site manager's quiet smile, they found two apartment managers willing to work with our office to provide housing for refugees. One was on the south side and the other was on the north side, across from the old north side Walmart store.

Finally, we had made all the preparations for their arrival: an apartment was booked for the two men and furniture delivered. They would share the apartment to save money and lower utility costs. There was (and still is) a list of mandatory household and food items for stocking each apartment or house and Peter had done the shopping. I went to help with organizing the apartment. When Peter went to pick up the new arrivals at the airport, Jennie gave him donated warm clothes to take right to the airport, since it was winter and they probably would not be prepared for cold weather. And boy, it was a cold winter that year!

I don't know what exactly I was expecting, but when Bouake and his roommate, Lionel, arrived, I was surprised to see that they did not look any different from other people in the United States. Of course, they were African, but otherwise, you could not tell from their appearance that they were "refugees." They looked a little haggard, but that may have been from the long and tiring flight. Two skinny men in their thirties, they were dressed in plain blue shirts and black pants. They both had their white plastic bags with the blue and white International Organization for Migration (IOM) logo, where all their documents and important papers were stored. They were in the waiting room of our office when I met them next morning coming to work. As I had to do resettlement planning with them a few days later, I introduced myself and we had a little small talk right then and there—although, I was mostly guessing what they were saying in response, as their English was hard to understand.

Peter had already told me that they did not come with much luggage—just a little duffel bag each. That was something to think about. When I moved to the US to live, I had sent several boxes ahead of me and came with three big suitcases. Both of these men came almost empty-handed, with no belongings at all. The IOM gives every refugee a quota of how much they can take with them, but Lionel and Bouake had not even met that. Later, I learned that many refugees prepare for the journey to their new country by giving away their personal belongings, like clothes and shoes, to refugees who stay behind in the camp. The ones who are about to come to the US are the lucky ones who will have a chance to get new things, while those who stay behind need all the help they can get.

Looking back, I think I was a little disappointed to see that our first refugees looked just like everybody else in town. Had I expected African clothing? I don't think so, but I had thought that they would stand apart in some way.

CHAPTER 2

Refugees and Their Stories: Who Participated and Why

T HE IDEA TO WRITE this book grew out of numerous conversations with refugees during my resettlement agency days.
Refugees often shared their stories with me about events that had
happened in their lives, and at first, I did not ask them why they
were doing it. I simply thought they had stories to tell and wanted
to share them with me, maybe to establish a better connection with
me as an agency worker.

With time, I noticed that the refugees had their own agendas
and used the stories as "tools of persuasion." Some wanted to make
sure that I saw the urgency of their requests while others wanted
me to believe that their cases were the most compelling and needed
special attention. I remember one refugee woman who confided her
hopes of finding a long-lost relative and told me her sad story about
a relative who got lost during their family's flight. I had known her
for several years, but she shared this story only when she needed
me to help find the lost relative.

After hearing some of the stories several times, I realized that
they belonged to a "refugee repertoire" they each had created and
recreated on multiple occasions when storytelling had to serve
a specific goal: at the UNHCR interviews, Overseas Processing
Entity (OPE) interviews, or in conversations with IOM employees.
In the US, these stories could be the ones that were shared in college or high school classrooms or with new friends, volunteers, and
coworkers. So, why not with an agency worker like me?

Here, I do not question the veracity of these stories or claim that
they were "fabrications" or "false"—no, far from that. They were as
true as any story could be, since we all remember events in our lives

in our own ways, repeat them from memory, and gradually add or omit things as needed. In these stories, refugees had structured their past events for themselves and for those they took into their confidence. They were persuasive tools successfully used in refugee resettlement interviews. After all, the storytellers were in the United States now, which meant their stories had been persuasive enough to qualify for resettlement.

Refugee stories brought me into this fascinating realm of storytelling I decided to explore in more detail. I gave up my job in the agency and embarked on a new project: a refugee storybook. As resettlement agency staff, we thought that we knew quite well what life in a refugee camp was like and how the resettlement process worked; that's where our training and experience came in. But why didn't we ask refugees themselves about their lives before and after resettlement? We just relied on our agency knowledge, but was this knowledge sufficient?

Now, in the new role of a writer (and not an agency worker anymore), I expected that everyone I contacted would be very excited about a chance to participate. After all, so many already had shared their stories with me quite happily while I was the IRC staff member. To my surprise, I got diverse responses when I called refugees: not everybody wanted to share their stories anymore. But they had done it quite comfortably and voluntarily just a few months ago! I began to realize that refugee storytelling had a pragmatic goal at the agency, while sharing the same story for a book was very different. Also, stories shared at the office would be kept confidential. For the storybook, their stories would become public, and this fact brought on new concerns.

I invited about fifty people, carefully selecting the potential storytellers based on their ethnic group, age and gender, with a goal to equally represent each one of them. I gave preference to those whose life stories could serve as "the most typical" representations of the respective group, thus contributing to the cultural variety presented in the book. About a half of them embraced the invitation, saying it was "a great project" and offered to participate right away. About a dozen others were a little more cautious and said that they would do it "to help me out" because I had "helped them a lot" as an agency worker or we had developed a friendship since we met.

Storytellers had no other incentive for participating since I did not pay them nor offer any other rewards. We held most of the storytelling sessions in my office, which I rented for this specific purpose, although I always offered to visit them in their homes or meet in some other public space. Most of them chose to come to my office as it would provide a quiet, comfortable space to sit and talk. When we met, I usually offered the tellers a choice to be recorded or not, and if they chose not to be recorded, I took extensive notes. Mostly, people were okay with recording, although some did not feel comfortable with it. Also, I explained that they could decide whether to appear with their original names or use a pseudonym. Here, I had about a fifty-fifty split; some said that it was fine to use their names as they were, but others wanted their names changed.

After I wrote down the stories from my notes or transcribed the recording, I invited all participants to review the resulting text for accuracy and to offer feedback. Several asked me to take out some facts that would lead to identifying their family members in their home countries. Also, some stories had to be "shelved" because of concerns about the well-being of friends and relatives still living in the country of origin.

What motivated them to share their stories? First, many enjoyed the thought that their story would be read, not just by those in the community of Abilene, but throughout the US. Refugees from the younger generation (early twenties to midthirties) embraced the idea most willingly, even though they were the busiest, with daily schedules that often involved full-time college studies and part-time or full-time jobs. I believe they found time to share because they were more open about their lives and experiences and were more used to the idea of "going public" with their stories, as I am sure they had done in high school or college. Telling personal experience stories gave them a chance to reflect on their lives, how they wanted to construct their pasts, and what they wanted from their futures. From their point of view, they were in America and "nothing was impossible"; the future was in their own hands. I think of them as the "Facebook generation," actively communicating with daily postings, photos, shares, comments, and all kinds of interactions. Being used to sharing their experiences on social networks may have been part of the reason the young refugees were so willing to share their stories with me for the book.

When younger refugees reviewed the stories I had written down from my notes or transcribed recordings, several of them commented, "Yes, that's me." It seemed they were looking at their story as if it were a "selfie." When asked what made them share their stories, several answered that they did it "to inspire other refugee kids" who were still in high school "to do the right thing," "to go to college," or "to stay away from bad things, like drugs and drinking."

Another group willing to share their stories was in their late thirties to fifties, and the majority of them remembered their lives in their countries of origin quite well. They were considerably more uncertain about their future in the US, and some of them mentioned that "it may be a little late to start a new career" here or expect new success. These storytellers often remarked that they "had to focus on their children", or that they "came to the US so that their children would have better future." Many noted that they had been treated unjustly in their "old countries" and they had lost everything there. These storytellers were willing to share their stories "for the sake of a greater good" so other people would have "a better understanding of the refugee plight in the world." They also wanted the injustice in the old country to be exposed, made public. They seemed equally interested to have their stories affect the "old country," hoping for policy changes there. Their focus was on the suffering and hardship that needed to be made public so others here would understand.

For this more mature group, another reason for participating was to help US readers better understand refugees as their "fellow citizens" and "neighbors." This role was new but especially important since many of the refugee arrivals had lived for decades in asylum countries where citizenship remained a distant dream. They hoped their stories about their lives and aspirations in the new land would enlighten their new American coworkers and neighbors. These were stories told specifically for "the new neighbor" to hear—not so much about refugee past suffering, but about their cultures, dreams, and current life. The stories would contribute to a mutual understanding among the cultural groups right here in the United States, making readers understand that refugees are human and complex personalities like everyone else.

For many of the storytellers, the country of belonging often was more imagined than real. Stories came from Liberians who were either born in Ivory Coast or spent all their young years there, some younger Congolese raised in Kenya, Bhutanese born in Nepal in refugee camps—the list could go on. Their life stories often transcended reality and invoked elements of magic or the supernatural in descriptions of near-death experiences and lucky escapes. Some attributed survival to the hand of God, while others just said, "I don't know how it happened. I guess I was lucky." Magic also pertained to their having been selected for resettlement, since everyone was willing to go, but only a few people were selected (only about half of 1 percent of all refugees are approved for resettlement). In the stories, overseas case workers or interviewers often acted like "magic helpers" in fairy tales: they offered valuable advice, asked that special question, or simply took a personal interest in a refugee's case. In short, they did something more humane, something more than expected, or something dramatic that changed the storyteller's life.

While overseas workers helped in a variety of capacities, some storytellers refer to "special feelings" about the US resettlement agency that helped them initially, claiming that there was a special bond between them and agency staff who became "their mother." One chapter explores this bond further by presenting the thoughts and feelings of refugees and agency workers and includes my own memories and observations.

While each story is unique, it also shares many traits with other refugee stories, such as a happy childhood, a good life before the conflict or war, flight and loss, life in a refugee camp or asylum country, the resettlement process and being approved, coming to the US, and the new life in America. Abilene and its residents are mentioned in almost every story as their new hometown and their "new neighbors" that shape the storytellers' current lives. Some of the stories are told with the "new neighbors" in mind, be it other new ethnic groups or long-term Abilene residents.

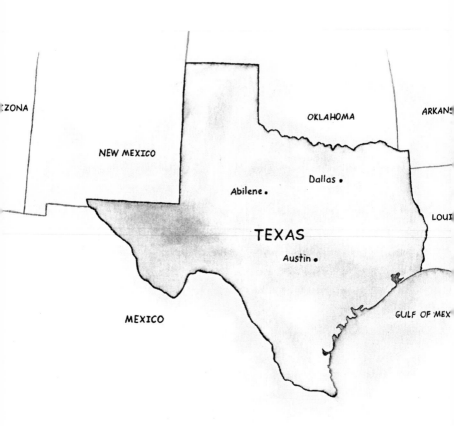

CHAPTER 3

Refugees and Abilene

W HEN THE IRC ABILENE resettlement office opened in the fall of 2003, it did not make the headlines. Moreover, the managers did not want to make it "big news." After the first couple of months, we had an open house for invited newspaper and TV reporters and staff from a few other nonprofit agencies, but even this event seemed to be done more for the sake of our office reporting (*Open house, check! Outreach done? Check!*) than to generate public interest.

I remember the open house was held on a cold and grey winter day when everybody just wanted to stay home and be warm. And yes, those days happen even in West Texas. Maybe that was why the turnout was not too high: a few people from our office building came in, curious about what was going on; a few personal friends and family members stopped by; and one or two nonprofits made an appearance.

I had bought some fruit and crackers for snacks, and as I was putting those on the table, a newspaper reporter arrived a little earlier than expected. Our directors were still in their meeting behind closed doors, so I showed the reporter around the office and told her all I had learned about refugees and our programs in my short time with the agency, hoping that I knew enough to tell the story straight, since I could have easily ended up being quoted word-for-word in the paper. Then, the Dallas director, Linda, came out of her meeting and took over the conversation, and I felt relieved because I really did not know that much about refugees yet. The expected TV crew never made it to our open house, but the local paper had a nice write-up about the IRC effort and refugees the next day.

We had two more guests from the IRC Dallas office: volunteer coordinator Lizzie and employment coordinator Thomas, both of whom had come from Dallas with the director. They told us captivating stories about refugees and how resettlement was done in Dallas, and we listened in disbelief: they resettled about six hundred refugees every year, and their office had been open since 1975. In Abilene, we would start with just one hundred refugees per year. Since there were only three of us here, and we had not resettled a single refugee yet, stories from the "Dallas people" sounded like fairy tales to me. They had more than fifteen employees and more than forty volunteers, and one refugee family had recently received a donated car! And *their* refugees had ethnic communities around them and often family members who had lived in Dallas for many years, and they all helped the newcomers by "taking them places." They even had refugees who had bought cars and who could go to work by car. Those stories were inspiring, and I caught myself wondering when the time would come that our town would have a "refugee community." I was not sure if it would ever happen in Abilene.

Now, it is the middle of 2016, and many of those "fairy tales" have come true: we do have multiple ethnic community groups in Abilene, and almost all new arrivals have some people from their culture in town to help them and to offer friendship. Plenty of refugees drive their own cars and help one another with rides, so new refugees often just have to make a phone call or two to get to places in town. Since 2003, the office has resettled more than 2,500 people from various cultures and countries. This number does not mean they all still live in Abilene, since refugees often like to explore different parts of the US. Some have moved away to be with friends or extended family in other states, while a few others, especially younger people, have chosen to live in bigger cities, such as Dallas or Houston. On the other hand, quite a sizeable group of refugees have moved from their original resettlement locations to live in Abilene and are mostly satisfied with their jobs and the feeling of a small community. That's how life is: refugees come, finish their resettlement program, and then are free to do as they wish—stay in town or move elsewhere. Many refugee storytellers mention—and praise—the freedom the US offers them, as does a young Burundian storyteller who says, "I felt that we were going to start a real life, a life with freedom. We would be like all other people: we could work, go to school, or do whatever our hearts were set on."

Now, looking back to that beginning, I realize that the IRC was intentionally cautious about making "big news." Abilene is part of the rural West Texas area called the Big Country, where people are predominantly conservative in their views. So, it was difficult to guess how "average" Abilene residents would react to the news that strangers from all over the world would soon start to settle in their hometown. It was better to keep a low profile while people got used to the idea. We at the IRC had to work with many other nonprofits, church volunteer groups, and government agencies in town, and nobody wanted the refugees to be looked upon as "more poor people brought to town." Overall, the notion of supporting "refugee resettlement" was and still is more acceptable to liberally minded people in the US than to those with conservative values, so it made sense to proceed slowly. The IRC also chose to proceed carefully to let new refugees feel safe and maintain their privacy, and making their arrival "big news" would have destroyed the peace and safety they sought.

Even with "moving slowly," our refugee program did not run very smoothly in the first couple of years: it was a time of learning and adjustment for both us and the Abilene community. Our site manager Jennie regularly visited directors of different nonprofits and leaders of church groups to explain the resettlement program and to advocate for the refugees. As the agency's rank-and-file staff, we advocated for our newcomers in a different way (and on a different level): as we took refugees for services to various places in town, we interacted daily with clerks and officers of diverse organizations. When we took them to apply for social security cards, we dealt with social security office staff, answered their questions, and explained refugee documents. When we went with refugees to open bank accounts, we had to introduce the refugee program to the bank tellers and their managers and so on. Refugee documents were unknown to town residents, refugees themselves looked different, and most of them could not speak English, so we had to keep explaining who they were and why they were here. Looking for employment for refugees involved convincing HR managers and business owners that "yes, this little paper gives this man or woman the right to work in the US legally."

All those daily interactions gave us a good idea about how local people felt about the refugee program and the newcomers. Some agencies were not too excited, since the new arrivals would increase their workloads. Some church groups were happy about refugees and eager to help them but felt frustrated with our organization because they thought that the IRC was not doing enough to help the new arrivals. We often heard, "What are they going to do when the resettlement program is over? You cannot just leave them like that." We truly could not be everywhere for every single refugee, since then each one would have to have a personal case worker; as we explained, that's where the volunteers and mentors would come in. We were resettling about a hundred people per year, and although it was not a large number, we could not spend time with them 24/7.

One or two charity groups had concerns about refugees in general. Why were refugees coming to Abilene exactly? Would refugees take away jobs from local people? Coming with nothing, would they just add to the number of poor people in Abilene? A few people questioned the refugees' religious beliefs. Those who were Christians fit right in, and one of the larger churches immediately offered to send their buses to pick up refugee families so they could attend their Sunday services.

Hindus and Buddhists only started arriving later and were accepted reasonably well, but Muslims were initially viewed with suspicion. When resettlement of the predominantly Muslim Meskhetian Turkish refugees started in 2005, several volunteers voiced concerns: "Muslims—and so close to the local Air Force base? That is dangerous." Things got better when actual Meskhetian Turkish refugees and volunteers met and got to know each other. The objections were forgotten, and the same volunteers got busy helping them. The same concern came up again when Iraqi refugees were about to arrive, but it died down quickly since the first Iraqis had been granted refugee status because they had helped the US military during the Iraq war. I remember one phone call from a former US military man who asked if he could speed up the arrival of an Iraqi refugee: "This man saved my life, so I will do anything I can to help him now."

One agency that was particularly cautious with the newcomers was the city's school district. I can only imagine how the teachers and administrators must have felt when all of a sudden, the schools had to figure out what to do with dozens of new students who could not speak English at all but had to be enrolled and taught in classrooms. Our case workers only helped refugee children get enrolled and take the initial test, which was offered in either English or Spanish. If the new student was not fluent in either one of those, no subject knowledge could be evaluated. After initial enrollment and orientation, the kids and teachers were on their own, since the IRC case manager's role ended there.

Only when the new kids sometimes missed their school buses would a frantic call from one or another school come through: "We cannot reach the parents of so-and-so," or, "We don't understand what so-and-so's parents are saying. You have to come and take that child home!" And we often did just that, as it was easier to go and take the child home instead of going into a debate with the teacher or administrator. With time, it turned out that tests could be obtained in other languages as well, and in a year or two, schools had set up Welcome Centers for all limited English speakers and had added positions for teacher's aides to help with interpreting.

When the refugee resettlement program started, some of the educators were simply not ready to deal with other cultures, the language barrier, and unusual customs. But teachers would not be teachers if they did not love kids and teaching, so soon, the majority of them were won over by one or another "very special" refugee kid who "was smart and bright and needed help," and after that, the others were embraced more easily. It must have been quite a challenge, since the language barrier was overwhelming and many of the refugee children had not been in school at all or had had long lapses in education.

I remember one fifteen-year-old Burundian girl whose cause united school district staff, volunteers, and our agency. The girl was an orphan and came with her uncle and his family. She had stayed home from school to help with the uncle's children until she came to the US. She had maybe completed a year or two in a primary school. Unfortunately, it is quite common in many African countries for girls to be deprived of education first should a family's resources get scarce. Anyway, here she was: a Burundian teenager who could hardly read or write but had to attend high school because of her age. The noble cause of helping her succeed united many teachers, volunteers, mentors, and the IRC employees, and with all the help, she got a "fast-track" education. I am sure it was not easy for her, but after several years, she managed to catch up with her age group and graduate. Last I heard about her, she was attending college. Such cases brought together the IRC staff, volunteers, and educators. Only by working together could each learn more about what the other was doing and experience the refugee resettlement from each other's perspectives.

Another relationship that initially did not go smoothly was with the local health department, where all refugees had to go for health check-ups and vaccinations. Now, things have been ironed out, but it took several years to find a way to work together. At the start, neither partner was ready for the challenge. It seemed that nobody had adequately notified health department staff about the initiation of a refugee program in Abilene, nor had anyone explained what it would be like to work with limited English speakers. I believe that the refugee health coordinator from the central offices in Austin should have done so, but it had not happened by the time the first refugees started arriving.

From our agency's perspective, the health department had to find their own interpreters and also had to learn how to interact with people from other cultures. Our job was to pick up the new refugees, transport them to the health department, and make sure they understood where they were going. After that, the nurses and doctors had to take over. For the health department staff, the central question was, "How do we communicate with new arrivals who do not speak English?" The nurses and doctors thought that a quick answer was right there—just ask our assistant case worker who was fluent in several African languages, including French. From the IRC's perspective, this was not a good idea, since the assistant case worker had his own duties, and interpreting for the health department was not one of them. The site manager could not simply let the health department "borrow an employee."

She asked our coworkers in Dallas how their health clinic solved such issues. "Tell them to call the language line," they answered. We knew that organizations or individuals could call an AT&T Language Line and order interpreter services via telephone. We even had business cards with the language line number on them. Still, no one was clear about how exactly the language line would work. "What language line? What are you talking about?" health clinic staff wondered.

For a while, the assistant case worker was pulled in both directions. When he took refugees to the health department, the nurses and doctors tried to keep him for interpreting, but when he returned to the office, our manager chided him for not being back on time. We often received phone calls from the health department demanding that "an interpreter be sent immediately." The issue got resolved when the health department received funding for a refugee program and hired a staff member whose duty was to schedule the screenings and provide interpreting. Also, the language line mystery eventually got resolved, and refugee appointment scheduling became a routine matter.

Even with these initial mishaps and conflicts, Abilene has proved to be a caring and receptive community for the refugees. Individuals and organizations have donated and volunteered in various ways. If I can paraphrase the proverb about "needing a village to raise a child," I would say that you need "a receptive community to resettle a refugee."[9] The program could not have succeeded in Abilene without community support, since resettlement staff are overworked and cannot afford too much daily "handholding." The refugee issue is more complex than just a matter of "liberals being for them" and "conservatives being against them." In Abilene, people have done what their hearts have told them to do, each for their own reasons.

Abilene is a very religious town—also quite typical of West Texas. It is dotted with churches of all kinds and sizes, from tiny clapboard structures to huge brick and stone edifices. Half-jokingly, local residents often say that Abilene has more churches per square mile than any other place in the US (over a dozen other towns from various states make the same claim, though). The church as an institution provides a social network and many friendships and business contacts. Although handbooks about American culture often advise against asking American friends about their political views or religious beliefs, this advice would not work in Abilene, where the question, "Which church do you go to?" is often used as an "ice-breaker" with a new friend or neighbor or as an appropriate conversation starter at a dinner party.

I think that Christianity has played a positive role in welcoming refugees, not so much because "people go to church" and therefore adhere to biblical teachings about "showing hospitality to strangers,"[10] but because religious teachings predispose people to be more caring for those less fortunate. Most of the churches have small groups, Bible study circles, and youth teams looking for new service projects. In Abilene, several churches offer English classes and mentoring for new arrivals. As one group leader told me, helping refugees is "like a mission trip, but right here in Abilene. Why go to the other end of the world when you have refugees here you can help with so many things?"

Making personal contact, I believe, is another key to acceptance. Abilene is quite small, so it is easier for residents to take notice of refugees and sometimes just strike up a conversation with them in a grocery store or the post office. It is one thing to read about the refugee crisis in newspapers but quite another to get to know actual people. I have an elderly friend who opposes immigration overall but enjoys donating to refugee causes and has a special attachment to one immigrant family about whom she always speaks with love and care. I remember a youth group from a local church befriended refugee teenagers through performing music together. As they played, sang, jammed, and performed in church services, the abstract notion of "refugees" took on new meaning and turned them into "real people"—"our friends David and Roger and Eric." After that, it was just one more step to becoming good friends, playing soccer together, or stopping by to check on one another.

Helping refugees, however, is not just a church effort; many people do it on their own or as part of the resettlement agency's volunteer and mentoring programs. Almost all refugee storytellers mention a special person, usually a volunteer or an "American friend" who helped them at the beginning, and many cherish those friendships even now, several years later. A Rwandese storyteller fondly remembers "her volunteer" who taught her to drive and helped her sister with schoolwork, while a Bhutanese-Nepali storyteller praises his volunteer, who befriended him and his family when they were new to Abilene and the US. When he was looking for a job, the volunteer introduced him to her son, who offered employment to him and even paid for his driving school.

People choose to work with refugees for a variety of reasons, including faith, a desire to help, curiosity, a way to fill free time, or to connect with international cultures. While working at the IRC, I met a small group of women who had befriended Burundian refugees and were teaching them English. They enjoyed their class and their interactions with the students. When I asked what motivated them, I was expecting to hear that they did it for charity, but instead, they said they "had always enjoyed international things" and "different cultures."

How do refugees like Abilene as their new home town, and what were their first impressions when they arrived? Did "America" turn out like what they had imagined?

All refugee storytellers remember the day they saw the United States and their new hometown, Abilene, for the first time. Usually, these first impressions were made on different days, as almost everyone came into a big city first, such as New York, Chicago, or Miami, on a long international flight, rested overnight in a hotel, and then traveled on the next day. Inevitably, the refugees compared what they saw to the images of "America" they already had in their heads. Their stories affirmed that cities like New York or Chicago matched their expectations of what the US should look like.

When it comes to Abilene, the first impressions were not as favorable, and more than one storyteller mentions that it "did not look like America." Those who had lived in truly remote areas without access to TV and newspapers often had pictured America as a dreamland where "everything was wonderful" or as "a land of plenty," although what it was like exactly was left to each person's imagination. A young Burundian storyteller, who grew up in a remote camp in Tanzania without TV or movie theater admits that she thought "all of America would be under one roof, like a huge building" and that it would be a place "always filled with light and happy people." Storytellers who had lived in cities or towns where TV and movie theaters were readily available imagined "America" to be like the places they had seen on TV series, such as *Walker, Texas Ranger* or in action movies like *Die Hard.* They all thought America would consist of "big cities, lots of traffic, and tall buildings everywhere."

Refugees who had lived in large cities, like Nairobi, Kenya, or Abidjan, Ivory Coast, may have had a somewhat more realistic image of the US but still expected that they would live a "high-class life" in America, with brand-new appliances in their apartments or houses, the latest model cars, and pockets stuffed with money. It did not work out that way. "Everything in my apartment was worn out," states a young Burundian woman from Kenya. "We even found a dead cockroach on the floor. It was not as I had seen in movies. It was not like a fairyland." Only a few had heard about the downside of "American living," such as paying bills and going to work every day.

Landing in Abilene, thus, did not seem too glamorous for many newcomers. Actually, only one Bhutanese-Nepali storyteller notes that when she "saw all the bright lights of Abilene upon landing in the darkness," she was amazed at the beauty and realized that "she had come to America." Other storytellers' memories are different. A Liberian storyteller's first impression of Abilene was "mud and dirt everywhere." A Tanzanian Burundian refugee remembers how surprised she was when she finally landed in a small town "with no trees," and her mother had to reassure her that she had come to the right place. She had expected "America" to be all under one roof and people would push a button to get transported from place to place.

Several storytellers from different cultures admit that after traveling long hours and going through crowded airports in big cities, Abilene had the feeling of being "at the end of the road," a place where there were "no people on the streets and empty sidewalks downtown." Some state that Abilene seemed a disappointing place for starting a new life, all the more so because "we had struggled so much to come here." Moreover, the triple digits of summer heat do not make it more endearing.

Only with time does a different view on small-town living emerge, and new residents find its advantages. Things happen slower in Abilene, and it is easier for the newly arrived to "catch up" with everything. Here, people often stop to offer help if you seem to have lost your way or have car trouble. Many storytellers remark that they have started to appreciate the feel of a small town, although their initial impression of Abilene was not exactly "America." Since refugees are free to move to other locations, those who have stayed have done so of their own free will. When asked why they stayed in Abilene, several acknowledge the peace, safety, and the convenience of everything located nearby. Many value the ties with members of their ethnic groups living next door, and others are content to be in a place that is "safe and quiet." Abilene is often referred to as "a good place to have family" or "to raise your children."

A storyteller from Rwanda acknowledges that the Rwandese community in Abilene is friendly, even though there are topics that cannot be discussed. "In Abilene, we are a mixed community of Tutsis and Hutus. We live in peace here, and we are friendly. I know that the people here are not the ones who killed my family, so I can see them as friends."

A Burundian refugee who had moved to Abilene from Portland, Maine describes his first impressions and thoughts that seem to sum up most of the town's benefits: "When I came to visit a friend, I was surprised to see a small city here where people lived in peace. And I thought, life would be easier here, my wife could drive here, and everything would be closer. I would have more time for family, and I would not be tired from long driving every day. If I need to go to the hospital, it is close, and my work is close. People from Dallas may not like Abilene and may say that 'it looks like countryside and does not have big buildings'...but I tell them, 'Those big buildings you see in Dallas, they do not belong to you.' I need time for my family. Our kids go to school, and we have time to follow up on how they are doing and spend time with them. That's why I moved here. That's why other people are moving to Abilene from big cities."

As I am writing this, refugee resettlement in Abilene is ongoing. The newly arrived now have other people from their ethnic groups around them as soon as they arrive, and town residents are better informed about the refugee program. The unaccustomed cultural diversity has had a positive impact on Abilene, especially as people have become acquainted with refugees personally as their "new neighbors." The refugees themselves, although coming with different expectations about America, now find members of their ethnic group living in Abilene, making it easier to settle in, to feel at home, and to fine-tune their versions of the American dream to the realities they encounter.

PART TWO

Refugee Stories

Nick Kloster

Nick Kloster

Faces of Liberia: Jackie Karnley (top) came to the US in 2004 as a teenager and is now the mother of two beautiful daughters. Amos Hardings (bottom) arrived in 2004. He now has a family and a career in manufacturing.

CHAPTER 4

Liberian Stories

R EFUGEES FROM LIBERIA WERE the first to arrive in early 2004. Most of them were displaced by the First Civil War that broke out in Liberia in 1989. It was soon followed by a second conflict, which prevented Liberian refugees from returning to their homeland. Before resettling in the US, the refugees had lived in the neighboring countries of Ivory Coast or Guinea for about ten or fifteen years. Thus, the younger generation really did not remember their old homeland, but knew it only from the images created by their parents in stories and reminiscences.

The Liberian Civil Wars will be remembered for their widespread use of child soldiers, who became both victims and perpetrators. Sandy, one of the storytellers, briefly mentions "child soldiers," saying that she "has heard from her mother about them and all the terrible things they were forced to do." The recent years of peace that brought relief to the devastated country were interrupted by another disaster – the Ebola epidemic, which has since subsided but whose outbreak not only brought about human losses and suffering but also created major set-backs to the economy of Liberia.

The country is stable now and the Liberian storytellers agree that the "Lady President is doing a good job" with uniting the numerous tribes living side by side, promoting economic development, and handling the Ebola crisis. Still, every narrator mentions current food shortages and the high unemployment, both intensified by Ebola. When I ask Sandy how her sister, who lives in Liberia, was doing after the epidemic, she says, "It is still nothing like it used to be. We just send her money as much as we can."

Sandy G: "We Really Get Busy Here"

Sandy G is a young woman in her late twenties who came to the US as a Liberian refugee in 2004. When Sandy and her family arrived, we at the IRC helped them get settled, find their first jobs, and, as Sandy says, "learn the system." "You taught us what to do, for example, when we wanted to change jobs, or when we wanted to go to college," she said. "How things have to be done in this country."

We both recall the days when her family had just arrived. Sandy remembers the exact date of arrival as a "nice birthday present for her brother" because the family came to Abilene on his birthday. I remember that day, too, but for different reasons: one was that we at the IRC were extremely busy on that day, as we had to make everything ready for the arrival of more than ten refugees—all on the same day. As our office was newly opened, we didn't have much experience; we had only resettled four or five refugees so far. That day also turned out to be one of those rare "snow days" in Abilene, when a layer of snow covered everything, making driving slow and scary. I had just learned how to drive and was quite relieved that I didn't need to help with airport pickup that day.

Sandy arrived with her mother, her siblings, one cousin, and a little niece. There was no mention of Sandy's father. I did not dare to ask too many questions about the absent father, since I was not sure what answer I would get. What if their father was killed in the war or missing? I did not want to bring up sad memories for them, but I wondered about "the man in the family." So, it was quite a surprise when Sandy's dad came to visit them one day a couple of months later. He had been living in one of the big cities in the US for quite a few years already. The family was happy to reunite with him, although Sandy's mom told me at the time that she wasn't sure if she "would take her husband back" because "he was gone for too long." But after another month passed, Sandy's dad moved to Abilene to be with the family.

I remember how we worked with Sandy to get her through the College of Cosmetology. She had always wanted to become a hairdresser, and even when she arrived, she was excellent with African-style hair braiding. But to officially have a job as a hair stylist, she had to get a Texas license. The school in Abilene accepted Sandy's high school diploma from Ivory Coast, and her English was already very good. After all, she was from an English-speaking country and had learned English in school in Ivory Coast, too. So, she needed just eleven months to graduate and be qualified for a well-paid job in one of the many hair salons in Abilene. Her school expenses were covered by financial aid; Sandy only needed pocket money.

Sandy's family was not very excited about her going to school, since they would have to help her pay her portion of the rent and utilities. And for new arrivals in a new country, eleven months seemed like forever. I talked to Sandy's mom, sister, and brother several times trying to convince them that Sandy's training would be a good thing for them in the long run. Why not support Sandy now so she could reciprocate and help them pay their bills later? But no, all my talking fell on deaf ears.

At the time, I was quite upset since I had spent a lot of time enrolling Sandy, helping her get financial aid, and making other arrangements. I did not want to give up so easily. I understand the family better now; the fear of not being able to pay the bills surely weighs heavy on every arrival's mind. Also, Sandy's other siblings may have felt slighted, since they had to be the ones to work while Sandy was given a chance to get an education. After a week of classes, Sandy told me, "My family wants me to quit the school and get a job."

I pleaded, "No, Sandy, please don't. We have invested so much in your cosmetology school already!"

Sandy said, "I don't even have any money for the bus fare or to buy school supplies because all my refugee assistance money goes for rent and utilities."

"How about a part-time job, after the class?"

"Yes, that would work. Otherwise, I have to ask my family for money, and they say, 'No.'"

We spent that afternoon applying for part-time positions and landed an interview for Sandy at the local Alzheimer's Care Center, but even there, the manager picked somebody else for the job. Time was ticking away, and Sandy was about to quit the school if I did not help her find a job. I think I was more desperate than she was since I wanted her to succeed and graduate from the school.

That same day, I went home after work but kept thinking about Sandy. What to do? I sat down to dinner with my husband, and he was telling me how tired he was doing all his own copying work in his office and how he *really needed to hire somebody to help with all those oil logs. My husband had a small oil company in town, and the business was doing quite well.*

I told him, "I think I might have found you an office helper. You just need to train her how to use the copying machine!"

He agreed, and Sandy's situation was resolved. Soon, she was making her own money. She worked in my husband's office in the evenings after her classes were over, and the evening CityLink bus took her home. Sandy is still a hairstylist, so I guess all the scheming did some good, after all.

When I met with Sandy more than ten years after she came to live in the US, I asked about her family, and she said that they all are doing fine. Sandy mentioned that as a family, they have been talking about buying a house in Liberia, since her parents may retire to Liberia when they get "really old." Sandy is busy as a hairdresser these days and plans to open her own hair place sometime soon. Sandy starts her story by describing a recent trip she took to Liberia. As Sandy did not want her story to be recorded, I took detailed notes.

YOU HAVE TO BE very careful when you go back to your old country and how you visit. Why? People may envy you because you have a better life now; you live in America. Say, you are an American now, live in a nice apartment or house in the US, have a fancy car, and go to school, but they have to live in Liberia where the living standard is very low. They can put something in your drink or food that will make you sick, so you would feel bad. Or, you can even die from it. It can be pieces of dried crocodile gut that contain poison, and it will make you sick. Or, they can put nail clippings in your food or drink. So, when going back, you have to be very careful who you visit and make sure that your old "friends" are really still your friends. And when you go out to a restaurant, never leave your food or drink unattended. But if you have to, like if you are in a restaurant and need to use the bathroom, do not touch your food or drink after—get a new one. That is true. Why would people do it? You know, they live in misery, and they would be happy to see someone bragging about life in America get sick. Then, those people could point to you and say, "Hey, now you are not doing that great anymore, huh? Now you see what it means to suffer, too."

But let me tell you about what happened to me and my family. I was just a little girl when the war broke out in Liberia. It was in 1989, I think, and we left Liberia at the end of 1990 when I was about four years old. At that time, fighting was everywhere, and it was too dangerous to stay. It was a lot of shooting, and people got scattered, ran and fled, and lost each other. Then one day, my dad was gone from home; he had left, and we did not know where he was. It all happened very fast. All I knew was that my dad was not with us anymore. We lived like that for a while, and it was hard. Then, all of a sudden, he sent a message for us through other people. The next thing I knew, my mom was saying, "We are going to Ivory Coast."

I remember my mom used to tell us, "I don't know where Dad is, but we'll find him in Ivory Coast." My mom was all by herself with us children in Liberia, and our dad was not there. So, we left for Ivory Coast. At that time, children could be kidnapped in Liberia, taken to the army or gangs that made them fight. I am telling it now, but I know it only from my mom's stories, as I was only four years old when we left.

My mom knows more; she remembers all the terrible things that were going on in Liberia at that time: child soldiers, little kids taken to serve in the military and given guns and drugs and then made to shoot their families or neighbors. Liberia has sixteen tribes, and the war was against the old president but, at the same time, also among the tribes. The Gio tribe was in power, the Krahn was in power before, and then there was the Mano tribe that wanted the power. And Mandingos and Krahn were attacked.

I even do not know what was happening exactly. I was little back then. You would have to ask my mom and dad—they would tell you more. Thank God, it is over now, and Liberia is doing alright. The woman president is doing a good job.

When we reached Ivory Coast, our dad was there. But it was not easy to get there. We settled in one of the neighborhoods of Abidjan, the capital city of Ivory Coast. Our neighborhood was called Riviera Trois. We did not live in a refugee camp or anything like that. We lived in a housing "compound," and it had a big fence around it. The entrance gate had a watchman there at all times, so we felt safe inside. And initially, life was good in Ivory Coast—until the unrests and war started.

With a few exceptions, people were friendly there. I remember one woman who was always shouting at me and other refugee kids just because we were from a different country and not born in Ivory Coast. And we could not do anything—could not shout back or say anything back—as we were refugees, and we did not want to make matters worse.

But otherwise, life was good, and we stayed in Ivory Coast for more than ten years. I practically grew up there because when I came, I was about four, and when we left, I was seventeen. I attended a small school called Rainbow Academy, and it was just for Liberian refugee children in Ivory Coast. The school was located in a little village called Akoudo. We lived in Riviera Trois, and I could walk to school in about twenty minutes. I could walk to the Air Force base and go through the base, or I could go the other way around. And I could also take a "walawala," which was like a taxi cab but without a meter. The driver used to charge one dollar for a ride, and then I could get to school in just five minutes. So, sometimes I walked, and some other times, I went by walawala.

We had an American school right across from our compound entrance, on the other side of the street. It was all in Riviera Trois, including the Air Force base. It was all close together, like we are in Abilene, and then there are little towns around Abilene, like Clyde and Sweetwater. So, they were separate villages, but all within Riviera Trois, and the big area was called Riviera Cocody. Like Dallas—you call it all "Dallas," but what you have is a lot of suburbs: Plano, Arlington, Irving.

After school, I helped my mom sell vegetables and other things on the street side so we could make a living. The school was free, so we did not have to worry about making money for school.

Things got a lot worse when the unrest and war started in Ivory Coast in 2002 and 2003. Things got worse little by little, and our neighbors were packing up and leaving, one by one. Refugees were fleeing across the border again, this time to Ghana. And about this time, my dad left again, and we did not know where he went. Our mother may have known more, but she did not tell us.

And you know, my dad, he was always lucky, and he was one of those people who did not want to stay long in one place. But when he planned something, he did not tell anyone, or otherwise, his plans would not work out. And I don't know if it was for better or worse, but he was never around when the war came. That's why I used to tell him that he was always lucky.

So, I was left in Ivory Coast with my mom, my sisters, my brother, and my cousin. My older sister was not there. We did not know where she was. We lost her while still in Liberia. There was Libby, and my brother John, and my cousin Aimee, and Josie, and myself. And we asked questions about Dad to our mom, but she just said, "Oh, I don't know."

So, we did not know if Dad had abandoned us or something had happened to him. But I guess it was all for the best, as he later turned out to be in America.

By then, a curfew hour was in effect. Initially, it was for 8:00 p.m., but then it was moved up to 6:00 p.m. So, there was practically no time after school to help my mom sell produce anymore. And if you went out, you would be stopped and questioned, and the question would come: "Why are you here when you are not from Ivory Coast?"

It was scary. Food was hard to find, and when you found it, it was very expensive. It was really difficult to make ends meet then, as there was almost no time to sell and make any money. People around us were all leaving, but my mom refused to go. She said that she was tired of running, that she had been on the run for too many years. All our neighbors urged us to go, but my mom said, "No."

There was lots of fighting and shots fired, and people stayed inside their houses out of fear of being shot or captured. But my mom said that God would help us, and if God wanted us dead, then we would be killed. So, she left our family future in God's hands. Every day, she used to say, "Everything will be ok, will be ok," and, "Where there is life, there is hope."

So, we stayed in Ivory Coast. Then, the Ghana border was closed, as Ghana did not want to accept more refugees, and the ones that had made it into Ghana already were accommodated in big tents, like you see in photos or movies.

Going to school had become scary, too, as shots could be fired at any time on the street or some kind of violence could happen. School hours were cut short as everything was closed due to the curfew. Local people often rebuked us for "being from Liberia" and "bringing war to their country." But shooting and violence were the worst. We had a high fence around our compound, and I remember how we used to climb up the big tree in our backyard to see what was going on outside when we heard grenades or shooting.

Then, something terrible happened to me on my way to school. Let me tell you about that day. I took a walawala to school that morning. From Riviera Trois, the fastest way to school was by walawala. So, the walawala came, and other people were in it already, and we all paid one dollar to the driver for the ride. But the walawala had to go through a military checkpoint, where all cars had to stop and people had to show their documents. They had guards there, and they used to make people pay money to let them pass. So, we stopped right at the checkpoint, and the guard told us, "Get out of the car, everybody, and give me your ID cards." And I gave my student ID card; I was the only student in the car. And I was the only foreigner in the car—the only Liberian in the car. We all got out of the walawala, and the guard took all the IDs. He looked at every single person and gave back all the IDs—except mine. He told all the passengers to get back in the walawala, but to me, he said, "Wait."

And the guard was there—a big man in his thirties—and I was in front of him. He had a machine gun on his shoulder, so I could not scream or run. If I did, he would have shot me, and I would be dead. He could always say later that I was "a rebel kid" or I was "resisting arrest," whatever. He told me to stay and wait. The walawala went on with everybody else inside, and I was alone with the guard at the checkpoint. The guard asked me, "Why are you bringing war to our country?"

I said, "No, I am not bringing war to your country. I am just a teenager, a student. I go to school here. I practically grew up here."

"Are you from Liberia?"

"Yes, but I don't know Liberia. I have been here for a long time, and I have not done anything bad."

Then he said, "Well, I could kill you right now, and nothing will come from out of it."

"Oh, God, no!"

A hot flash went over me when I heard him say that, and I froze. He told me all that stuff, and I could not argue; you never ever argue with a man in power. And this guy was from the military. At that checkpoint, the guards checked people's IDs, but most of all, they wanted people to give them some money. Everybody used to give the guards a dollar or two, and they would let you go. But they also checked for suspicious activities, like somebody carrying drugs or something like that.

At first, he told me to wait, and he kept my ID. He said he needed to think about what to do with me. So, I was standing there and praying to God, "Oh, my God, let me get out of here, please."

It was so scary; the guard could make up his mind to shoot me or not. After some fifteen or twenty minutes, he gave back my ID and told me, "Okay, you can go now!"

I was still frozen with fear, but I asked him, "Are you sure?"

He barked at me, "Go before I change my mind!"

I started walking away, but I kept looking back, as I was afraid that he would shoot me in the back. But he did not; he just let me go. And then I got to a place where the road curved, and I started walking faster. He could still see me, so I did not run as I thought he may find it suspicious. I just walked easily—walked on to school, although I was late for my classes. And after school, I did not go home through the checkpoint. I went back through the Air Force base. That afternoon, I told my mom about what happened at the checkpoint, and it scared her. She told me, "You are not going back to school anymore."

But I said, "No, this is my last year at school. I want to finish school."

It was in 2002, and I graduated in 2003. It was the last year before we came to the US, and it was a really bad time in Ivory Coast. People were captured or shot on the streets, the curfew was pushed up to earlier hours, and a lot of people were leaving the country. But I was still able to graduate from Rainbow Academy. There were just six students left, as all the other Liberians had already fled from Ivory Coast. Soon after I graduated, the school closed down because no refugee children were left in Ivory Coast.

We were really lucky to get in the resettlement program and come to the US. I don't know if we would have found out about the program by ourselves, but we had a family friend whose name was Abraham. We just called him AB. My mom was very nice to our neighbors, and she always fed everybody who was hungry. AB came one day to tell us about a program that helped people go live in the United States. He worked for the office that signed people up for it and asked us if we would be interested.

At first, we were not sure what to do, as we were afraid that it could be some kind of trick to get us out of Ivory Coast, but AB convinced us that it was for real and that we had to fill out all the forms if we wanted to be considered. AB helped us with that, and it was just one form for my mom and us, as we were her children. We all were on her form. Then, AB took the form to the agency or wherever he had to take it, and after a few days, he came back with good news. My mom had just prepared dinner, and when AB came, he said, "Good news, but give me some food first." Then, he said that our family was on the list for resettlement, and we went to see it with our own eyes. And yes, AB was right: our names were on the list, and now we had to wait until we were called for an interview.

By the time the interview invitation came, that office had moved to a bigger location; it was now in the middle of a football field with a fence around it. The resettlement agency's tent was in the middle of that field, but outside that fence, lots of people were pushing and shoving, trying to get in. When the interview day came, my mom was asked questions, and then we were all sent for medical tests. The day before leaving, the agency workers told us to dispose of all our things and to keep just what we would carry with us on the plane. Then, they took us to a different place to stay overnight before the flight. They put us in a hotel and gave us medications that made all of us sick. On the day of travel, we were still sick. When the plane was taking off, we all were sitting in our seats thinking, "What if this flight is taking us back to Liberia, instead of America?"

Travel by plane seemed scary to me, as I was afraid of flying. We went from Abidjan to Brussels, then on to Chicago, then Dallas, and finally to Abilene. I was both happy and sad: sad to leave behind the place I had called home for more than ten years, my friends, and the life I was used to. But I was happy to be going to live in America. Now, I am so grateful to God that he made it possible. And I learned a lesson from this: always keep your faith up and never give up. It felt good when we found our dad and then, later, when my missing sister turned out to be alive and well. You know, I am from Liberia, but because of the war, I am here in America. Many people ask, "How did you leave the war?"

Maybe it was God or fate or whatever, but hey, that's what happened to us. In Liberia, it was war. We went to Ivory Coast, and we stayed there for thirteen—almost fourteen—years, and then the war started again. So, we could not stay in Ivory Coast and had to find some way to leave. And it so happened that the resettlement program came up. We were not thinking about getting in that resettlement program. God made a way for us. It took us just three months since the program started, and we were here in America.

Some people could still be back in Ghana or Ivory Coast. And for some, it took ten years to come to America on the same program. So, everybody is not the same. God works in mysterious ways. You know, you can leave from one place and go live in a different place, and people ask, "How did you do that?" But you don't know what to say, you just don't know. And as I said, that's life. If it is not "your time," you cannot do anything. When I was in Ivory Coast, I never thought I would be in America. But the war came, and "one, two, three," we were here.

And here we are.

August 8, 2014

Issa: "I Have Plans for My Future"

Issa is a twenty-year-old Liberian woman who came to Abilene in the spring of 2005 with her mother and younger sister. She was only twelve at the time. As Issa's mother was from Liberia, the family were considered Liberian, although Issa and her sister were born in Ivory Coast and had never been to Liberia. The family had lived in Ivory Coast until the war broke out there, and then they fled across the border to Guinea. Issa and her family lived in Laine refugee camp in Guinea for a few years before Issa's family got approved for resettlement in the US. At first, they lived in Abilene, but after five years, the family moved to Dallas, where Issa graduated from high school and started nursing school.

Now, when we talk on the phone, Issa tells me that she has recently given birth to a baby boy, Thomas, and has taken time off from school to be at home with him. She says that she plans to go back to school when Thomas gets a little bigger.

Issa's story adds a new perspective on a refugee's life, one that contradicts all the assumptions (remember, "never assume"): Issa states that she enjoyed her life in the refugee camp in Guinea. The conventional wisdom is that all refugees hate camp life because the conditions are usually terrible, the food is scarce, and opportunities are very limited. And in many cases, that is true, but Issa's story offers a different view, showing that camp life can be more than a sum total of poor education, limited freedom, and harsh living conditions that include beds made out of loose soil covered with straw, fetching water with a bucket from a community water pump, and surviving on substandard food. A refugee camp is also a network of friends, familiar surroundings, enjoyable and familiar cultural activities, school activities, helping moms cook and trade, and attending Friday evening dance and song parties. People feel connected to one another in the camp, as they usually come from the same cultures and have been through the same hardships. They make friends and develop daily routines. It is their lives. Refugee storytellers often remark that they were happy to come to the US but were also sad to leave their friends behind.

Issa's story is written from notes.

MY NAME IS ISSA, and I was born in Ivory Coast. I had friends and family there. I always knew that I was a Liberian, though.

And then the war came to Ivory Coast, and we could not stay there anymore. I was about eight years old at that time; I think it was in 2000. One night, our mom got tipped off that the war may be starting, so we knew. It was because our mom was always nice to other people when we lived there, always feeding the hungry, giving food to other people. Late one evening, some rebel soldiers came to our house and told my mom that we should get out as soon as possible. They said, "Get out right now—tonight, because the war will start in the morning."

When we heard that, we were very scared. My mom told us that we were leaving right away, and we did not take much with us. We left in a few minutes, in the darkness of the night. We knew that if the war broke out, we would be killed. So, we walked all night and day, and we did not stop for rest. No rest, no breaks for food or drink. We just kept walking. Then, a group of rebel soldiers saw us. They stopped us and started questioning my mom, asking who we were and where we were going. When they heard we were Liberians, they wanted to shoot us right there, but my mom was pleading with them, saying that she was "just a mom with two little children," and thank goodness, they let us go. She begged them for something to eat, and the rebels gave her some food. She gave it to me and my sister, but I could not eat; I just took some water. I did not feel hungry the whole time we were walking.

The rebels had shot three soldiers right in the place where they had stopped us. The soldiers were lying on the ground, and we had to pass by their dead bodies. My mom told us girls to close our eyes while we were walking by, and I did, but I could still see them. It was a terrible sight, and I had nightmares long after that. They were just there lying dead on the ground.

Later that day, we reached the border of Guinea. A crowd of people were at the border crossing point already, wanting to get into Guinea, as Guinea was safe. They were all pleading for the border guards to let them across. The border between the two countries was along a big river. On one side, it was Ivory Coast, and on the other side, it was Guinea. I think a lot of people had already entered Guinea, and the guards did not want to let more people in; it was just too many.

All the people were standing in a long line, and there was a crowd of people around that line. The border guards would wrestle the people back, not letting them cross the border into Guinea. I remember one man was up in front of the line, pleading for them to let him in, saying that he was in danger. But the border guards told him to go back to the end of the line. The man did not go, and then the border guards took him behind the house and shot him. We heard those shots, and then we saw that the man was dead.

My mother went to talk to the border guards and plead our case. She also begged for some food, because we did not have any, and we were very hungry. We stayed there waiting for about half a day or longer. My mom went to the river to wash up and wash our clothes, and the rebels in Ivory Coast threw a bomb in the river, close to where she was washing. A big splash of sand, rocks, and water hit my mom right in the head. She was injured and bleeding, but the situation at the border was so bad that she did not pay much attention to her injuries, just cleaned up the blood and wrapped a strip of cloth around her head wound.

After long hours of waiting, the guards finally let us cross the border. I think they let us in because my mom still had a house in Guinea. Before the war started in Liberia, my mom was a businesswoman and often traveled from Liberia to Guinea and back, as she used to own a restaurant and a house in Guinea. The house was still there, and my mom was the owner, so we had a place to stay. My mom told that to the border guards, and we were allowed in. It was already evening when we finally entered Guinea, and we went to our mom's house, which was not far from the border. There was one man, a friend of my mom's, who was looking after the house while she was away. That man met us at the border and took us to the house. It was in a town called Guinea Border. There was a family living in the house as tenants, renting from us or something like that. The friend who was taking care of the house offered to tell the tenants that they should leave the house, but my mom said, "No, no, let them stay. We will just stay in the living room for a few days. Let them keep their rooms and beds."

That's how nice my mom was to other people. So, we slept on the floor in the living room, and my mom let the family keep the house. We had blankets and food; my mom's friend brought all that to us.

The next day was the day of Ramadan, and the people in town were celebrating. You know, many people in Guinea are Muslim, and Ramadan was a big day there.

My mom went to a doctor, who treated her head injuries, but we stayed at home. Then, she went to the market and bought new dresses for us—nice dresses—and brought back some food for us. I think that the UN people who were at the border had given her some money to live on. Then, our mom's friend took us to a restaurant to eat breakfast, and it was a very good breakfast with plenty of food, like eggs, sausages, bread, and drinks. But I could not eat anything; I just had a little drink because I could not get those dead soldiers we saw out of my mind. I could remember them too well—they were in front of my eyes, and I could not eat. Then, our mom told us that we were all going to the river, as it was a nice and warm day with lots of sunshine. We were hoping to go swimming in the river. It was the same river that made up the border between Ivory Coast and Guinea. We all went there, and my sister and I started playing in the water. But all of a sudden, our mom shouted, "Girls, come out of the water, quick!"

We rushed out of the water and got up on the riverbank to see what was going on. We were a little higher up on the coast, so we could see really well why our mom had called us to come out: dozens of dead soldiers were floating down the river. It was so terrifying! All those dead bodies were noiselessly floating in the water, going with the river stream. Even such little kids as we were, we did not plead with our mom to let us back in the water; we knew that we did not want to go back in.

I heard adults talking about the war in Ivory Coast getting worse. They sounded concerned that the war could come over to Guinea, which was just across the river, but at the moment, everything was still peaceful. We could just see more soldiers than usual at the border; that was all.

Our mom did not want us to stay long in the house, as it was in the border zone, and she was afraid that the war could come across the river to Guinea. Since we were not from Guinea but were

Liberians, we could easily get killed there if some unrest broke out. So, after about a week, we set out on the road again. We went to live in a refugee camp in Guinea; it was called Laine refugee camp. It was a long way to travel, but when we reached the place, I saw many people already living in the camp. We were shown to a shelter, and somebody took us to a place where we could get food. At the beginning, we lived in a large tent with many other people. We had blankets but had to sleep on the ground; there were no beds or any other furniture. We could cook on an open fire outside the tent.

Not very long after that, a team of missionaries built a house for us. They helped many families with children, and our family was just the three of us—we did not have our dad—so I think that's why they gave us that house so soon. Living in the tent was hard, as we had to be with many other people all together in one large tent and it got cold in the tent at nights. But the house was really very nice. We had a living room and a bedroom, and then we had the kitchen and even a backyard, where my mom planted vegetables. And we had a fence around the house. We made beds from dirt and covered them with cloth and also made pillows that way. And we had blankets—real blankets—so we were living comfortably. It rained a lot in Guinea, but we had a good house to stay out of the rain.

My mom was running a restaurant from the back of the house. She would cook different foods, and people would either come to eat the food there or buy and take the food to their houses or tents— wherever they lived. My mom started out with frying doughnuts and selling them in Laine village, which was about half an hour's walking distance away. Every Monday, she would go there with doughnuts and sell to people in the flea market. Laine village was quite a big place—I call it a "village," but it was a big village. And then, she would buy snacks there with the money she made—like chocolate bars and other candy, chewing gum, snacks, and fruit— and bring it all back to the camp to sell to people in the camp. When she had raised some money, she started cooking bigger meals, and camp people would come to eat at our place. My mom was a very good cook. She was even hired as a cook for the camp kitchen, she was so good at it, and they paid her money for the job. People knew my mom in the camp as an excellent cook. And when she started cooking for the camp, I had to do cooking for our restaurant after school to keep the business going.

I enjoyed my life in the camp. We had a school there, and I went to school every morning. Here in the US, you wait outside the classroom until the teacher gets there, but in Guinea, we had to be in the classroom before the teacher came in. And then, we had to get up from our seats to greet the teacher when she walked in, to say "hi" to the teacher. If you were late for the class, the teacher would spank you for it, so you would be thinking about it when you came late next time. You didn't want to be late. I was late a few times but tried to be on time to not get the spanking. You could also get spanked when you were not doing well in class.

We used to go to school in the morning, come home for a lunch break, and then go back till late afternoon, till about three or four o'clock. We could buy food on campus or go home to have our lunch, and I usually ate food on campus, as I did not want to be late after the break. After lunch, everybody just ran back to the classroom. School started between seven and eight in the morning, lunch was at noon for about one hour, and by about three or four in the afternoon, school was over. And then we went home and did our homework. I usually had a lot of homework, and I used to do a lot of activities in school and also in the camp. I was really involved: I was in cheerleading and drama in the camp, and I was in cheerleading in school, too. I was in drama classes, and we even learned computers.

We had lots of activities in the camp. On Saturdays and Fridays, we used to have refugee parties. On those days, you could skip a class or two at school; it was okay on that day. I had a lot of friends in the camp. Now, I really miss all those activities we had in the camp, and I miss my friends. You know, since we came here, I have not been in touch with any of them. I would have liked to be in touch, but I cannot do it from here; I just don't have a way to communicate with them. I have heard though through other Liberians that many of the same people are still in the camp. Not many have left.

Our family was one of the few that got a chance to come to America. You may ask me how we got to be the lucky ones. The thing is that our family was supposed to come to America a long time ago, before my father died. Yes, it was really an awfully long time ago. I think I mentioned to you one white man named Kevin who helped us get our house in the camp. He worked in Laine camp, but before he came to work there, he was in Ivory Coast at the same time we were there. I think he worked with a refugee agency in Ivory Coast before the war started. During the war, it was too dangerous to stay there, and he came to Guinea.

As I said, we were supposed to go to America, but everything stopped because my father died. I don't know exactly how it happened, but my mom told me that my dad died in the war. So now, in Laine camp, we met the same man, Kevin, who was the one to bring refugees to America from Ivory Coast.

Kevin recognized my mom in the camp and asked her, "Mary, why are you still here? I thought you were supposed to be in America?"

And my mom answered, "Yes, but my husband died, and everything stopped."

But Kevin had all the records of our family case. He pulled those papers out, looked at them, and said, "You were supposed to be in America a long time ago."

I don't know what had happened, but we were still in the camp and not in America. So, Kevin told my mom to go for another interview, and she went, and they talked to her and asked her questions. The old case had all our family in it, but now, it was just my mom with the two of us, as my older siblings were not in our camp, and my dad was not living anymore. It seemed like somebody had tried to ruin my mom's case, her papers. When my mom was interviewed, some guy in the camp just came out of nowhere and claimed that he was my mom's husband. But my mom said, "I don't even know your name. How can you say that you are my husband?"

I think it was because people wanted to go to America really bad. Yeah. In fact, I remember two people who tried to ruin my mom's papers. This man was one of them. But Kevin said, "I knew Mary's husband. I know what he looked like. What's going on here?"

Then, we had another woman in the camp who also tried. This woman had the same name as my mom. My mom is Mary Kamara, and the other woman's name was also Mary Kamara. When my mom was called for an interview, the other woman said, "It is not for you—it is me who they want to interview!"

But Kevin told the other woman, "No, Mary, it is not for you. I am talking about the other Mary, the one who is in the camp with two little girls."

We were very lucky that Kevin was there and helped us through the refugee process for the second time. We got approved to go. After we got the good news and were getting ready to go, some friends threw a party for us to celebrate. We were going to America! And almost everybody in the camp turned out for the party.

The next day, we woke up early and were ready to go. I remember that I took some of my clothes to my friends in the camp; they needed them more than I did, as I was leaving now. We took the bus from our refugee camp to Conakry, the capital city of Guinea. It was a long bus ride, about two days on the road. But Conakry was the city from where you went to America.

When we got to Conakry, they had a big place for refugees there. It was a camp, but it was really very nice. We had a house with a living room, restroom, showers, and everything. Once we got there, they gave my mom money to buy food for us, they gave us pocket money, and they gave us food to eat. We went through an orientation, and then we took the bus to Lola. I don't remember the place too well, but we had another orientation there, and we had another interview. I don't remember much, but they asked me if my mom was really my mother, and I had to say, "Yes, yes, she is my mother."

Then, they asked my sister the same question, and she also said, "Yes."

And they said, "Okay, then."

I was really little then, so I don't remember that much. Then, one day, we were done with all that, and they put us on the plane to go. It was a little scary to be on that plane because it was my first time to travel by plane. And it was a big airplane. It was a flight from Conakry to Atlanta. When we landed in Atlanta, I think we had missed our next flight to Dallas, so they made us spend the night in a hotel in Atlanta. The next day, we reached Dallas, and it looked nice.

But from Dallas, we had to go on to Abilene, and we got confused. We did not know how to find that flight, so we just sat down for a while. There was this lady sitting not far from us. She was an American lady, and she was watching us. Then, she came up to us and asked my mom, "Are you alright?"

Then, she sat down next to us and asked my mom and my little sister, "Do you want anything to eat?"

My little sister asked my mom, "Mom, what is she saying? I don't understand what she is saying."

Then, the lady said, "Wait for me here." She went to McDonald's and bought hamburgers, fries, chicken nuggets, and drinks, and then she brought the food to us. She was very kind. When she brought the food to us, my little sister and me, we ate. And she gave some food to my mom, too. My mom ate a hamburger. That was my first time to eat a hamburger and fries, and it did not taste too good to me, especially that tomato ketchup. We were wondering what that was; it looked and smelled so nasty. Yuck. We did not know what we were eating. Then, the lady asked my mom where we were going, and my mom said, "I don't know. We are lost here."

The lady looked at my mom's ticket and said, "Oh, you are going to Abilene, Texas. That's where I am going, too. I live in Abilene, Texas."

My mom said, "Really?"

Then, the lady introduced herself to my mom. Her name was Leyla. She wrote down her phone number on a piece of paper and gave it to my mom and said, "Call me when you reach Abilene."

So, we were riding the same plane. Yes, that's how we traveled from Dallas to Abilene, Texas.

When we got out of the plane in Abilene, it seemed to me we were someplace else, not in America. It looked like Africa to me. Mr. Peter picked us up at the airport and took us all the way to our apartment complex. I told my mom, "This place is different. I don't think America should be like that."

It was the month of May when we came, and it may have been after a rain or something, but everything looked really messy. Mud and puddles…it was not like America at all. It was so different from what I had thought America would be like; this was just like Africa.

The apartment we had to stay in was a problem because we had to live with a roommate at first. The agency had put us together with another lady from the camp named Alice. We had lots of troubles with her. My mom went to the agency and told them, "I cannot stay with this lady because she is too messy." Then, they found a different place for us.

I did not get to go to school that year because school was almost over, so I had to wait until next fall. I had nothing to do all summer. I made many friends fast, though, as we had many other African refugees in the same apartment complex. I was very confident, and we all went to the same school in the fall. So, it was not really too hard. But later on, they started turning their backs on me—all of the other African kids who lived in the same apartments. They were mean to me in school; only Jeanne was nice. She was the only person who would talk to me. But the rest of them were mean to me at school, and they were talking bad about me behind my back. I don't even know why they were so mean to me.

Then, during the summer after my sophomore year was over, we moved to Dallas. It was at the end of the summer of 2010. We found a high school in Dallas for me, Lake Highland High School. On my first day at that school, I was feeling low; you know, I was all alone, and I did not know anybody at school. But then, like out of nowhere, this white boy came up to me and asked, "Can I ask you a question?"

And I said, "Yes?"

He asked, "Are you new to this school?"

I said, "Yes, I am new."

He said, "I know how it feels to be new at school with no friends. I have some African friends around here. I can introduce you to them, so they can be your friends, too."

And I said, "Thank you."

And he did. That's how I met my African friends in Dallas, and all of them were very nice to me. We even had an African club in school, and I used to stay after school with my friends. I graduated in 2012.

I met my baby's father in my junior year. We are engaged now and have a baby boy. We have not made firm plans for a wedding yet, as I need to finish college first. After high school, I started nursing school; I just took a break to take care of my baby. I want to be a pediatric nurse and take care of babies. Right now, I am taking time off from school, but I am going back in a few months. My mom is helping with the baby, and my fiancé helps, too. Everybody is here for the baby.

The best thing about America is that we have many opportunities that we would not have in Africa. Here, you can go to high school for free, and it is easy to get education. In Africa, you pay for high school and also for college. I appreciate the opportunities. I have plans for my future.

February 5, 2014

A View from the Office

"Liberian English"

Talking to Liberians today reminds me of my agency days in early 2004 when Liberian refugees just started arriving. I had a hard time understanding them, and it was not just me; it was hard for all of us in the office. Then, with daily practice as the months passed by, my understanding of Liberian English improved considerably. Now, I feel a little rusty again, since I do not talk with Liberians often anymore.

Although English is the official language of Liberia, the majority of people speak different dialects and tribal languages. English proficiency depends on the speaker's level of formal education and exposure to English speakers. I would say competency typically ranges from total Creole, which would be mostly the person's tribal language sprinkled with a "dash of English" as a spice and would not make any sense to English speakers, to Liberian English, which is close to American English and is spoken with a slightly different accent and does not create any difficulty. If I imagine a scale from one to ten, where "one" is totally Creole and "ten" is standard English, then the language our first Liberian arrivals spoke was somewhere in the middle.

Lionel would be at about five or six, Sandy at solid eight or nine, but our very first arrival, Bouake, would be around four. As a result, we all went through a "crash course," doing the best we could before interpreters for Liberian English were available. Then, 2004 was over, and with it, our "Liberian days" were over, too: we started getting refugees from other ethnic groups.

In 2005, we had a lot of Meskhetian Turkish refugees coming from the Krasnodar area in Russia, and thus, we had to have somebody to help us communicate in Russian, a language which the majority of Turkish refugees could speak in addition to their native Turkish. Because of this new group, a case worker assistant, Vadim, whose native language was Russian, was hired. He had an excellent command of English but, unfortunately, no experience with Liberians and Liberian English. Vadim was in charge of the "front desk," which was actually just a service window where refugees stopped to ask questions as they entered our office. Vadim was properly trained to seek help with interpreting if he could not communicate with clients, so he occasionally came over to our employment office to get help with other languages. I could help him with Spanish for Colombian clients, while my coworker, Andre, was fluent in French and could help with French speakers. Our office staff was still quite small at that time—just five of us, including the manager—and we naturally helped each other out when needed.

One day, as I came in through the front lobby where clients usually waited, I saw Anna from Liberia waiting in the front. She had recently moved to Abilene, where her friends lived, and I knew her because I had helped her find a job and fill out application forms. This time, she was not here for me, so I just said, "Hello," noted her presence in my mind, and went on about my business.

After a moment, Vadim came into our room to get help with French. He said, "There is this lady out there at the front window, and she is saying something, but I cannot understand her. She must be speaking French."

Andre looked at me inquiringly to see if I would nod and say, "Yes, please, go ahead, help Vadim out, alright?"

I was about to say exactly that, but then it dawned on me. "Are you talking about Anna, the woman in the waiting room?"

"Yes, I think so," Vadim said. "She is the only one there, but I could not catch her name."

"If that's her, she does not speak French, either," I said. "She is from Liberia, and what she speaks is Liberian English! Andre, just a minute. Let me go see."

I went out in the lobby, and true, it *was* Anna. To Vadim's surprise, I could communicate with her just fine. I was surprised myself that I could understand her; I guess the "crash course" in Liberian English had truly helped. Anna's question was answered—I have forgotten what it was—and life returned to normal.

Greg Kendall-Ball

Greg Kendall-Ball

Faces of Congo-Brazzaville: Anicet McKinney and his wife, Sylvanie Samba, pose for photos a couple of months after their arrival in Abilene, Texas, in November 2008 (top). The couple came from Mouila, Gabon, where Anicet had taught English and Spanish languages in a local school, but Sylvanie had a small business. Before the coup d'etat, Lazare Boulingui Goma (bottom) used to be the mayor of a city in the western part of Congo-Brazzaville, but here he has found a new home.

CHAPTER 5

Stories from Congo-Brazzaville

THAT WINTER AND SPRING of 2004, our next refugees to arrive were Congolese from Congo-Brazzaville. The country's official name is *the Republic of Congo*, but it is not often used in daily conversations. Instead, the country is referred to as "French Congo" or "Little Congo" or "Congo-Brazzaville." Congo-Brazzaville is indeed a small country in Central Africa with about 4.5 million people, and beside its neighbor, the huge Democratic Republic of Congo (or so-called "the Big Congo" or "Belgium Congo"), Congo-Brazzaville shrinks by comparison.

The first Congolese refugees we resettled came from Ivory Coast, where they had lived since the Congo Civil War of 1997 to 1999. Then, in the fall of 2008, another Congolese refugee group came from Gabon. The Congolese who had sought refuge in Ivory Coast or Gabon were supporters either of Pascal Lissouba or Bernard Kolelas, both presidential candidates who had competed in a general election when the pre-election events turned violent and led to the civil war that resulted in a military coup, bringing the third presidential candidate, Sassou Nguesso, to power. Congolese here often acknowledge that the situation in Congo has not changed much since those days because Sassou Nguesso is still in power.

Congolese refugees seemed quite different from Liberians, both by character and background. The majority of our Liberians were very dynamic, talked loudly, and gestured a lot, and they often seemed confrontational when in fact they were just talking.

One of our volunteers had noticed it as a cultural difference: "When you see Liberians talking to one another, they are so loud and stand so close together that you start watching out, wondering if they may get in a fight. But then you hear them laugh and smile, and it turns out they were just having a friendly conversation."

The Congolese left a different impression; they had a milder manner of interaction and seemed more ready to compromise. Overall, they appeared to be better educated, since schooling had been more available throughout Congo and the living standard had been higher than in Liberia. Liberians came from different walks of life: some were highly educated and used to city life, but some others had lived in the deep countryside and were illiterate.

All Congolese were French speakers, and the French language endeared them to the community of Abilene, whose residents, like many others in West Texas, seemed fascinated by all things French. Perhaps it was the Statue of Liberty that the French gifted to the US or the French fries that so many Texans like so well. There is a strip mall named "French Creek" in town, a French Market, a hair salon and an art shop "Objet D'Art," and a bakery named "Sweets Du Jour." Even though the relationship between the US and France has had its ups and downs, and "French fries" for a time turned to

"Freedom fries," people still like the French charm and the sound of the French language.

Now, let me introduce two refugee stories from Congo-Brazzaville. Let's start with Emmanuella.

Emmanuella: "We Came to America Too Late"

It is a quiet Sunday afternoon, and I am in my office with Emmanuella, who has agreed to share her story. I have known her husband, Andre, longer than her, since he was one of our first refugees, and Emmanuella joined him about two and a half years later. We have become good friends by now, although I still do not know why they did not come together. Emmanuella does not want to be recorded, so I am taking notes as we talk.

I remember quite well the confusion we had when Andre told us during his first office visit that he was married and would like to petition for his wife. All the paperwork listed him as "single." Looking back, it seems like a small thing: many people arrive by themselves first and then file petitions for spouses or children. But back then, we were very cautious, since we were told that those who had gotten married after the resettlement interview had to notify the overseas agency. The same was true if a baby had been born. The spouse or child had to be added to the case, which meant more paperwork for the overseas agency and also a couple more years of waiting for resettlement. In a way, the refugee would lose his or her place in line if changes were made. So, in real life, overseas agency staff would often advise the person to just go ahead with the resettlement process and file a petition for the family member from the US. At least, that's what many refugees have told me.

At that time, we were not sure what to think of Andre's "marriage." A few months passed by, the marriage turned out to be a real one, and with our manager's help, Andre filed a petition for his wife. Finally, after about two years of waiting, the day came when "Emmanuella was coming." We at the IRC were happy for them both. By that time, Andre had made so many friends at church and work that a crowd of people were at the airport to greet Emmanuella and celebrate Andre's reunion with her. Since then, a lot of things have happened in her life.

M Y NAME IS EMMANUELLA, and I come from a big family. My parents had eleven children, but one passed away, so now we are ten siblings—four brothers and six sisters. Before the war, life in Congo was good: we were all attending school, we had a house, and everything was going quite well. Our family lived in Makelekele, which is one neighborhood or "block" of the city of

Brazzaville. You know, Brazzaville is the capital city of Congo, and it has nine neighborhoods or blocks. My mom used to sell traditional wine in the market. It was white wine made from palm trees, not from grapes. Farmers from villages would make this wine and then come to the city to sell it, and my mother would buy from them in bulk and then sell that wine. She had her own space in the market, and she used to go there every day. And she was making really good money with it.

My father was a school teacher, although he is retired now. But he was not doing well because he liked alcohol too much. Only when we grew up did we find out that my father had taken to drinking because he was very jealous. Really jealous! He did not like that my mom was selling wine in the market because people were coming and going in the market all the time, and he was afraid that she would find another man and leave him. Because of that, he neglected us, the kids. He would not buy food for us nor pay for our schooling. Our mother was the one who paid for everything with the money she made in the market. Yeah. And although my parents lived together in the same house, they were arguing and fighting all the time.

Every day while my mom was selling in the market, my dad would go there and watch her from around the corner. And when she came home, he would yell at her, "Hey, who was that guy in the red shirt, the one who was talking to you? Now tell me, who was he?" And he would start a fight, and my parents would argue almost every day. It was bad, but we children did not pay too much attention to these arguments, since we played outside most of the time.

My dad changed for the better when the war started in 1993. This war was only in the South of Congo where the Lari tribe and the so-called NIBOLEK group of tribes lived. The NIBOLEK group supported President Lissouba's party, UPADS (Pan-African Union for Social Democracy), and included people from the tribes who lived in the Niari, Bouenza, and Lékoumou areas—that's how the group got its name, "NI-BO-LEK." The Lari tribe supported Kolelas' party, MCDDI (Congolese Movement for Democracy and Integral Development). So, the two groups went to war because of their different party allegiances. Most of the time, wars in Congo were between the southern and northern parts of the country, but this was all in the south, and I think it was really stupid for the Lari people and the NIBOLEK group to fight like that.

My parents were from two different tribes: my mom was Lari, but my father was from the Lumbu tribe that was part of NIBOLEK group. We lived in the part of Brazzaville that was mostly a Lari area, although many people from other tribes used to live there as well before the war. So, I could say it was a mixed neighborhood. We all lived in our father's house. The day right before the war started, my father went to the water faucet to fetch water. As he was lifting up the water bucket, he felt a sharp pain in his back and he could not stand up straight anymore. He had injured his back really badly. He got back home only with great difficulty, and he was in so much pain that we took him to see a doctor right away. But the very next day the war started, and Lari people with guns were walking from house to house, looking for people from my father's village! My mom said, "We need to do something. If the fighters find your father, they will kill him."

My mom decided that we should bring my dad to the NIBOLEK side, where he would be with his own tribe. To get there, we would have to take him to the big road that divided the Lari area from the NIBOLEK part of town. If we could just get there, my father would be safe. The question was, "How to do it?"

In our neighborhood, everybody knew my mother. She was safe because she was Lari, and we children were safe with her. But my dad was from the Lumbu tribe, and things were different for him; that's why we had to get him out. We decided that the three of us would go: my mom, my father, and me. My mom put on her party uniform so everybody would see that she was Lari, and we started our journey. We got through the Lari side without any trouble. But when we reached the big road where the NIBOLEK area started, things got out of hand. We were standing in front of one building, and across the road was "the other side." The NIBOLEK people were protecting their area; they were out there with guns. When we tried to go closer, their militias started shouting at us, "Hey, where are you going? Go back, go back!"

My father had an X-ray done in hospital, and I was carrying that big, black X-ray with me. I started waving it up in the air, shouting, "We are going to hospital! We need hospital!"

That X-ray may have looked suspicious to the fighters, or something else, but the militias suddenly opened fire at us. Oh, my God! We forgot everything and dropped to the ground. Then, the shooting eased up a little, and we got up again, but we did not try to go close to the other side anymore; instead, we hid behind the building. It was getting dark, and we could see bullets coming in our direction. They passed us in the dark like red lines of fire. The militias were still shooting at us! That was really frightening.

Then, we took a different route that was a long way around, and finally, we reached my father's cousin's place. Thank goodness, the cousin was at home, and we left my father with him in safety and went home the same way we had come. That day was really scary. But my dad came home after a few days, anyway, and said, "I'd rather get killed here where my children are than be in the safety without my kids."

And he started crying. Then, we saw that my dad truly cared for us. After a while, he went back to the north to be with his ethnic group again, but we stayed at home with our mom. Some weeks passed and we had not heard from my dad, so one day, I told my mom, "I think I am going to go and see my father."

The militias were still fighting, but overall, the situation was not that bad. It was just that people from the Lari side could not go over to the NIBOLEK side, and from there, they could not come here. Roadblocks were everywhere, and cars could not get through. The militias would stop everyone and question them, "Who are you? Where are you going?"

So, on that day, I went to look for my father. At the roadblock, militias stopped me like everyone else, and since my last name was a Lumbu name, I thought that they would let me pass. I was in the NIBOLEK area checkpoint, ready to go through, when one of the guys in the line pointed to me, "I know that girl—she is Lari!"

And the militias were like, "Oh, she is Lari, what is she doing here?"

One of the guards told me, "Go to that wall! Who are you? Why are you coming here?"

I tried to explain, "I am here to visit my father. He broke his back, and he is walking with a cane now. I am his daughter. I just wanted to see how he was doing."

The guards told me, "No, we know you are Lari!"

I said, "My name is Mahoundi—it is my father's family name, and he is from your tribe, too."

When they tell you to go to the wall like they did to me, it is bad news. You are at the wall, and they can kill you right on the spot. I was very scared. But in situations like that, God always comes to help. So, there was an officer who seemed to like me. He was looking at me in a flirting way, and then he started a conversation, "What's your name? Where do you live?"

I started flirting back, just to save my skin. And it worked: he let me go from the wall and walked me to the bus station and said, "Go."

So, I just got on the bus and went, just to get out of there, although I did not know where I was going. Finally, I reached my own home, but later, it took me about a month to find my father. But in 1993, war stopped after a few months, and President Lissouba stayed in power. It was the year I graduated from high school and passed my graduation exams. So, when the war was over, the bravest people from the other tribes started coming back to our neighborhood to rebuild their homes. Yeah.

But many of them did not come back. Even my father decided not to return; he would just come to visit us, stay a few days, and then go back to his village. He was from Banda village, and that's where he went back to live. I went to visit him there in 1997, right before the next war started. That war was a much bigger one, a really bad war, and a lot of people got killed in it.

But let me tell you first how I met Andre. It was before the first war; I think we started seeing each other in 1990. We have been together for a long time. I have a niece who was one year old when I started dating Andre, and she is twenty-five years old now. But it started this way: I used to see Andre when I was coming back from school. I was in middle school then; it was called "college" in

French. He was in high school. When I was coming home, he was going to school, and we always passed each other in the same place every school day. I did not like him because he was always staring at me. He was looking at me like—I don't know! I even told my sister, "I always see that guy on my way from school, and he must be strange or something because he is always staring at me when we pass each other."

Andre was looking at me, but we never talked. Then, a young girl in our neighborhood died, and there was a wake for her one evening. In Congo, when somebody passes away, people go outside, put mats on the ground and sleep there, and sing and play music to pay their last respects. That's what was happening that night. I had known that girl, so I went to her wake. It turned out that this girl had lived in the same place where Andre lived, so he went to the wake, too. I saw Andre and thought, *Oh, that's the guy who is always staring at me*. But this time, Andre came up to me and started talking. He asked me what my name was and where I lived. We talked for a little bit. Then, he said, "I'll come visit you tomorrow."

And I said, "Okay, come!"

Then, I went home and told my sister, "Remember the guy I was telling you about, who was staring at me all the time? He is coming to see me tomorrow!" So, Andre came, and we talked and went walking; we walked a long way. Just walking, talking… After that first date, we started going out regularly. And now, twenty-five years later, we are still together and married. That's the story about Andre and me.

But the big war started on June 5, 1997. Andre and I were both downtown, and I don't remember now why we went there on that day. The war took us by surprise. We were there, downtown, walking, and all of a sudden, we saw people had started running, and we heard shooting, gunfire, and thought, *Oh, something is going on here, let's get home quick!*

We took the bus back home. At that time, I was living with my mom, and Andre lived with his parents, but our homes were not far from each other. People were telling us that President Lissouba's forces had gone to the former president Sassou Nguesso's place and woke him up with shooting. I think that Lissouba had found out that Sassou was planning a coup in the country, to overthrow the president or something like that. They had surrounded Sassou's house and wanted to arrest him. But when they went, Sassou had been ready with his helicopters and his own army. So, it was a war again.

When we got home, we tried to find out what was going on. And you know, in Africa, people are always outside, in front of their homes, walking around, talking, always crowded…But this time, there was nobody outside, nobody! It got so quiet, really quiet. No cars, no people, nothing. And we were staying indoors, looking out of the windows. You could see police vehicles passing by. Militias were walking around; we saw a lot of young people in uniforms and with guns, and they would walk around looking for people. We all kept to our homes, without going outside. People were scared to be on the street, and everything was closed—schools, colleges, everything just stopped. Just stay home, lock the door. Maybe try to peek outside, to see what was going on. And all of a sudden, shooting would break out, and the fighters would be looking for the best positions and would overrun your neighborhood. It was terrible.

After some time, the fighting was over, and Sassou Nguesso was in power now. But he was seeking out people who had supported other parties. So, Andre and I decided to leave the country and go to Ivory Coast. We had our reasons: Andre had been in the party, and everybody knew that, so he had to leave. And I was his girl-friend and in the same party, too, so it was better for me to leave as well. Andre went first with his older brother, and I followed him later. It was in 1998, I think. Andre went in May, and I went in October. I took a plane to Abidjan. I had saved a little bit of money and could afford to buy a plane ticket. At Abidjan airport, I got off the plane and took a taxicab to Andre's place. The house was really tiny; maybe the whole house was as big as an office cubicle, only a little longer. It was just one room, and that's where Andre and his brother lived. When I saw it, I said to myself, "Oh, my God."

In Congo, you don't really see houses like that. It was like many tiny houses squeezed together and surrounded with a fence. And we did not have water in our house; some of the old tenants had not paid their water bill, so the water was cut off. We had to go to our neighbors to buy water. In Congo, we had running water in the house. But here, water faucets were outside, and our house even did not have water. It was tough. In my father's house in Congo, I had my own room. But here, we had just one room to share among the three of us: Andre, his brother, and me. We divided the room with a curtain in two parts, one for Andre and me, and the other for his brother, who was sleeping in the side where we were cooking. We cooked in the same room, since we had no kitchen, just a little stove.

The money we had ran out very fast, and after that, we did not have any money at all. It was very hard at first. Andre was calling his cousin in France to send money to help us, and he sometimes did, but not much. We had no way to make any money because we did not have the right documents to get a job. So, we could hardly find enough to buy food or pay for the water. I could not even afford to buy women's hygiene pads; I was using up my old underwear for that. Oh, it was awful. It took us two years to find a job, and in the meanwhile, we lived like that, in extreme poverty. I used to cry almost every day at that time, wishing to be back at home.

But I could not return to Congo. I could not go back and admit that I failed. My parents and siblings in Congo were proud of me for going to Ivory Coast for a "better life." A neighbor would ask, "Oh, where is Emmanuella?" And my family would say, "She went to Ivory Coast to have a better life." And the neighbor would be impressed: "Oh, yes. That's great!" If I went back now, everybody would ask about me, "Oh, is she the one who went to Ivory Coast? And is she back now? How come, what happened?"

And everybody would say that I'd failed. It would shame my family, and I could not do it to them. Because I left for "a better life," I could not go back and show that I failed. As I said, it took us two years to find a job. In Ivory Coast, people could tell that we were not local: we looked different and even spoke French in a different way. French in Ivory Coast was different, and when I lived there, I tried to speak like them. Otherwise, you would get, "What are you saying? I don't understand you." Sometimes, even little kids on the street would say, "Is she speaking English or what?"

Then one day, Andre met a guy who told him about the plastic shoe factory, and Andre went there and got a job. He applied for me and for his brother, too, and we all got hired and started working. The owners were immigrants themselves, and they did not care if we had documents or not, but we had to work very hard to keep the job. That's where my experience in production work came from. When I came to the US, my first job was in the cookie factory, and it was hard, but not as hard as in that shoe factory. But we could not get a better job because we did not have papers. So, we were quite happy for this chance to make some money. Finally, we could pay our own rent and buy groceries. Oh, God, it felt so good! The rent seemed really cheap now when we had some money coming in, and we were grateful to have a job. Then, Andre's brother got lucky and left for France, and it was just the two of us in the little rental house.

Before Andre's brother left for France, he and Andre had been to UNHCR and had told their story and got refugee documents, which meant that they were accepted in the refugee program. I think they found out where to go because many refugees lived in our neighborhood and advised them. I went to UNHCR to apply as well, but my application did not go as well. One woman who worked there obviously did not like me. You know, sometimes women are like that to other women, especially in Africa. I like to do my hair nicely, dress up a little... so, I went there nicely dressed, and when she saw me, she asked, "Are you a refugee?"

And I said, "Yes."

She looked at me and said, "No, I don't think so." And she made it really difficult for me. I had to go and explain my story again and again: what happened, how people came to our house and threatened us, and that I was with Andre, doing political things, wearing party T-shirts, and that I was in the party, too. Finally, I got approved and got my refugee card, but even then, my case was not moving along. Only when Andre came to America and filed a petition for me did I get invited for an interview at the embassy. But my refugee case had stopped. Many people came after me, and their cases were moving forward fast, but not mine. I called UNHCR about it, but all they said was, "Everybody's case is different. Just wait." But that waiting took too long!

When Andre found out that he would be going to America soon, we decided to get married. Our wedding was really simple; we could not afford anything big. Of course, I was wearing a nice outfit, and we took a taxicab to the town hall. There was a big wedding planned to take place after ours. The waiting room was full of people. All the family and guests for that wedding had come early, and they all were sitting and waiting. But we did not have any family or guests; it was just Andre and me, his brother, and two more friends. All those people were so amazed at our simple wedding that they started cheering and clapping. It was so nice that I still remember it. A little thing, but it made us really feel good. They said, "You made it really simple, but that's how it should be. That's what a wedding is all about. It is so nice how you are doing it, so great."

Yeah. They really made us feel good. After the ceremony, we took our taxicab, and all those people followed us to see us off. And we came home and had a celebration with all the neighbors. I cooked some food, and we all ate and had a good time. It was not a big thing, but we both enjoyed it, and now, it is a good memory. Then, three months later, Andre was off to America. And I thought, *Oh, no, now I'll be all by myself...*

I stayed for two and a half years all by myself, and it was hard to live alone. And you know what happened? As soon as Andre left, the roof of the house fell in! It was a stormy night with torrential rains and lots of thunder, and the roof just collapsed. A good thing was that Andre found a job soon and started sending me money, so I could move to a different place. My new house was nicer and it had more space; I had my own bathroom and living room and a kitchen. I bought a TV and some things for the house with the money Andre sent. All the neighbors knew that my husband was in America, so everybody was like, "Oh, can I watch TV with you? Can I borrow some money from you?"

When Andre left, I thought I would continue working in the shoe factory because I wanted to have something to do. But the owners and managers of that factory were really mean. Sometimes, they could just slap you with a shoe. Yeah. Then one day, when a young supervisor talked down to me, I had had enough. I just told him, "I quit."

So, I left the factory job, and I just lived on the money Andre sent me from the US. Overall, life was not expensive in Ivory Coast.

Andre was sending me one hundred dollars of pocket money, and then he used to send me rent money, about thirty-five or forty dollars per month. For the US, one hundred forty dollars is not a lot. But for Ivory Coast, it was very good money. I could live on it and buy a lot of nice clothes and shoes and other things. When I went to church, I was always dressed up so nicely that somebody in church even asked me, "Are you a seamstress? Do you make your dresses yourself?"

It felt really good to have some money at last, after all that misery at the beginning. Yeah. I did not wish anymore to be back at home in Congo. I was just waiting on my papers to go through so I could be with Andre again. But there was nothing to do, just wait. And it was a long wait, too. I could just pray for it. I used to go to church every morning and pray. I talked to my pastor, and he said, "It's going to be okay. Believe me, you're gonna go."

And then one day, the embassy called me: "You have to go to the doctor and interview." Finally, the day came for me to travel. Before I left Ivory Coast, Andre told me on the phone, "All my church members want to come to the airport to meet you!"

When Andre said that his church people would come out to greet me, I thought, *Oh, my God, what am I going to do when all those people will greet me? They will be speaking English!* How would I know what to say? The church I was attending in Ivory Coast was a Nigerian church, and they were preaching in English and interpreting in French. I used to carry a notebook with me, and sometimes I was listening and making notes—that's how I started learning English.

But when I got to the Abilene airport, Andre was there, and the case worker from the IRC was there, and Andre's brother with his wife and their baby daughter...so I had some people who spoke French. Andre's church members—many people—they all were at the airport, too. Since I could not say much in English to them, but in Ivory Coast people always hug one another, I began hugging everybody, just like we did in Ivory Coast. And hugging turned out to be the American way, too, but I did not know it yet. That arrival was really good. Andre brought me flowers but forgot all about them because we both were so happy to see each other. Only after a while, somebody reminded him, "Andre, the flowers! They were for her!"

Andre still had those flowers in his hand. We had not seen each other for almost three years, and it felt a little different at the beginning. I was looking at Andre and thinking, *Is that the same guy I married?* We learned to live together again, and we had new friends, and we were in a different culture. In Africa, you would never see Andre upset or worried, but here, I could tell he had more stress, worrying about bills and rent payments.

The time soon came for me to start working, and my first job was at the cookie factory. That job was stressful, mostly because some of my coworkers acted like they owned the place. These ladies were really bossy and did not treat us Africans well. They would not even call you by your name, although they knew your name. They would just holler at me, "Hey!" if they wanted me to do something. I hated it.

And then somebody told me about the plastic factory PWP, that they were taking people. I went and got hired, and I liked the new job better, and the pay was higher there, too. The job was easier: it was two people on one line, both packing. It was really easy compared to the cookie factory. And coworkers were nicer. After some time, I thought that I did not want to stay in production forever and decided to try the medical field. There was a class for certified nurse aides, called CNAs. One hospital in town was doing this class, as they were short on nurse aides. And I thought, *Why not?* My mom had always wanted me to be in the medical field. I could get a certificate for this and work in a hospital. So, I said to myself, "Okay, I'll try."

So, I started the CNA class there. It was not easy because the English level was a little high for me. The nurses who were teaching, they would be talking fast, explaining. Sometimes, I had to write, so it was not easy, but I tried to follow. Every day, we had an assignment, and I remember one time, I got 75 percent for my assignment, and there was one girl who was from here, and she got just seventy. I was proud that I could do better than her, who was born here, a native English speaker. I was reading the books they gave us to study from and really liked them. I thought that I could pass the test because they gave us a pre-test, and I got a good grade—way over the passing level. I thought, yes, I am going to make it. Then, before we finished the class, the hospital put us to work because they were short-handed. I started working in that hospital in the morning shift. In the morning, I did not have any problems, but then they asked me to do the night shift. And I said, "Night shift is okay. I can do it."

I was thinking that it might be a little quieter during the night, so it would be easier for a beginner like me. I started doing the night shift. I had twenty-one rooms all by myself, and I had to check fever, blood pressure, and blood sugar and help the people who wanted to go to the bathroom. I also had to clean them, help make the beds, and change bed pans—things like that. It was a lot of work to do because when you start with room one and then go on to twenty-one, it is quite a lot. And I had to do it fast because I had to do it all every two or three hours. So, I had to go back to every room again and take the vital signs. One time was at midnight and then at three o'clock at night, and so on. The patients may have been sleeping, but I still had to go in and check the vital signs and write down each patient's bowel movements and so on. It was a lot of work. But I enjoyed the job because some of the people, especially older ones, started to like me, and I was enjoying them, too. I started to look forward to seeing my patients. It felt good because I like helping people.

But what I did not like was the nurses; they were really unfriendly there. I would come in to my shift and say "hi" or "good evening" to them, and nobody would reply. Yes. How come nobody would return my greeting? And nobody was really showing me where things were. Like, the hospital had one room where the supplies were kept. But nobody took me there to show what was where and explain. Sometimes, patients needed one thing or another, so I went to this room and started looking, and when you did not know where things were, it would just take a long time to find. The nurses were there, but nobody would come and show me anything. Except for one nurse—she was really nice to me. When she was there on her shift, she would talk to me, and sometimes she would come and help with patients. But the other nurses did not pay any attention to me. They were on the computer all the time, not even talking or laughing. I always heard that nurses made a lot of money, but how come they always seemed so unhappy? No smile, no laugh, nothing. I was looking at them and thinking, *No, I don't want to be like them.*

For some patients, I had to write down how much water they drank. They each had a water pitcher in their rooms. In one room, I made a mistake and wrote down what was left in the water pitcher and not what the patient had drank. I was new to the job and made a mistake. The nurse that was on duty started screaming at me, "Is that the water this patient drank?"

I did not realize that I had made a mistake, and I said, "Yes."

And she went on, "No way she drank so much water. I have known that patient for a long time! She does not drink that much water!"

I was confused because I did not realize yet that I had written down the water that was left in the pitcher. So, I said, "Yes, that's what she did."

The nurse said, "No way, she could not have had so much water! And nobody taught you that you have to sign every day? Nobody told you to do that?" She was really screaming.

I said, "No, I did not know that."

"How come you did not know that? You are supposed to sign everything every day in the rooms. And you have to sign the book!"

She was screaming so loud that other nurses came out to see what was going on and joined in. "Oh, what did she do? Oh, my God, it is horrible!"

It all made me cry. It still makes me cry when I remember it. It was a mistake, I admit, but it was just water, and it was easy to correct because we knew how much water was in the pitcher at the beginning, and we knew how much water was left, so I could have corrected the entry. But that nurse just wanted to give me a hard time. I had just started working as a nurse's aide, and I had not even taken my test yet. And nobody had told me that I had to sign those papers. I had twenty-one rooms, and I had to check everything—fever, blood pressure, sugar, and empty the pans. Nobody had told me to sign! I started crying, and the other nurse who liked me was in that night, too. That nurse followed me into the kitchen and said, "You don't have to cry, you know. You don't know what I went through when I started. It is just like that. You have to deal with this; it is not easy."

But I was crying about the attitude. The good nurse tried to calm me down. "Oh, don't worry about that other nurse. It is going to be okay."

All this had happened toward the end of the shift, when it was almost morning. I stayed on working, but I had made up my mind. I told her, "I am not going to work here no more, no. The way that nurse screamed at me and the others acted, it does not look like they want me here. I do not feel welcome."

After the shift was over, I went outside and started crying even harder. Andre came to pick me up, and I was crying. He was worried. "What happened?"

And I said, "I cannot tell you right now, but for one thing, I am not coming back."

Andre said, "Oh, you cannot leave like that. We have bills to pay and everything!"

But I said, "Just give me some time."

I did not want to talk about it right then, but I knew that I was not coming back. At that moment, I just wanted to leave everything and go home and forget about the CNA job.

The next day, two ladies called me from the office. I was on schedule for the night, but did not go in, so the day after, they called. I explained what happened, about that nurse, how she made me feel. And the test was coming up in two days. The office ladies said, "No, do not leave like that! At least come for the test. Just come for the test."

I said, "No, I am not coming for the test. I am not doing the test because of that nurse. She made me feel so bad that I do not want to be a CNA anymore."

Then, the office lady gave the phone to the other lady, who asked me, "How was your experience at work? Was everybody treating you like that nurse?"

I said, "No, there was one nurse who was very nice to me, very helpful."

You know, I did not have a problem with that nurse who was helpful. It was just the other one who had screamed at me and put me down. I had really invested a lot in that class, staying up late every evening to read for it and do my homework. I was reading all the time and studying abbreviations; many things were new to me. I was ready for that test. But that nurse was so mean. I told myself, *If I see that nurse again, I will go and tell her what I think.*

I was not sure what would come out of my mouth, but I would not leave it like that. But now, years have passed since this incident, so I don't even remember what she looked like.

So, I went back to work in production again. They sent me to work at the warehouse. I started again in plastic factory. And you know, my job has always been an extremely important thing in my life—we spend too much time at work to have it any other way. But life is different here, and some of the things are stressful. Like, we did not know what bills were until we went to live in Ivory Coast. But here, you have to worry about bills almost every day. And most of your money goes for the bills and to pay your credit card, you know. You have to think about it every day, worry about not getting into debt, things like that, and it is really stressful. But you are now in America, and you have to send some money home. We do not really send much, but we have to do it regularly. If I was still living in the apartment, it would be more restful, but for a house, you have many more chores to do, like yard work and watering the plants. But it is a good feeling, too, to have our own house.

And I really thank God that I could come and live here. We have made a lot of friends, in church and also in the African community. Sunday in church is really "the hugging time." It feels like family now.

But I am thinking that when I get really old, I would like to go back to Africa and live in Ivory Coast. Somehow, I do not want to go back to Congo; it just does not feel the same after the war. Andre does not want it, but I think I have my roots still in Africa; I cannot forget Africa. I really liked the people in Ivory Coast and low prices, too. The people were friendly, and life was good after we started working. It was easy to live there. So, when we retire, we could save money and live in Ivory Coast. Just sit outside in front of my house and watch kids running, playing, all the people walking and talking outside. And when I get tired of Africa, I can come back to the US. I am sure I will miss my life here, but we could go back and forth.

I am not sure what else I will do here, but I am sure I do not want to stay in my current job until I retire, no…I am thinking of doing some online training sometime in the future. I enjoy working with children, so I thought maybe I could do something with kids, help kids who are struggling. Like social work, but with children. But I do not want to go to class every morning, no. But I could do online training from home. Like teacher's aide, translate for kids into French, something like that, and be paid better, more interesting. I like my job now, I am on my own, work and take breaks when I want, and have my own pace.

Sometimes Andre tells me, "We came too late to America. We are too old." I could have gone to school if I was in my twenties. But now, it is too late to go back to school. When I went to college, I was in journalism class, but here, it would be too difficult because of the language. But I am sure that I can still find something; life is not over yet. So, I am not just waiting on the check to pay the bills. It would be good to have my own business. Then, you are your own boss. But I will think about it. We'll see.

April 13, 2014

Moise: "What Business If You Don't Know English?"

Today, I have unexpected visitors: Moise comes in with his countryman, Paul, who wants to consult on immigration matters, and Moise will help with interpreting. Both men are from Congo-Brazzaville, and I have known them for many years, since the early days of their resettlement. When Paul's questions have been answered, I take the opportunity and ask Moise if he would like to share his life story for the storybook, and at first, he sounds somewhat hesitant, saying that he "was just a student at the time" and "has not accomplished anything big" in Congo. Then, I explain the intentions of the project in more detail, and Moise agrees. He will take Paul home and come back for the storytelling session. He declines to be recorded, so I will take notes.

What I remember best about Moise is how we both went job searching and how I helped him save his job. When Moise first arrived, we both went around town looking for employment, and he got two job offers: one with a food service company and the other in production. It was Fehr Foods, Inc., a production company in town that makes cookies, and Moise started working there, first as a production worker and later, he got promoted to a machine operator's position. But during his first months with the company, Moise almost got fired.

What happened was this: Moise had a knee injury and was absent from work, since he had to go see a doctor one day, and he was not yet well the next day and did not go to work on that day, either. According to company policy, he had to call in sick if he missed a workday, and he also had to bring a doctor's note if his absence was more than one day. But the workplace rules were new to Moise, and some "got lost in translation," so he had not called in sick nor reported having seen a doctor. When Moise showed up without any doctor's notes two days later, the HR manager was about to let him go.

It was good that I happened to call her exactly the same day, and she gave me a heads up about Moise's pending termination. I pleaded with the manager to give him a couple of days more time to get that doctor's note, explaining that he must have misunderstood the rules. Right after my conversation with the manager, I got on the phone with Moise.

"How can I go to the doctor's office when I have to be at work?" Moise wondered. "You know I have to go by bus to that doctor's office, and it

takes almost all day to get back and forth. I will miss another day at work!"
It was a challenge to travel around town by city bus, which ran once an
hour and went in circles. But when Moise realized how serious the situa-
tion was, he somehow managed to get it done, and his job was saved.

Since those days, more than ten years have passed, and Moise is still
with Fehr Foods, Inc. and has been promoted to a better paid position, so
it was the right decision for the HR manager to let him stay. When I hap-
pen to see Moise these days, he looks happy and content with his life in the
US. He occasionally brings me a box of cookies to remind me about the job
search we did together and to say, "The cookie factory is the best!"

I HAD A VERY GOOD CHILDHOOD. Sometimes, I remember
those days, and I feel happy. They were really nice. My dad used
to work for a manganese mining company, and the house that we
lived in was provided by the mining company for free. And that
house was really very nice. Every summer, when we had school
holidays, I got to go to "colonie de vacance," like summer camp
for children. Each family could give the name of one child for the
camp, and then the kids would all go to one place for a month of
holiday. They would live there, but from that camp, we would go
to different trips, visit different places in the country. It was really
great. It was for children between six and twelve years of age, so
I went when I was probably eight or nine years old. The summer
camp was in Makabana.

The mining company was really generous, and they gave toys to
the kids of their employees every Christmas; we got soccer balls
and guitars, among other things. And they paid good wages, too.
When my dad retired from the mining work in 1990, he bought
a house in a big city from his savings in Pointe Noire. There were
five children in the family, and I was the youngest. I had two brothers and two sisters, but the eldest sister passed away a couple of
years ago. One of my brothers lives in Gabon—he is a mechanic
there—and the other brother lives in Congo. He has never been
interested in politics, as he is a religious man and has always stayed
away from politics. My dad has always been for President Lissouba,
but his brother has been a Sassou's supporter, so we never talked
about politics in our house when my uncle was around. My dad

knows quite well that his brother is for Sassou, but they just do not talk about it. At least, they can have good family relations this way.

During the civil war, I tried to get out of the country and cross the border to Gabon. But it was close to the time when the war was over, and things had started to settle down, so Gabon border guards told me to turn around and go back. They said, "War is over in Congo. Now it is peaceful, and you can go home."

So, I went home and was not really thinking of leaving again. But when I came back, my dad told me how my brother almost got killed, and I thought, *No, I cannot live like that. I better try to leave in one way or another.*

My dad also encouraged us both to leave. He said, "You are young. Go while you can. You see, everybody here knows that we voted for President Lissouba, so it is just a matter of time before the new president's people come for you. And don't worry about me. I am old, I will be alright. Sassou's men don't need an old man like me, but they will come looking for you both. I don't think it is safe for you to remain here."

So, my brother and I both left. My brother went to Gabon but took a different route, not the one I had tried before, and he managed to get to Gabon and reach Libreville. But me, I bought a plane ticket and flew over to Abidjan, Ivory Coast. But what happened to my brother in Congo, why I changed my mind about staying, was this.

It was during the last months of the civil war. One evening, my brother was coming home from a different district, and he was carrying two huge canisters of palm oil, maybe about fifty liters each. He had come in by train, brought that oil in by train, and he was looking for a taxicab to get those canisters home. At that time, just after the civil war, palm oil was very hard to find, and it cost a lot of money. It was essential to have, as we used it for everything: cooking, for light—it was totally indispensable in any household. He was so happy that he could get this palm oil in some remote area, and he had paid fifty dollars for each of the containers. It was a lot of money for us in Congo. You could do a lot with fifty dollars, like live for one month on it! While he was there looking for a taxicab, a soldier from Sassou's army stopped him and pointed to his palm oil canisters. "Give one of them to me!"

My brother said, "No, man, I cannot give you one, because that is a lot of oil. This oil is not just for me but for our whole family, my parents, wife, and other brothers to use. But I can give you half of one canister. Just come with me, and we'll split it."

But the soldier told him, "No, half will not do, and since you refused to give me one, now I am taking both of your canisters!"

And my brother said, "No, how can you take the canisters from me? You cannot do it! Is this how you are protecting us? You are here to keep peace, not take things away from us."

During that time, military people were in the streets to keep peace and order, to prevent any riots and the like. It was Sassou Nguesso's forces. When the soldier heard what my brother was saying, he got angry and pulled out his gun. He pointed it at my brother. "How do you dare to talk like that? I know you are Lissouba's supporters, all your family. I will shoot you!"

He was about to pull the trigger when a military jeep rolled by with a senior officer in it. The officer stopped the jeep, leaned out of the window, and yelled at the soldier, "Hey, what do you think you are doing here?"

And the soldier pointed at my brother. "This guy, he is 'Lissouba,' and he is refusing to give that oil to me, so I will shoot him!"

But the officer said, "No, you are not here to shoot people. Stop it right now!"

So, my brother was spared, but it was just by sheer luck because that officer happened to pass by exactly in the right moment. After hearing what had happened from my brother, I told myself, *No, I better get out of this. Here, everybody knows about everyone else, who each one voted for, and that will not lead to anything good.*

So, that was what happened, why my dad told us both to leave the country. As I said, my brother got across the border safely; he went to Gabon, and he still lives there. He works as a mechanic, and he has some legal papers from Gabon, like resident's papers. He does not really like Gabon, but I am not sure what he can do. He cannot go back to Congo after what happened. I am thinking about filing for him to come to the US to live. I know you told me it would be a very long waiting time, but I may still do it sometime in future.

Sometimes, I remember the days when Lissouba was the president. As you know, many people had to leave Congo when Sassou Nguesso took power by force. At that time, Lissouba was our first democratically elected president, and the majority of people supported him. When the first election took place in 1992, everybody was excited about Lissouba, and everybody voted for Lissouba. Like I told you, my brother said that he was not interested in politics, that "politics was not his business." But at that time, my dad told him, "But this house is your business!"

So, even my brother voted for Lissouba. I remember how all the people were really involved, happy, and everyone was going to meetings, talking, discussing things. Pictures and posters of Lissouba were everywhere, and people were holding vigils, drumming, and dancing at fires all night. Crowds of people were singing songs about Lissouba, girls dancing, people up all night, celebrating. It was democracy for the first time in the country, and people were really excited. All people liked him at that time. When time for new elections came closer in 1997, Lissouba would have won again, but Sassou arranged a coup because he wanted the power for himself. So, what followed was the civil war, and Sassou is still in power now.

Now, I have been in the United States for more than ten years, and I am a US citizen. At present, I want to finish my GED class, pass the test, and then go to college for baking science. But to be good at baking, you have to know how to do calculations, understand all the chemical processes, and know how to do equations. I may go to American baking school in Kansas, since they have indicated that I could get a scholarship there. I like chemistry, and baking is a lot about chemistry. And then, I want to find a good job with baking. I may stay with the same company or find a different one; it all depends what they can offer.

But I have also always wanted to become a medical doctor and study for that. I am forty-one years old now, so maybe after some years, I will save up enough money to go to college full-time and go through medical school. I am really good at chemistry and biology, and these are the hardest subjects in medical school. And anatomy is not easy, either, as you really have to memorize a lot. But I think I could handle those.

But now, I want to tell you about our Congolese association. It also started the same summer of 2004. At that time, it was just the three of us here from Congo-Brazzaville: me, Andre, and his roommate Ray, who also came to work in the cookie factory. A little later, Ray's wife, Reine, came to live with him. I had the idea to start a Congolese association, and I talked to Andre and Ray about it. And they both said, "Oh, yes, it is a good idea, let's go ahead with it."

At that time, we were not sure how to make it official, so we decided to just start doing something and leave papers for later. For starters, we agreed to do a welcome party for each new Congolese refugee who arrived to live in Abilene. Arthur was the first to arrive after us, and we did a welcome party for him. I asked him, "Do you think a Congolese association is a good thing? Would you like to join in?"

He said he liked it. Then, Andre's brother arrived, and we welcomed him, too. I think we had a meeting in the house the church gave him when he came. So, everything was going well at the beginning. In our first meeting, we had decided to do two things: "welcome" everyone who was newly arrived and also focus on learning English. We used to get together on Saturdays for an English class, and we would talk English during that time. One of us would read an excerpt from the Bible in English, and we would discuss it in English to practice the language. So, the first two years, everything was going well, people were coming one by one, and we welcomed them. Fresnel came next, and then somebody else arrived, I forget who, but the first two years were good.

The trouble started at the end of 2006, when Lionel and Frederic arrived. Then, Paul and his relatives arrived in 2008—another trouble. As I told you, when we first started, we agreed on doing welcome parties for all new people and to focus on English language. Our goal was to integrate Congolese into American society. But when Frederic and Lionel came, nothing could be decided anymore because they opposed everything. We just had meetings, and every time, it was like, "We are running out of time. Let's leave it for our next meeting."

By that time, our numbers had grown, and we were about to make the association official. But some people did not like the mission we had chosen—namely, that we should learn more English. They just wanted to push for business and making money. I told them, "What business? How can you do any business here if you do not know English?"

Another issue that we were struggling with at that time was who would be the president of the association. We needed somebody who was respected in the Congolese community, somebody who was smart and honest and who knew how things worked in the US. I did not want to run because I felt that I was too young; we needed somebody more mature.

At first, we thought that Lionel would make a good candidate, and he was eager to get that job. But then, we saw that he was always behind on his household bills, always fighting with his wife, and—the main thing—he really did not want to keep a job. It seemed like he wanted to be on food stamps forever. So, no, we thought, he would not be the right person for the president's position. And then, the thing with the lottery happened, and Lionel got in trouble for it. I am sure you have heard about it.

Remember what happened? How he "won the lottery?" It was a scam, and I knew it from the very beginning, and I told him that. But Lionel did not believe me. He thought I was just talking out of jealousy and wanted to take away his "chance of the lifetime," as he said. I think he went to see you at the IRC after all that had happened, but it was too late.

What happened was this: Lionel had received an email saying that he had been "randomly selected" in a lottery and had won half a million dollars. Also, he had received money orders or cashier's checks in the mail, and that was supposedly the money that the lottery organizers "gave away" to him to help cover the income tax for the lottery winnings. To get his half-million, he had to deposit the money orders in his bank account, cash them, and send it all together with his own savings to somebody by Western Union. Lionel was so excited, but all this did not sound right to me, and I did not believe that it was a true deal. I truly had doubts.

I told him, "Lionel, it does not sound right. Something is fishy about this email and this lottery."

But he said, "Oh, Moise, come on, this will bring me so much money. Just help me handle that."

Lionel had cashed the money orders and withdrawn all money from his bank account to send it away. His English was pretty poor then, and he asked me to help interpret. The lottery people had told him to call before wiring the money. So, I helped him call the number they gave in the email, and some lady answered the phone. She spoke English and a little French, and she told us that she lived in Great Britain, that she was British. But her accent was not like one from Great Britain. I know how British people talk, and I could tell on the phone that it was Nigerian English from Africa.

So, I told Lionel about my suspicions to warn him, but he said, "No, everything will be fine." He just wanted that money so badly that he was not listening to common sense! I refused to interpret for him, but he found somebody else to do it. All this lottery business took several days, so at that time, I even called Andre's brother, who was the pastor, and asked him to help me talk Lionel out of this lottery. I told him, "You are the pastor, and you should help me talk Lionel out of this. Even the Bible says not to gamble, not to play risky games."

But he did the opposite. He helped Lionel cash the money orders that turned out to be fakes. I guess even he did not catch on that it was a scam. In the end, Lionel did not get the half-million; his money disappeared together with money he got from the bank for the fake money orders, and he had to pay the bank back the money he took out from money orders. The bank reported him as a criminal. When he realized that it really had been a scam, he went to you at the IRC for help, but nobody could get his money back or catch the scammers. They were long gone. The money he sent was taken out at the other end of Western Union, and that was the end of the story.

I remember how Lionel and I went to the district attorney's offices to explain the situation and propose a payment plan for Lionel. Before that,

I had talked to the bank several times and had written a letter to the board pleading to write off Lionel's losses. After all, the man had taken out all his family's savings plus cashed in fake cashiers' checks that now had to be paid back, so he was totally broke. I was sorry to hear that the board had not approved the request and made him pay back in full. Surely, I thought, they had more money than Lionel and could have shown a little charity.

It was a very sad situation, but I cannot understand how he could have believed it. So, after this, we decided that we should wait to fill the president's position. Some of the Congolese advised to wait until Paul arrived. Paul had been an elected government officer before Sassou came to power in Congo. He was not here yet, but we had heard about him and decided to wait until he came.

In 2008, Paul arrived through the resettlement program like all of us, and we called a meeting for all Congolese interested in the association. But that first meeting with Paul did not go too well. Paul came, but he talked down to everyone. When I asked him questions about the future of the association, he got upset and shouted at me, "Who are you? I don't even know you! Why are you asking all these questions?"

That meeting did not bring us closer to selecting the president. By the way, do you remember Jean, the Burundian guy? He got the idea about an association from us, but while we were still talking and talking, he went ahead and set up the Burundian association. He basically "took" my idea and put it to practice.

But for us, the hardest part was to agree on things we wanted to do. Some of the people wanted to get involved in politics, especially the ones who were of older age. They were not as interested in learning English and integrating into the American community; instead, they wanted the association to get involved in politics and try to make it really big, like a national association, and write to President Obama to get help with restoring democracy in Congo again. Like Lionel and Paul, they had good jobs under the old president, so if Congo became democratic again, they could go back and not worry about integration.

For example, Paul was an elected city official under the old government, and Lionel was one of president's drivers; he was part of president's driving fleet. Also, Frederic was involved in politics in the past. They all are here now but hope to go back when the power changes. Like Paul was saying the other day, "I don't want to die here with Sassou still in power in Congo." If they stayed, they would have to study hard to improve their English. And even then, it would be hard to get well-paid office jobs like the ones they had in Congo. They are not that young anymore, so it would be really hard for them to go back to school. So, no wonder they were not so keen on learning English!

But I am thinking of the younger generation, the ones who were not in high political positions. For us, it would be best to learn more English and go to school. Through the association, we could offer additional resources to teenagers and young people who have just arrived and are in high school or are thinking of college but have gaps in their education because of incomplete previous schooling. Also, for adults: pushing for English and integration into the local community through education. But when I proposed that, others were like, "No, we don't need that."

So, it was difficult to agree on things that we wanted to do. We all are from different parts of Congo, with different political views and ethnic affiliations, and that does not help, either.

Then, after some time, it was Danny who finally registered the association. He came in 2008, and I think he was a teacher in Gabon. He even gave the name to the association, "The Hand of God" (or "La Main de Dieu" in French), and we elected the board. We all had to sign a document that we would abide by the rules of the association. At last, we had a temporary president elected and the treasurer. We were collecting membership dues, and people could get money for dental and medical expenses, relatives' funeral expenses, and things like that. We also let some people borrow money without interest, but that borrowing money got us in trouble. One of men borrowed money but never paid it back. He kept saying, "Next month," but then he moved to another state, and we never saw that money again. I forget exactly which one did it.

And the issue was not just this lost money; the main reason the association did not succeed was that people were fighting among themselves. We still could not agree on the goals of the association, and some were critical that the money the association gave out to help was too small. Somebody's wife was invited to join without letting the husband know about it...It was a lot of small things like that, and after a year or two, Danny said to me, "I am tired. I am giving it up."

At that time, we still had some little money in the association's bank account, but we decided not to divide it up among the members, not to create another fight. So, it is just sitting there in the bank and waiting for better times. And the same with the association—it may come back to life one day.

March 30, 2014

A View from the Office

"Roommates"

October 2004

Today, my phone rings. "Hi, Daina, how are you? I have a problem here."

It is Moise. He is from Congo-Brazzaville and has been in Abilene for about six months. He has a roommate, Joseph, who is quite new here and from the "other" Congo. Joseph lost his job not that long ago, and both roommates do not get along very well. I expect it will be about Joseph, and it turns out I am right.

Moise sounds unhappy. "I cannot live with a roommate like Joseph anymore. You really have to do something! I swear I will cover all the rent myself. Just help me do something about him."

They have had their ups and downs, but this time, it does not sound too promising. Moise lives in a two-bedroom apartment on the south side of town, has a full-time job, and there is no doubt that he could afford the apartment by himself, if needed. It is different with Joseph. Adjusting to life here has not been easy for him after years in a refugee camp, although his English is commendable. I am wondering what happened between them this time. Maybe the friction started when Joseph lost his job? He has probably been spending more time at home…

I want to give Moise some time to think everything through, so I ask him to come to the office tomorrow to talk about it in person.

"Okay," he says and rings off.

I get back to my job scouting. Not long after, my phone rings again, and this time, it is Joseph, the roommate.

"Could you do something about Moise? I cannot live with him any longer!" Joseph's English is very good, so he can tell me his side of the story in every detail.

I say, "Well, you both signed the lease, but let me see what I can do. We'll need to find you another roommate."

The next morning, Moise comes in, and we sit down to talk.

Moise says, "Do you know how it is to live with him?" Of course, he means Joseph. And I don't, so I can only listen. "Yesterday, he took our house phone with him to the library."

I am puzzled. "Why would he do that?"

Moise goes on. "You know, I have a full-time job now, and I wanted a better phone for the apartment. So, I went and bought one, and it is a cordless phone. When I brought the phone home, I showed it to Joseph and explained to him that it only works in the apartment. That it is not a cell phone. But he did not believe me, I think.

"So, he said to me, 'I am expecting an important call from Africa tomorrow.'

"And I said, 'That's fine—you can use my phone.'

"But imagine, in the morning, I woke up, and there was no Joseph nor phone in the apartment. At first, I thought that Joseph or I had misplaced it, and I looked and looked. But in the evening, when I came home from work, the phone was back in its place. I asked Joseph, 'Did you take the phone with you this morning?'

"And he said, 'I told you that I needed the phone—that I was waiting on an important phone call.'

"Then, I asked Joseph, 'And how about your important phone call? Did your call come in?'

"'No,' he said.

"And I told him, 'And do you know why? Because I told you that this is not a cell phone. It will not work outside the house!'"

I think that what Joseph did sounds unusual, but it takes time to learn all the new things. Then, Moise goes on, "And you know that he lost his job in the factory, don't you?"

I say, "Yes, in fact, I am looking for something new for Joseph. Maybe a cafeteria job this time…"

Moise says, "Okay, but let me tell you how it happened. When he got hired, the managers told Joseph that he is on probation time for three months and that he has to call in if he is sick and cannot make it to work. But Joseph just did not want to go to work every day, no. So, one morning, we went to the library, and at 12:00 p.m., I told him, 'Let's get going, or we'll be late for work.'

"We have to be at work at 3:00 p.m. for the shift. And from our apartment, we have to catch the 1:30 p.m. bus to get to the factory on time.

"But Joseph said, 'No, you go ahead. I want to stay longer here. I have something really important to finish up.'

"Then, I said, 'If you don't get there on time, they may fire you. You'll be late for work. Remember what they said? That you are temporary, on probation.'"

"But Joseph said, 'Oh, no, we are in America now. They will not fire me like that. People are nice here. I will call and tell them that I cannot come in today because I need to stay in the library.'

"So, I left him at the library and went home. When I clocked in at the factory, the manager told me that Joseph had called in sick today.

"I said, 'I don't know, maybe he has a headache or something.'

"Then, the same thing happened the next day—he did not go to work, just called that he could not be there. And his job was really easy, just to stand at the line and watch the cookies and push those that were broken to the floor. Then, the next day, he was fired. Joseph was shocked, and I said, 'Joseph, you see, it is not like you thought. People have to work hard in America.' And I am worried about him now—how is he going to pay his part of the rent?"

I assure Moise that I will find a new job for Joseph soon, although I note to myself that I first need to talk to Joseph again about work discipline.

I ask Moise, "Do you think you could still live together until your lease is over?"

"Sorry," he says. "It is not just his job and the telephone. You know, a volunteer donated a little TV to Joseph. And he watches it himself quite fine, but when I want to watch something, he touches the top of the TV and says, 'Oh, it is heating up too much now. I am afraid it will explode.' And he switches it off or even takes it away in his room. And when I explain things to him, like how to flush the toilet or how to get water in the shower, he would not listen. He is stubborn, too. I cannot live with a roommate like that. No. One of us has to go."

The roommate situation seems beyond repair, so I better start thinking about new arrangements. We agree that I will talk to Joseph as well, and then I will need time to find him another apartment. Since it was Moise's apartment before Joseph arrived, it would be fair that Moise stays and Joseph moves.

Next, I have a meeting with Joseph, and I hear his story about living with a roommate like Moise. "He pushed me," Joseph says. "And he dropped my bath towel in the commode, just because I forgot to put it back on the towel rack after shower!"

It sounds to me that Joseph is also ready for a new roommate, too. When both slighted parties have gone back to their shared apartment, I scroll all of the refugee names in my head. Who could use a roommate? I stop at Andre, whose roommate recently moved out of town. Yes, I will have to call Andre.

After initial chitchat, I ask him, "What do you think about having a roommate? That would save you quite a bit of money, since he would pay half of the rent and utilities."

Andre says, "Let me think about it."

The next day, Andre calls me back. "Who is the guy you were talking about?"

I tell him about Joseph and the situation, and Andre agrees. Then, I call Joseph. "How about moving in with Andre for a while?"

Joseph is happy about the solution. Andre helps Joseph take his things over to the new place, and now Moise lives by himself again, and Joseph has a new roommate. I assume that they are getting along alright, since I do not hear from either one of them.

One day, I run across Andre when I am walking around in the apartment complex where they live. I ask him how things are going.

"Everything is going alright," he says, "but, oh … well, I wanted to ask you something."

"Okay, what is it?"

"You know, that new guy, Joseph, brought some strange device home, and I want to know if it will use up a lot of electricity. I don't want to pay too high electric bills."

I ask him what the "thing" is, and from the description I hear, it must be a microwave oven.

"No, I don't think so," I tell him. "It can even save you electricity if you use it instead of the stove top for warming your food up."

"Are you sure?" Andre sounds serious.

"Yes," I assure him. "Every house here has a microwave, or almost every one."

Andre looks relieved, and we both go our own ways. Another "little issue" is solved, and I can get back to the job search.

Nick Kloster

Nick Kloster

Faces of The Democratic Republic of Congo: Kiza Biringanine (top) came to the US in 2014, after sixteen years in Nyarugusu Refugee Camp in Tanzania. She works full-time and is a full-time college student, as well. Storyteller Ali Mitachi (bottom) stands with his wife, Miriam, and their children in their back yard. They arrived in the US in summer of 2007.

CHAPTER 6

Stories from "The Big Congo," Part I

Since the opening of the IRC office in Abilene, more than two hundred refugees from the Democratic Republic of Congo have arrived and settled in this town. While other refugee groups have come in "waves"—that is, the resettlement started as a response to some specific emergency and afterwards the program closed down—Congolese resettlement had started years before our Abilene office opened. It is still ongoing more than ten years later. Our first Congolese refugees came in March and April of 2004. They were from various ethnic groups, except the Banyamulenge Tutsis, whose resettlement started only in 2007. I have dedicated

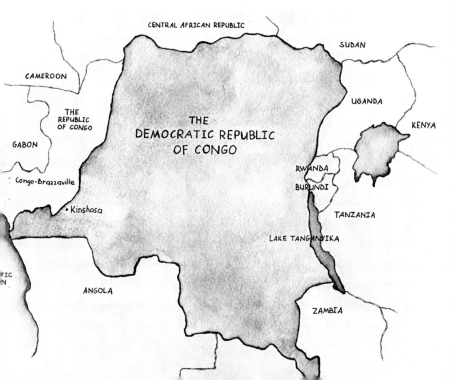

a separate chapter to them, since this distinct cultural group has often been marginalized by the government of the Democratic Republic of Congo and sometimes by other Congolese for not being "true Congolese," a situation that led to their resettlement to the US.

The Democratic Republic of Congo (or so-called Congo-Kinshasa, Congo DR, or "The Big Congo") is the second largest country in Africa. It is the home of about two hundred ethnic groups. It has a wealth of natural resources, including diamonds and many rare metals, a fact that obviously attracts the attention of various military groups and rebel formations who fight over access to this great wealth. Ethnic conflicts add to the fight for resources and power in certain areas of Congo, and armed conflicts seem never to stop. Neighboring countries often provide military aid to one or another side, and that's why political observers note that the country is not just perpetually waging a civil war but has been the center of "Africa's world war" for decades. Rwanda, Uganda, Zambia, Angola, Hutu militias from Rwanda, Mai Mai militias, and the M23 rebel group are among those involved in the fighting.

Congolese seek refuge in neighboring countries: many live in Kenya, some in Burundi, Rwanda, and Uganda. Civilians cannot feel safe anywhere in Congo DR, especially in the eastern provinces of South and North Kivu. While peace-keeping missions maintain a constant presence in the country, their help is minimal because the country is large and their resources are quite limited. So, the way out is to seek refuge status and hope for resettlement to another country.

Mado: "Fitting in the Circle"

Mado calls me to get directions to my office, since it is her first visit here. I stand by my window overlooking the parking lot and see her car approaching. After Mado parks the car and gets out, I wave to her and rush out to meet her in the lobby. Then, we settle down on the sofa to chat, and Mado starts her story. She is okay with her story being recorded.

I have known Mado since February of 2005, when our office resettled her and her family. She arrived from Ivory Coast with her uncle, her two younger sisters, and her cousin. Mado was a teenager then. Since I worked in the employment department then, for me, Mado was just "another child in the household whose school schedule had to be considered" when looking for jobs for the adults.

Eight years later, in 2013, Mado accepted a job at the IRC office as a case worker assistant, and I met her again. I was surprised to see that the teenager Mado, whom I had barely known, had turned into a dynamic young woman, optimistic and cheerful. I knew that Mado's parents had passed away a long time ago and that she had lived in Ivory Coast with her uncle, who was Mado's mother's sister's husband. Mado's aunt was not with them (she had somehow ended up living in Great Britain). Mado went to college at the University of Texas at Arlington, and during her study years, she had developed a close relationship with a foster family here in Abilene. Since those college days, Mado has graduated, started working, and leads a successful, independent life. But now, Mado is here, and she starts her story.

MY NAME IS MADO. I remember my first day in the United States very clearly. It was a very cold day—we arrived in February. We lived at Fairmont Apartments at that time, and I remember waking up there from some noise coming from outside. I thought I was still in Africa, and I looked out of the window: somebody was cleaning the road with a machine that was making so much noise that it woke me up. It was very cold outside, and everything was totally different.

The first person I remember was the volunteer who came to our house. His name was Gary, and I am sure you know him; he was everywhere. When Gary was speaking to me, somehow we could communicate, although I did not know any English. I was speaking French and he was trying to understand what I was saying. It was much easier with him, and I don't know how it happened, but he could talk to me and I could talk to him, even though we spoke different languages.

I remember how we walked to Walmart to buy groceries and how we carried all the grocery bags on our heads on the way back as we had no car, and people were looking at us. We soon met other refugee families who had come here before us, and it was pretty exciting to see them and hear how they were getting on in the new place. They were the happy moments! But the whole new system of living in America and trying to make new friends was a little difficult.

We were refugees from the Democratic Republic of Congo, but we came to the United States from Ivory Coast. We used to live in Abidjan, the capital city of Ivory Coast, before we came. We did not live in a refugee camp; we just lived there in our own house. And I enjoyed Ivory Coast, because it was a place where I grew up, and it felt like home to me. I was just six years old when I moved to Ivory Coast, but we could not go back to Congo because of the war. I went to school in Ivory Coast, and my entire youth was there; I had a lot of friends around me. I liked it, although life was a little bit challenging at times.

I was very excited when we found out that we would be coming to America. I was happy to go! As little kids, we used to play a game where we each had to pick a country we liked most, and then other kids would call you by the name of that country. And every kid always wanted to be "The United States of America." We used to say that America was the most powerful country of the world, and we always watched the movies about America—all these things—so I was very excited that I would have a chance to go. And also the coup d'état had taken place in Ivory Coast, so it was scary to stay there. But I also felt sad to leave our church and my friends. I wished that I could take them with me. Otherwise, we would be moving on, but they had to stay…But overall, I was more happy than sad.

I remember how we found out that we were going. It was in our church; our uncle was the pastor there, and he informed the whole church that "his family was going to the United States." He never told us children in advance; we just found out about it in church with everybody else. He was the kind of person who would not tell you anything while things were still in process. But when we got approved, he told to everyone in the church and us, also. When he found out the exact day of leaving, he just told us, "We are leaving on this day. Start packing."

That's how we found out exactly what day we were leaving. And I was like, "Oh, I guess we are leaving for real, then!" He did not tell us anything before because I think he was very conservative and wanted to keep things to himself. He did not like to tell people what was going on. And not everybody had to know that we were applying for the refugee program, so he kept it quiet until the very end, when he really knew that we were approved and going.

When I think about it, I realize that it is an African thing, too. When you want to do something, you are always afraid that somebody could do something against it and ruin it, so you actually do not talk much about your plans in advance. In this way, you are able to achieve things you have intended. I am different; if I know something is about to happen, I always share it with all my family and friends. I tell my closest people, those who help me in the process. Like, when I applied for college, I talked about it to all my friends and the people who helped me.

But before coming here as refugees, we all had to go through resettlement interviews: my uncle, his daughter, and me with my two little sisters. I remember our interviewer was a huge African-American guy. He was so big that when I looked at him, I felt very intimidated—oh, my God! I was very scared. And my uncle had told me beforehand, "Tell him everything, and look at him when you speak."

And that made it even scarier. The interviewer was a big man, he had his eyeglasses on, and we had to face him—so, yes, it was intimidating. He started asking us questions, like why exactly we wanted to go to America, and he asked about our biological parents and what happened to them. I told him that my parents passed away; they had died, and we were living with our uncle. And my little sisters started crying, and I cried with them. The interviewer started crying with us.

Then, it took quite a long time after that to receive approval. I do not remember how long it was exactly, but I recall my uncle complaining that he was not in America yet because of us—blaming us for that. He said that he had to wait with us, although his brother and sisters were in America already. The immigration office did not want him to go with us because he was not our official legal guardian, but my aunt—my mom's sister who was his wife—was in England. We had to wait for a really long time; then, finally, they said that we could go with him because we were underage, minors.

Then, the day came when we had to travel. We were going in that big plane, just like we had seen in the movies on TV, with all these air hostesses coming to you and asking what you wanted to drink and eat...for me, it seemed so unreal. You know, I saw all those Caucasian—or African-American or European—women offering me things, asking me questions. It was like in a movie! I remember I was asking for water, but I did not know how to say it in English, and they kept bringing me different drinks—Coke, coffee—but I kept saying, "No, sorry, I don't want Coke."

Then, they brought me coffee, and I was saying, "No, no, I don't want any coffee."

Then, somebody who spoke English and French interpreted for me, and the flight attendant said, "Oh, I see, she wanted water." And then I got my water. I guess it was hard on the flight attendant; she kept going back and forth until we got it. It was very interesting.

But the flight was a great experience, and we landed in New York. I saw snow for the first time. For me, it was something unbelievable. I had seen it on TV, and I wanted to touch it, but I could not because we were in the airplane. Then, in New York, the airport was so huge that we did not even know where we were. We could see a lot of people walking around, and we went to a hotel. I remember the lady who was taking care of us. She was one of the people helping in the hotel, bringing us food and drinks. She kept talking very fast, and it was in English, so I had no idea what she was saying. I was just nodding, "Yes, yes." It was very funny.

I remember that I was watching TV that was switched on to the Disney Channel, and since then, we have all fallen in love with the Disney Channel. It was a young African-American girl on the show, and we've liked this show since then. It was a good experience.

I am happy with my life now. I am twenty-three years old and have a degree. I am enjoying it, and I am happy. I feel I have achieved a lot. And I always tell the younger kids in the African community that they can do it, too. And I am proud to hear that their parents tell them, "Look at Mado. She went to school, and now she has graduated, has a degree, and has a good job." I feel good that the parents look up to me as a role model for their kids, that my achievements set an example for them. I think that the youth are also looking up to me.

I am proud to be an American, and I am proud of what I have achieved, given the things I have been through. I did not let those things bring me down; instead, I focused on what I wanted to achieve. I am working, I have my degree, and I am planning to go back to school for a master's degree. And I have a great American family that takes me as their daughter.

My foster family has helped me a lot, especially in my freshman year in college, when I was just by myself and I had nobody there yet. They were supportive until I graduated, and even now. I needed their support because when I was living with my uncle, he did not want me to go to college after I graduated from high school. He wanted me to stay here in town, but my main focus was to go to a four-year university outside of Abilene. It was challenging, as my uncle was not helping at all and I had to do everything myself.

No, it was not easy. I remember calling him and asking for money to buy my college textbooks and school stuff after I was admitted to UT in Arlington, but he pretty much rejected me. I was the kid in college with nobody, all by myself. I was just waiting on financial aid to come in, and it was pretty challenging until the foster family found out what was going on and stepped in. They started helping me out. My freshman year was very hard because of what was going on in the family. When it came to academics, I was okay because I received a lot of support: I had tutors, people who came to help with homework, and I could use the library, so I was passing all my class tests. And overall, I had done well in high school; the only thing that had been difficult was the TAKS test [the standardized test all students must take in Texas before graduating from high school].

This test was hard for all refugee community kids. We did well in classes, but we had no experience with that type of testing. You know, American kids start taking those tests when they are really young, like in elementary school or in middle school. But for us, we were already in high school but had never taken those tests, so we had so much pressure on us and we did not know what to do. We were all studying hard, but the actual test was completely different from what we had studied. More common sense questions, I think.

But I loved high school. If I could go back to high school, I would go back anytime! We had great teachers at Abilene High School, where I was a student. My new experience with school was very different from the one in Ivory Coast. The first thing was that big yellow bus, the school bus. That was different; we had never seen a bus like that before. Also, the time we went to school was different. In Ivory Coast, we went to school in the morning, maybe 8:30 or 9:00 a.m. Then, we came back home at noon, and after lunch break, went back to school at 1:00 or 2:00. After that, we stayed in school until 5:00 p.m. or 5:30 p.m. If we had any school activities to do, we stayed even later. But here, we had to go very early in the morning—like, the bus picked us up around 7:00 or 7:15 a.m., and the school was over around 3:00 p.m. This schedule seemed very different.

Also, the food in the cafeteria; I remember I'd never eaten pizza, and none of us Africans ate pizza when we first came here. You have to present Africans with chicken or a hamburger: at least they can see the meat. But pizza, what is that? But later, I got used to pizza, although some of the other African students did not eat it. So, the food was different.

And something else was different, too: here, we saw other kids kissing in school. Back home, you would not see it, and if anybody tried, the teacher would say right away, "Get out of my class," or,

"Bring your parents." But here, it seemed to be okay, and I was very surprised. It was like, "Oooh," you know?

Another thing that was different from Ivory Coast was that here, we did not have to wear uniforms at school. In Ivory Coast, we had uniforms, and I hated them. Everybody could tell from your uniform if you were in fifth grade or sixth grade or any other grade; it was easy to place you. Other students would look down on you if you were in a lower grade, not in high school yet. So, I liked it better here because we could just wear our normal clothes, and nobody would know what grade we were in.

The system in school is different in the United States. I think everybody can be successful here if they want, especially when it comes to school. Back home, it is really difficult; you really have to study. But here, they give you all resources for your studies. The teachers give you everything you are meant to know for the exam. Over there, you are on your own, and you have to study from the beginning until the end of the year and find everything yourself. So, if you don't have notes from school, you are in trouble. But here, you get materials ahead of time.

Also, in Ivory Coast, we had to pay for school. And if we did not pay, we could not go to school. They would kick you out. And school was quite expensive. I remember one time we did not have enough money, and we could not go. I've loved school since I was a little kid, and I remember that when they kicked us out because we had no money, I went back the next day. I just wanted to be in school, and I could not understand why they did not let me come just because of money. School tuition fees were quite expensive, plus we had to buy our own uniforms as well. We could not wear just anything. As we were not able to attend for some time, it put us behind other kids because if we did not attend classes, we did not have any materials to study from, no notes, while everybody else had everything from the class.

When the test results came out, they were posted on the board. All students' names were there, and we could see if we would go to the next year or not. But if you did not see your name, it meant that you had to repeat the year again. That was another challenge that came with not being able to pay for school. Everybody else in school could see if your name was or was not on the board; that was pushing all kids to study harder. We had a time when we had to stay at home one semester because of money. We missed the semester right before we were coming here to live.

What I like about the United States is that here, we as women have the freedom to do whatever we intend to. We have the right to speak our minds, we can go to work if we want, and it is not always like that in other countries. In Ivory Coast or Congo DR, women stay at home if their husbands have well-paid jobs and tell them to stay at home. The woman will take care of the house and the kids, and that's pretty much it. Some of the women probably would not go to school because they have married very young and had kids, so they stay at home. But here, women have the opportunity to get education and focus on being independent. Back in Ivory Coast, it was very different, and quite a few women are without education because of having married early. The parents would also push their daughters to get married quickly.

In the US, women get married because they want to, but in Africa, it happens because your parents may not have the money to send you to school. Here, all education is free until you go to college. Also, you have financial aid here, and you may have to take loans, but at least you have a chance—you can get scholarships and financial aid, so it is easier. But in Africa, we don't have that much support. Mostly, if your parents have money, they would send you to Europe or America to study, but the parents who do not have the money try to get their daughters married off as soon as they can because they do not have the money to send them to school. And then it is just "make kids, stay at home."

Here, one thing I was especially excited about was "fitting in the circle." Let me explain. When I went to the University of Texas at Arlington, the school had a very diverse community of students— white, black, Hispanic—so I did not have just Africans around me anymore. In high school in Abilene, we had our "African circle": I had all other African kids around me, and well, it was just Africans. We even had a table in the school cafeteria where we all sat for lunch, and nobody else would take our table. That table was "for African kids." We used to sit there together, do homework, and laugh and talk and stuff. We spoke French together—we always spoke French. It was fun. Sometimes, we started dancing, and all the other kids would stop and look and clap.

But when I went to college, it was completely different. I did not have an "African circle" anymore in college, so I started having more Caucasian friends, and I made friends with students from other countries. I had some Indian friends, friends from very far-away places—like Korea and China—and I was happy that I could fit in that circle. I do not think it was very hard to connect because I am a talkative person, bubbly, and if someone came to me, I always wanted to make friends. I was involved in organizations, in the dorm life, and it was exciting.

When I started dating, my first boyfriend was white, which I never thought would happen. That was so exciting to me: "Oh, gosh, I am dating a white person!" It was very different, and when I came with him to visit my friends here in Abilene, other people in the African community were in a shock: "Mado, are you dating a white guy? Seriously?"

Nobody was expecting it, I guess. And some people did not approve; they would rather see me going out with somebody from our African community. I had a friend in college who had an issue with her parents about the same thing: they did not approve of her dating a white guy. They told her, "Stop seeing this guy right now, or you are coming back home." She was from Nigeria, and she had to stop. All I can say is that some people take interracial dating very seriously, but some others are more relaxed and say, "Whatever...do whatever makes you happy."

My foster parents often give me advice, and I listen to them a lot, but otherwise, I am pretty much on my own. And I know right from wrong. I have been independent since I was very young. But I take their advice because although I am American, deep down inside me, I am still an African. So, I try to be very careful. For example, in the African community, you cannot hold hands until you are married. And if other Africans saw me holding hands, they would ask, "Are you getting married?"

I have to be careful about the customs, although I am not in that African community anymore. And even if I am dating a person out-side that community, I still have to consider those African customs, things that I really cannot do. Like, I cannot be kissing around, you know. I still have to respect those things that are different. Like, I cannot wear shorts, cannot show my legs outside my home. When I tried once, one of the Africans asked me, "Why are you in shorts? What do you mean?" The African mentality is, "Who's going to marry you if you show your legs off to everybody?" And if I want to work out, I have to wear pants, not shorts.

I still have my friends' parents who take me as a daughter, like Clemence, who always says, "Mado, just be careful. Don't do this, don't do that." My friends' parents always tell me what to do and what not to do, and they always encourage me. They advise me as if I were their own daughter, and I take their advice.

But as for my uncle, I have not spoken to him since I went away to college, so it has been almost five years. But even when we were together, he would never talk to me like a father would. He was always quick to punish if we did something wrong, but he would never sit down and talk to us in a positive way, like, "Hey, this is what you are supposed to do as a woman, and this is good."

Now, I live by myself, I have my own apartment, and my foster parents helped me set it all up. I have a small place for myself. I am an adult woman now. My younger sisters are doing well: my youngest sister is in Cisco College, and she is on their soccer team, although she is trying to transfer to Arlington. And the middle sister is in university in Wichita Falls. She wants to be a lawyer and is in the criminal justice program. They used to live together with another foster family. We are keeping in touch; we talk very often.

But in the future, I want to go back for a master's program and get a master's degree in teaching. I would like to teach African students ESL when they come. And of course, I want to get married sometime in future. Now, I have a Hispanic boyfriend, and his family is from California. With time, maybe I can open an orphanage for kids in a country where they need the most support. I just want to give back to the community, to all those people who helped me and my sisters, and the best way to do it would be to do something for a country where there is a need. I am not sure what country it would be—it could be anywhere in Africa, but it could be somewhere else just as well, like in Haiti.

November 2013

Ali: "Life Has Been Good to Us"

Ali is a Congolese refugee and has agreed to tell his story. He would rather not get recorded, so I will take notes.

Ali and his family came to the US in the summer of 2008. I do not know exactly what ethnic group he is from, but I know for sure that he does not look like Banyamulenge Tutsis, although he was born and grew up in the eastern part of Congo, which traditionally has been "Banyamulenge land." He is in his midthirties, and overall, has done very well in the US. He has a good career at a hotel where he recently has been promoted to a team leader's position in the maintenance department, and he has started college to acquire credentials for the job. His wife, Miriam, has a production job, and they have recently bought a house that was built with the help of Habitat for Humanity.

Ali and Miriam's children are doing well. I believe the oldest one, Rejoice, must be about eight or nine now, and two more children were born after the family came to the US. They are all in good health, so what else could you desire from life? Ali truly wants to integrate into American society and enjoys the opportunities this country provides. He often helps other newly arrived countrymen and women adjust and learn their way in the new culture. While many refugees do not venture outside their ethnic community and often are shy about speaking English, Ali's English is fluent. He takes pride in work and education and does not side with those who advocate relying on food stamps.

I AM FROM CONGO-KINSHASA, OR some people may know it by name of "Zaire." That was the old name of the country. You need to know that Congo has 453 tribes and 455 languages. Most of the time, all these tribes live in peace, although at times, we have had war. My native language is Kibembe, and I am from the Hutu tribal group, but the name of my tribe is Babembe. We do not have many people here from my tribe. I can speak several languages: Lingala, Swahili, French, and now English.

When I was a child, my family used to live in the countryside in a village, and my parents had other children, not just me. We were from Suima, a small place not far from Ngovi in Fizi territory. And Fizi is in the South Kivu province in the eastern part of Congo. My parents were quite poor; they were working fields and had some goats and chickens. But overall, it was village life.

The best thing for me was that a Christian organization called Compassion stepped in and helped seventy children with school fees, clothing, and school supplies. I was among those seventy children. I don't know exactly why or how they selected me, but they did, and I could attend school. Otherwise, I am not sure if my parents would have had the money to pay for my schooling because school is not just the fees. You have to get the uniform and books as well, and we as a family could survive, but cash was very hard to earn.

So, I attended school, and I was done with primary school and already in high school when the war came. The high school was in a little bit bigger place, in a more developed village where about five hundred or up to one thousand people lived. When fighting started in our area, people got in kayaks and went across the lake to Tanzania. We also went, and it was already nighttime and dark when we were in the boats. The shooting and fire came right across us. I did not realize then how dangerous it was, but later, my dad told us about it, how close we were to being hit by bullets.

In Tanzania, we were hiding in the bush for about two weeks, living like that and watching what would happen. Other people were doing the same, and then we heard from others that help had arrived, that people could go to a refugee camp, so we went and got registered, and we were taken to Nyarugusu refugee camp.

They gave us a tent to live in and started giving out some food, but the food was really poor, just beans or peas, and this was all we got. There was no school at first, but after some months, they started a school. School was just very simple: students were gathered under open skies, and the teachers were other refugees who did the teaching as volunteers. As we had no building, we could not meet for school on days when it was raining. The war started in 1996, and that was the year we went to Nyarugusu. We lived like that for about two years. I was a teenager at that time, and I was really eager to get an education and go to school. I was very frustrated with the camp and the way schooling went there. But the main thing was that time was going on, but nothing better was coming; things were not changing.

One day, I decided to go back to our area in Congo to see if I could get a better schooling. From what people were telling us, it seemed like things had calmed down in South Kivu area in Congo at that time, but my parents were cautious and did not want to leave the camp yet. So, one day or night, I sneaked out and went back to Congo. My parents did not know what happened to me after that. I went back to Uvira, a town in South Kivu, and I was trying to register in school when the war started back again. Everybody went running, and I fled with others. The fighters had burned down Makobola village, hundreds of people were killed, and to get away, we had to cross the Makobola River, which was right next to that village. It was a very dangerous crossing because fighters were there and were shooting everyone trying to go across. But to escape, we had to go.

I was really lucky—God saved us—because the group who tried to get across before us were all killed, and then the group after us, they were killed, too, but we escaped. We thought that maybe we got lucky, as the fighters had gone for something or were taking rest, but I don't know for sure. But we got across and went on to Kalemie first and then on to Zambia. When I got to Zambia, I tried to go on, as I did not want to stay in Zambia. I met a driver who had a big truck, and he said he could take me. He was going to Zimbabwe, so I went with him as far as he was going. That's how I found myself in Zimbabwe in the end.

At first, I walked for many weeks with many other people—Congo, Zambia, we just walked and walked, on and on. We could find some food in abandoned fields, we dug up cassava root and made it into food, and also we could go in people's houses that were abandoned and look for something to eat, so somehow, we survived.

When I reached the border of Zambia with many other people who were fleeing, the border guards let us across. Some people stayed in Zambia, but many went on, and I went with them. When the truck took me into Zimbabwe, it was the end of my journey. I ended up in Mutare refugee camp. For a while, I lived in the camp, but then I went to live in town to be able to go to school. This camp was really good; we had good food, good housing. We shared the house with three other boys—or, I should say, young men—about my age. The school was good, too, and after I finished it, they sent me to a technical school in town. I was really interested in that.

Back in the camp, everything was going well, except my family did not know anything about me or what had happened to me after I had gone back to Congo. I tried to contact them, but I was in Zimbabwe and they were in Tanzania, so it was not easy. I let them know that I was alive and got news from them. But we could not talk on the phone or anything like that. I went to see them last year, and they told me that after I left to Congo, they thought that I had been killed at Makobola, and they were preparing to have funeral service for me.

I spent several years in this camp in Zimbabwe, and it took about three or four years to go through the refugee process (interviews and such). Not all people got this chance. I think God helped me, and maybe the interviewers liked that I was so focused on school. 2004 was when the interviews started, and then the second interview was in 2005, and then I got approved. I got married about that time.

I met my wife Miriam in the camp. I saw her, and we started talking, and we liked each other and started dating. I moved back to the camp while interviewing was going on and also to be closer to her. We got married soon after, and our firstborn, Rejoice, was born in Mutare camp in Zimbabwe.

The United States has been good to us. Miriam has been a wonderful wife to me, and I am sure she has her own story to tell. She has been of great help and encouragement to me. When we came to the US, the IRC and you helped us a lot. We had a good apartment, and you helped us find our first jobs. I started at the MCM Elegante Hotel as a groundskeeper and worked there for a while. Then, they had an opening in the mechanical department, and I moved to that department, mostly because I like that type of work and my education was in technical things.

After some time there, the supervisor from the mechanical department left, and my manager offered me a promotion. I was not sure about myself because it was a job with more responsibility, and Miriam was the one who told me that I could do it. I took her advice and accepted the job. My supervisor, Joanne, told me that I could do it, but at that time, I was not sure. But after talking it over at home with Miriam, I knew that I wanted to try. Now, I can say that it has worked out very well; I know that I am doing the job just fine.

I am attending Cisco College now, and I want to finish HVAC specialty and get certification for it. I am going that direction. Also, we have a good house now, and we are all enjoying it. The Habitat for Humanity program gave us this opportunity. So, life has been really good to us.

February 2015

Nick Kloster

Nick Kloster

*Faces of Banyamulenge Tutsis: Storyteller Berthe Kanyabitabo (top) has
recently reunited with her daughter, Angelique, after being separated
for thirteen years. Adrien Nkurunziza (bottom), originally from the
Democratic Republic of Congo, came to the US in 2009. He has become a
well-known singer of African gospel music.*

118

CHAPTER 7

Stories from "The Big Congo," Part II: Banyamulenge Tutsis

Richard comes by my office today to check on his dad's paperwork, and somehow, we start talking about his old homeland—the Democratic Republic of Congo, or the so-called Big Congo. Richard is a young man

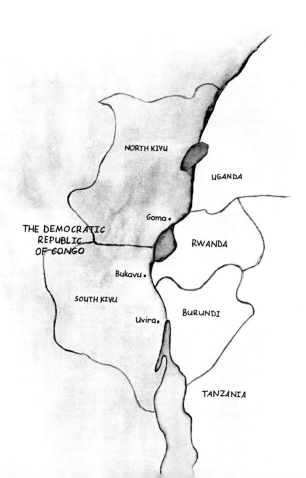

who belongs to the Banyamulenge Tutsi ethnic group living in the eastern part of Democratic Republic of Congo—namely, in the North and South Kivu provinces. Banyamulenge Tutsis have a very distinctive culture and traditions and a love for land, cattle, and pastoral life. It is quite unfortunate that wars and fighting have plagued their Kivu lands for several decades, and some of the conflict may be attributed to the presence of natural resources, including diamonds.

As we are chatting about this and that, he brings up the subject of diamonds. Yes, you heard me right—diamonds. He tells me that the area around his former hometown of Kalemie is known for its wealth of diamonds, and people can easily find these precious stones almost anywhere, lying on the ground or even in topsoil. What is more, North Kivu province, just north of Kalemie, is even richer. Richard's "diamond story" is a good introduction to the political situation in eastern Congo, so I decided to share it here.

WHY DO YOU THINK Congo has been at war for so many years? It is because everybody is after the diamonds, especially in both of the Kivu provinces, which are our—the Banyamulenge—part of the country. This is really the right place to look for diamonds, and it is easy to find them there. When you find a diamond for the first time, you may not even know that you have it; it just looks so much like a simple stone. If you have it and want to sell it right there in Congo, you will not get much for it because diamonds are everywhere. But if you take your diamond across the border to Rwanda, the price goes up right away. It is different in Rwanda.

Sometimes, cattle can dig up diamonds while they are grazing. My uncle told me this story about a farmer who my uncle personally knew. It could have happened to anybody in Congo. But the story is like this: that man's cows were grazing in the pasture, and they were slowly moving here and there. The pasture area was rolling hills, up and down. The cattle were going down a little hill, and when cows go downward, they tend to dig their hooves into the soil deeper than when they are going up—to keep their balance, I think. So, one of the cows dug her hooves in the dirt and kind of got stuck. She could not pull her hoof out of the mud.

The man—the owner—came to see what was going on. He helped the cow to get her hoof out, and he saw that something was stuck between the claws of the hoof, like a big piece of mud. The man loosened it up to get it out, and it was a large stone covered in mud. Then, the man started looking at it, checking and cleaning, and it turned out to be a large diamond, alright! It just needed a good cleaning and washing, but otherwise, it was really big and nice. Then, the man took that diamond to Rwanda to sell because he could get a better price there. You may not believe me, but this is how it really happened. My uncle told me about it.

And it could have happened just about anywhere in Congo, as lots of diamonds just lay there hidden in the ground, and often they are really close to the surface. When people make roads and level the ground and take the top layer of soil off to spread the dirt, they get some loose stones and pebbles, and there is a good chance they will find some diamonds. You just have to know a little bit about how to tell them apart from stones. Often, they do not look like the diamonds you see in pictures or movies—they are covered in mud. Even kids sometimes find diamonds when they go swimming in a lake or a river. The diamonds will be right there in the sand on the bank, washed up by waves and wind. I have seen myself how people go looking in lakes and rivers: they walk slowly in shallow water with sieves in their hands and scan the water. If there was nothing to it, they would not be doing it.

So, I think Congo would be a good place to try your luck with diamonds. I just need to find out more about the paperwork that is needed to bring them into the US. And now, when my dad has come here, we could do it as business together.

February 2014

BANYAMULENGE TUTSIS ARE OFTEN marginalized as those who are "not true Congolese," a statement used by government militias to provoke ethnic conflicts and drive Banyamulenge Tutsis out of their area. The generally known fact that Banyamulenge Tutsis are related to Rwandan Tutsis serves as an excuse to claim that the Banyamulenge "do not belong in Congo" since they are "just Rwandese who migrated to Kivu areas some time ago," implying that they could just as easily "go back."

As one of my Banyamulenge Tutsi storytellers remarked, "They say we are not Congolese, but I do not know any other country." This often sums up the "refugee experience" in general. You are expelled from your own homeland for one reason or another. Due to constant rebel attacks and ongoing fighting in the Kivu provinces, large numbers of Banyamulenge people have moved to neighboring countries to find peace. Many of them live in Rwanda or Burundi, and some have moved to Kenya, Ethiopia, or even gone as far as India.

The Gatumba Camp Massacre in August of 2004 in Burundi, which left around two hundred Banyamulenge people dead and hundreds more injured, accelerated Banyamulenge Tutsi resettlement to the US and Canada. Different sources blame different military groups for this hate crime, but there are no clear answers; nobody has been tried for these attacks. There is little doubt that Banyamulenge Tutsis were the intended victims because only their part of the camp came under attack.

After news about this atrocity reached the world, UNHCR approached refugees from this group and started resettlement preparations. The first Banyamulenge refugees came to the US and Canada in 2007, which was the same year we also resettled around a hundred refugees from the Banyamulenge Tutsi group in Abilene. Although the main resettlement was over by the end of 2008, a few more families are resettled every year.

Jolie: "Social Work, Again?"

One day, my cell phone rings, and it is Jolie. Jolie is a young woman from the Banyamulenge Tutsi group who was resettled to Austin, Texas in 2007, when she was a teenager. The family moved to Abilene in 2010. I am surprised that she has my cell phone number, since we have had only a business relationship at the IRC office, but here she is on my cell wanting to know how to apply for a job at the IRC. When I tell her that I am no longer with the IRC, she is surprised and exclaims, "Why? You should have stayed!"

It turns out that Jolie has applied for a job there but has not heard back from the IRC for more than a month. Now, she is concerned that her application may have not been received at all. Jolie is a college student majoring in social work and is very interested in refugee case management. I advise her how to follow up.

Then, she asks me what I am doing now, and I explain to her that I am putting together a book of refugee stories. I ask her if she would like to share her story, and she says, "Yes, I would be happy to do that, but I live in Ranger now. I am in college in Ranger. But don't worry, I am coming home to visit my family this Friday, so I will be in Abilene and we can meet and talk."

Ranger is a small town about one and a half hours from Abilene, about halfway to Dallas on Interstate 20. So, when Friday comes, Jolie calls me in the morning.

"Hey, I am already in town. Can we meet now? I could come anytime."

Jolie arrives after half an hour. I notice her slowly driving around the parking lot of my office building, searching for the right entrance. I go outside to meet her. We hug each other after such a long time and settle down in my office to talk. It feels like meeting an old friend, although I have seen Jolie just once or twice in my life. I think it feels that way because of her warm personality. Jolie says that she is fine with having her story recorded.

MY NAME IS JOLIE, and I was born in the Democratic Republic of Congo in 1991. We used to live in the village when I was a child; yes, that's where we were. But by the time I turned seven, we moved to town. I do not remember much about life in the village, as I was very young then. I just remember a few things. I know my mom and my father used to work the land—they were farmers. And my grandma and grandpa, too. They had everything in their farms: fields, buildings, cattle, cows, all kinds of other farm animals, chickens, everything. They used to grow all we needed for food, or almost all.

I know that I lived with my mom and my dad in one house, and my grandpa lived in another house nearby. My uncles lived very close-by with their families. I remember that I used to know only my family members because we lived so close to each other, and we were so many people. That's how my tribe is; that's how we live. For example, all the people who are descendants of my great-grandfather—all his children—would build houses in the same place, very close to one another. The related families would live within about two to five minutes from one another. That's how we were doing it. That's what I remember best—that we were all close together.

I remember that when I was a little girl, we used to go for water from the well. This well was quite a long way from our house, or at least that's how I remember it. I used to go there with my aunt or with my mother. I was very young, so I had to go with somebody. And sometimes, we had to bring cassava home. If we went for cassava, my mom would go first to the field and get the cassava ready. She would put it together, and we had to go get it from her, as she could not do everything by herself. We had to fetch things we made fire with. I used to watch my mom and aunt doing it, but I did not do it myself. But I used to go with them and help them. When we went to fetch water, my mom or my aunt would give me a little bottle of water, so I could carry something, too.

The women used to carry water containers on their heads. They had really big vessels to carry, and they would carry them on their heads. It looked so pretty to me; I was amazed how they could balance the water containers just on their heads, without holding them with their hands. I wish I could do that, but I never learned how. We had these containers in three sizes: the big ones were for keeping in the house, the medium size you could carry, and the small ones for little kids. I was carrying the small one.

When I did not have chores to do, I used to be outside playing with other kids. We spent a lot of time outdoors. Then, I started going to school in the village. We were in Vyura village, and that's where my school was. My dad was a teacher, and I remember how I went to school my first year and how I learned not to be late. It happened like this.

One morning, I was sleeping. I was about six years old at that time. My dad tried to wake me up: "Wake up, Jolie, wake up, get ready, we need to go."

But I felt so sleepy that morning that I just mumbled, "Yeah, I am coming, I am coming," but I did not get up. And my dad left for school without me. Then, my mom tried to wake me up: "Wake up, time to go, your dad already left for school."

Then, I really got up and went. But when I got there, I was so late! I saw my dad waiting for me outside. That was not good because if we were late, the teachers would beat us with a stick. I saw my dad standing outside, waiting for me, and I thought, *Oh, my God, I am dying, I am dying!*

And I was thinking, *Should I go back home?*

But then, I thought, *No, if I go home, he's going to find me there, anyway, so let me just go on to school.* I started crying before I even reached him.

So, I was crying, and he asked, "Why are you crying?"

I said, "Because I am so scared!"

He asked, "Scared of what?"

"From getting a beating. I know you are going to beat me up."

I saw that he was holding a stick behind his back to hide it from me, and he told me, "Come here!"

I tried to plead for myself. "Dad, I am so sorry."

But he repeated, "Come here!"

And I said, "Dad, I am so sorry, sorry!"

As I was coming closer to him, he grabbed me by the hand and tried to beat me like that. But I turned around away from him, and he could not reach me with the stick. Then, he called the other teacher to come and help him. We had two elementary teachers in our school, grade A and B. So, he called the B teacher. My dad was holding me by one hand and the other teacher was holding my other hand. And my dad stepped on one of my feet and the B teacher stepped on the other. And he gave me a good beating.

Now, I know that it was mean of them, but I learned a lesson from it. I knew that I was not going to be late anymore. Because I knew that if I were late, the teachers would beat me up again. From then on, I was never late; I was the one who would wake my dad up: "Dad, time to get up, let's go to school." I was afraid of the beating.

Now, when I remember those days, I think that it was a good lesson to learn, although it was a beating. They did use a stick. I understand now that they tried to teach me a lesson, to tell me that I had to take school seriously, to teach me respect. You know, we had to pay for education in Africa. Parents had to pay for our school. So, your father paid money for you to go to school. But if you try to mess it up, play around instead of learn, they have to beat you up to tell you, "This is your father's money—don't mess with it. It is not a joke. You have to come to school and learn and be smart." I think that was the only reason they were beating us up.

When I was seven and a half years old, the war started. It was in 1998, and I do not remember who was fighting whom at that time. My family decided it would be safer in a city with other people from our tribe around us, so we moved from Vyura village to Uvira city, where many Banyamulenge people lived. We stayed in Uvira for quite a long time, I think about six years. Living in Uvira was okay, but in Africa, it is better to live in a village than in a city. In our village, we used to know everybody, and people did not try to cheat you in any way. But in the city, people tried to be smart and take advantage of you if you were not careful. But we had to go there to live for our safety. I went to school in Uvira for several years, I think until seventh grade. One thing I do remember from our Uvira days is when I went to visit my grandmother who lived in the mountains. It was in 2001, and I was about ten years old. That's when it happened.

In eastern Congo, we had a lot of mountains, and they were very pretty, those mountains, but very high, too. The problem was that you had to climb the mountains if you wanted to get somewhere in the mountains, as we did not have any cars that could drive up there, no roads there. So, you had to walk all the way. My grandmother—my mother's mom—lived high up in the mountains. I had been begging my mom for three years, "Mom, I want to go see my grandma. I want to meet her!" We often talked on the phone, but I did not know her in person. I had never seen her, as she used to live so high up in the mountains.

When I begged my mom to let me go see my grandma, she used to say, "No, Jolie, you cannot go to the mountains. It is too far, and the trip is too difficult for you."

But I kept repeating, "Let me try because I want to go see my grandma. I want to meet her." So, I kept asking my mom if I could go.

Finally, one day, my mom told me, "Okay, let me call your uncle. He will come here for you, and then you will go with him to see your grandma." It was summertime, and I did not have to be in school. I was very excited about my uncle coming to see us. "Oh, I will see my uncle! I will see my cousin!"

That uncle was my mom's brother, and he lived up in the mountains, close to my grandma. So, my uncle came, visited for a while, and then one day, he said, "Jolie, get ready. Tomorrow, we are leaving very early."

Oh, my gosh! We walked for many hours, climbing the mountains. Mountains and mountains! We went up one mountain, and then down, and then up another mountain and down again. After nine hours, I was so tired. "Uncle, uncle, are we there yet?"

But he shook his head. "No, we still have several more hours to go."

I was so exhausted that I sat down, and I asked him, "Could you go tell Grandma to come here to meet me? I cannot go any further!"

My uncle said, "You asked for it. You were the one who wanted to go!"

I said, "Yes, but I cannot go on, I am too tired."

Then, my uncle put me on his shoulders and carried me further. We kept going, and I was on my uncle's shoulders. We had left our house in Uvira at six in the morning, and we got to my grandma's house around eight or nine in the evening. It was about fourteen or fifteen hours walking nonstop, no rest. I remember while we were walking, my grandma called my uncle on the phone. "When are you going to get here? When are you going to get here?"

And my uncle said, "I think we are going to get to your house at ten or eleven."

My grandma said, "Do you want me to stay up till eleven?"

She said that because she used to go to bed early, at 9:00 p.m. or around that time.

My uncle said, "If you do not want to see your granddaughter, go to bed, then!"

My grandma said, "No, I cannot go to bed. I want to see her!"

When we finally got to my grandma's place, she was still awake, waiting on us. Oh, I remember it. She was so happy! She cried because it was her first time to see me. She cried with tears that night! And it was my first time to see her, too. I was ten years old, soon to turn eleven. So, we both cried. I was crying when I saw her, and she cried. I was not crying because I was sad, but I was crying because she was crying. She was crying and hugging me. We stayed up and talked for two hours. She was asking me so many questions. She was very old and could not remember things. You would tell her your name, and then after an hour or so, she would ask you again, "What's your name?"

And I would say, "Grandma, I just told you my name!"

She was asking me a lot of questions: what was my name, how old I was, how we were doing, and I was telling her all these things. Then, after a while, she would start over again: "What is your name? How many siblings do you have?" and like that.

My mom was her last born, and my grandma was quite old. She lived with her two sons—my two uncles—and my aunt, who was married to one of my uncles. They all lived close-by, high up in the mountains. But one thing that we do in our tribe is that grandparents often live with their grandchildren. Let's say, my grandma, she had two sons and three daughters, and they all had children, my cousins and me. And then when we got older, one of us would go and live with our grandma. It would not be right to let her live by herself without any help, especially if grandpa was not living anymore. One of her grandchildren would live with her.

And these days, she is very old, but she still calls my mom on the phone and they talk. My grandma would sometimes forget that she was talking on the phone and would just fall asleep while on the phone. My uncle would laugh. "Mom, wake up, you are talking on the phone!"

And she would wake up. "Hello?"

I think my grandma is in her nineties now. But the older uncle, the one who carried me, still lives with my grandma. The other uncle lives in Rwanda now.

But back then, I enjoyed my visiting with her. I was very happy and proud that I could make the trip. I helped them with milking cows and always went with them for milking. I stayed there for about a month because it was during summer break, and then I came back with my uncle again. Now, I feel like going to see her again. More than ten years have passed since that time, and I know more about life. I am grown up now. It is too bad that I cannot go back right now. I feel that I really want to go back, but I know it would be too expensive.

A couple of years after I came back from my grandma's visit, we started hearing about fighting again, and many people from our Banyamulenge tribe went to live in Burundi. It was in the summer of 2004. Our family followed the others to Burundi, and we settled in Gatumba camp with many other people from our tribe.

I was shot and injured while in that camp. It happened during the Gatumba Massacre on the night of August 13, 2004. The attack came in the middle of the night, while we were all sleeping in the camp. Our family—we were in our home. It was all quiet, and then all of a sudden, we heard people shouting and screaming, and we heard gunshots and saw fire blaze all around us. Armed men had gotten into the camp and were killing our people, shooting and setting houses on fire.

See, I don't even have my finger. Look at my arm where the skin is rough like that. I was injured there; a bullet went through it. It happened while I was sleeping, and I was holding my arms around me. I think I had embraced myself in sleep, and that really saved me. The bullet came here and went through my arm and my finger. My brother was injured, too. He was shot in the shoulder, but it was just a scratch. And my mom was injured, too. She was pregnant, then, just about two weeks from having a baby. She got shot in her stomach, and her injury was very serious. Imagine, she was pregnant, just two weeks from giving birth, and she got shot in the stomach. We all were saying, "Oh, my God, oh, my God, what's going to happen to the baby?" But the baby was fine.

After the initial attack, many of our people tried to escape. We did run, too. I was sleeping with my sister and brother in one bed when the shooting happened, and my mom was in the other bed. I remember hearing my dad yelling, "Get up, get up, if you are still alive, let's get out of here! If any of you are still alive, let's just run! We cannot stay here. They will come in and kill us all! Let's run!"

I told my dad, "Dad, I can't run, I got shot," but my dad said, "Jolie, try, please try, because you cannot stay here!"

My mom was not shot yet, so she helped me up and put some clothes on, and we got outside, ready to run. She said, "Please, be brave and stand up, and let's run. You are breathing, so let's just go."

My dad was in the front, holding my brother's hand, and he kept shouting, "Jolie, run behind your brother, don't stay. I know you are injured, but I plead you, follow us."

And I said, "Okay, Dad, I am coming!"

The attackers saw us running away, and they started shooting at us from the back. That's when they shot my mom, and she fell down. And I screamed, "Mom, are you okay?"

She said, "Yeah, I guess I am okay."

I shouted, "Mom, Mom, hold my hand, and let's keep running, we cannot stay!"

We were looking back now and then, and we saw the attackers following us, screaming, "Catch them, catch them, catch them!"

I said, "Oh, my God, Mom, I don't want them to catch us, let's just run, please!"

And she got up and ran, although she was wounded. We escaped like that. The attackers were following us, but we were running so fast that they could not catch us, and they gave up. Or at least, I felt that we were running very fast. Anyway, they did not catch us, no. When we got out of the camp, we ran in the bush and hid. While we were there, we saw a military jeep passing by.

We stood up and waved, "Please, help us! Help us! We need a doctor."

But they did not stop. Then, I saw one man approaching, shouting, "Is anybody alive? Is anybody alive?"

And we called out, "Yes, yes, we are here, please help us. We need help!"

And he helped us get out of there, and he took us to the hospital. He was one of our Banyamulenge people. He was just walking around, looking for people who may have survived the attack to help them. And he was on foot; he did not have a car or anything. And he came up to us and said, "Let's just be brave and walk to the hospital because there is no other way. I don't have a car. We don't have anything, but let's just go."

He helped us to get to the hospital. Yeah. But in the camp, about 160 people died that night, and 164 got injured. So, there were many people in the hospital who were injured and needed help. The hospital staff said, "We cannot treat so many people here. Let's take some to another hospital."

We told the hospital staff everything—how my mom was shot and injured, and that she was so close to having a baby—and they ran out fast and took her by ambulance to the city of Bujumbura. As she was pregnant and injured, they took her very fast. Yeah, and when she got to Bujumbura hospital, they found out the baby was fine. They treated her injuries and then waited for those two weeks, and then the baby came. It was my little sister, Louange. My mom and the baby were fine. And my mom stayed in hospital for two or three months—I think about that long. And then she was out.

But I stayed in the hospital for eight or nine months. They took me and a friend of mine to the other hospital in Bujumbura, in the city. It was a different hospital, not the one where they took my mom. They helped us a lot in that hospital. A bullet had hit my shoulder bone, and they had to take some muscle from my leg and put it over here, on the arm. They did many surgeries. And the hospital tried really hard to do everything right. They tried their best. While we were in hospitals here and there, my dad was around. He took care of my two sisters and my grandma. He was a pastor, and he had a church there. They all lived in an apartment in Bujumbura city. They had to wait because me, my mom, and my brother, we were all in hospitals.

After we all got out, we went to live in a different refugee camp in Burundi. It was called Mwaro refugee camp. By then, we were already in the process of coming to the US. And that's where we stayed for the next two years, from 2005 until 2007. Mwaro was a big camp; we were all Congolese there. We had people from three different tribes there, but it was only Congolese. I went to school there; we had a school. I think that UNHCR was helping with the school and food and everything there. Life was not really "*normal* normal," but we got help, and we went to school. So, it was not too bad.

Now when I think back about the attack, I still do not know why they attacked us. Why it was just people from our Banyamulenge tribe who were attacked. I think that one thing is that other people call us "Rwandan" because we speak the same language as Rwandan people. It is not exactly the same language, but we understand one another. And we, Banyamulenge, look a lot like Rwandans—there is almost no difference. And the language, overall, is the same. Other Congolese used to call us "Tutsis," you know. They would say, "You are Tutsis, you are not Congolese." And I think that's why they were fighting; maybe they did not want us to be "Congolese." But I don't know for sure why they called us "Rwandans," and I don't know where we had come from. Maybe many centuries ago our ancestors had come from Rwanda. But I know that if that was true, it was a very long time ago, centuries ago.

All I know is that we found ourselves already in Congo. I was born in Congo. Even history books are not sure about the origins of our tribe; we may be from another part of Congo, or somewhere else. But I don't know why they did not like us. Back then, Banyamulenge people were not that educated—they were just farmers, peasants, raising cattle in the villages, working the land. I cannot think of anything they had that other tribes could be jealous of. Our tribe lived in villages in the plains or settlements in the mountains; that's where my people were. They really did not have anything special, like riches or money.

When I came here in 2007, my arm was still not good, and I had a big scar here at my shoulder. At first, I felt very depressed because of that. I was thinking, *I am not like other girls, I don't feel comfortable. I am different.* You know, I did not feel comfortable. But my mom used to come in my room every morning and say, "Jolie, I know God loves you."

But I was so depressed because of the scars, and I did not have all my fingers. I thought that I did not look like other girls. I thought, *No, I am not like other girls, I am different.*

But my mom and my dad always used to tell me, "Jolie, you are normal."

I felt very lonely. And in school, everything was so hard at the beginning. I even did not know how to say "Good morning!" in English. But after one semester, I could speak English. It was not very good, but I could really speak English. It was good enough to make me a "peer mediator" in school. The peer mediator helps other kids who fight and mediates their disagreements in high school. So, I was like a student counselor. It was at the end of the ninth grade, and I did it for two years. When I was in my senior year, I did not want to do it anymore because I wanted to do something related to social work, so I went to a program that helped kids after school with their homework, and I did that for one year.

I picked social work in 2007 when I was in ninth grade. When we came to the US, I saw the case workers in the agency who helped us—you know, like the IRC, but it was a different one. We were resettled by Caritas in Austin, Texas. I saw what they were doing and I thought, *Oh, man, these people, they do everything that I want to do.*

Because they helped us, I think they do more than anybody else has been doing. They would tell us how to do things here. They would say, "You are new here, you don't know anything."

And they helped us with all the things. They helped us with school, transportation, and housing, and I was thinking, *Yes, that's what I want to do, too.* But I did not know what I had to study to do it, and I did not know that it was called "social work."

I have a friend who is like my sister. Her name is Caitleen Meredith, and she is a white person. She was helping Caritas with interpreting, and we met at the agency and became friends. She used to come to our house, and as she spoke French, we could talk.

One day, she asked me, "Hey, Jolie, what do you want to be when you grow up? What do you want to major in college?"

At first, I was surprised. "What? What do I want to be? But I am just in the ninth grade!"

She laughed. "Hey, you are in America. Here, you need to think way ahead about what you want to be in future, although you are not there yet."

I said, "Oh, I think I want to do case work. Work as a case worker. I want to do the same job as the agency workers are doing."

She was joking with me, "You know, you won't make much money with this job."

But I said, "I don't care, as long as I do what I want."

She was in the medical field, so it was different for her. Caitleen used to say, "You need to think bigger, like become a doctor or psychologist."

But I said, "No, I think I want to be a social worker."

I was in ninth grade when I decided what I wanted to do. I saw how the case workers were doing things, and I thought, *Yes, that's what I want to do.* Since then, I have been thinking about some other majors, too. Should I do counseling? Should I do psychology? But every time, I go back to social work. In my freshman year in college, I even thought about becoming a psychologist, but at the end of semester, I was decided: "No, I want to do social work."

So, when I told my dad that I want to do social work, he asked, "You, social work again?"

I said, "Yes, I think that's what I want to be."

And my dad laughed at me. "What happened to your psychology?"

I said, "I don't think I would fit in that."

He was alright with that. "Whatever you choose, as long as you love it, go for it!"

I said, "Dad, thanks for understanding."

And now, I am happy. I like my school and my social work major. I don't think social work will "go away." I think after I finish Ranger College, I will come back to Abilene to Hardin-Simmons University to get at least my Bachelor's in social work.

But after I graduate, I want to work with the United Nations, UNHCR. And I want to work outside of America. My first choice would be Kenya or Rwanda. I think I would pick Kenya, as there are a lot of refugees who live in Kenya, and the UN has more work in Kenya because of that. I don't know how I will get there, but that's what I really want to do. Or Rwanda—I really don't know why Rwanda, maybe because I have never seen it, but many people are saying that it is really beautiful. I would like to go and see it. But my first choice would be Kenya. You know, when I just came here to live, I came thinking that life would be much easier here. That everything would come easily. But now I know that it is not easy, and to accomplish something, you have to do a lot, make an effort.

What was the best thing for me in the US? I think the best thing is that I have learned a lot. I have grown up. Now, I am thinking as a grown-up woman. Since I came, I have experienced school and work, found my first job, gotten my first paycheck. I am leading the life of an adult. And I think it is very good. I am thinking responsibly, and I have my own life. Although I live with my parents and I share a home with them, I contribute to rent and utility payments. I help out as much as I can. I have a car loan, and I pay it every month, and it is a good feeling.

Life in the US is so much better. It is true that America is a land of opportunity. People always have a chance to think beyond what they are doing at the moment. Like in school, you think about your future. For example, I am in college now, but I am thinking that after two years, I will graduate and have a job in the social work field.

But back home in Congo, we do not have that opportunity. You cannot plan there, because maybe after one year, a war will break out, and you will have to give up everything and move away. But if we had peace in Congo, I would go back and work in Congo. There are so many things to do in Congo, and I feel it is my land, my country. But mostly because there is so much need. People live in poverty over there, and so many people need help, and I could help in any situation.

But the reason why we do not do much in Congo is that there is no peace. And you cannot go to some villages to do things, organize. But if there were peace, it would be the best place to be. But right now, I am not sure if the war and fighting will ever stop. Since

I was born, it seems like it is just fighting and fighting. And we all hope that one day, there will be peace.

When I came here, I was in my teens, and I was old enough to remember Congo. But my little sister was born here in the US, so she does not know about Congo. I don't know how she would feel about Congo. All my younger siblings were very young when we came, like my other little sister—she was two years old when we came, and she does not remember anything.

And it is not just Africans. If we are not born American, each one of us has some place where we were born and we consider "our own country." Like where your father or mother were born. And we feel, "Oh, this is my country." But I am an African, although I am a citizen of the US. And I feel I am an American, too. I am both, an American and an African. I feel I belong to both places. Time will show what will happen.

March 28, 2014

Berthe: "My Good-Luck Wedding Gift"

Berthe was resettled to Abilene with her husband and children in 2007, when the Banyamulenge Tutsi resettlement had just started. Actually, Berthe and her family were the first ones to arrive in Abilene. And not just the first ones, theirs was the largest family we had ever resettled—twelve people in one family! I remember all the pre-arrival preparations we made: we had booked two apartments to accommodate them all, and as a special favor, CityLink agreed to send their van to the airport to pick them all up at once. More than seven years have passed since that time, and Berthe and her family have done very well in the US.

Berthe is only in her midthirties now. She "inherited" the large family when she got married to a middle-aged widower who had eight children. The children's mother had died during the Gatumba attack in Burundi, and he had decided to remarry. Berthe's oldest stepdaughters were just a few years younger than Berthe when their father remarried. Since those days, Berthe and her husband have had three children together, and her oldest stepdaughters have grown up and have families of their own. Berthe may be one of the youngest grandmas in town. Berthe and her husband have bought a house, and everyone in the family has become an American citizen.

Today, Berthe comes for her storytelling session, but before we start, she asks me if I could help her with an immigration petition for her daughter. I am surprised because I did not know she had a daughter, even though I have known Berthe since 2007. Berthe explains that her daughter, Angelique, who is from a previous relationship, disappeared during the war in Congo. The daughter's father was killed in that war while they were fleeing together. Although nobody really believed that Angelique could be still alive, Berthe and her parents kept looking, against all odds. Now, almost fifteen years later, Berthe's father found her in Rwanda. Angelique is a teenager now. We discuss what documents Berthe will need for the petition, and after that, Berthe starts her story. She does not want to be recorded, so I will take notes.

I WAS BORN IN 1980 in Vyura and grew up there. Vyura is a village in the Kalemie area in the Democratic Republic of Congo. It is the area where we, Banyamulenge, used to live before the wars started. I don't remember my house, but I remember how I was going to school and how I was helping my parents after school. I was a really good student. My mom had a shop, and she was making clothes, like traditional dresses and pants, and selling them in that shop. People used to come to buy what she had made. My mom had a sewing machine, and she made all the clothes herself. I think she was good with sewing and people liked her clothes. I was helping her after school. I did not know how to sew, but I laid things out for her in the store to make everything look nice and neat. Her shop was in a big market, and she had her own place there, like a booth or stall. That's where her store was, and that's where we sold the clothes she made. I enjoyed helping her with that.

My dad was a Bible teacher. He was a pastor and taught in a church called Vyura Christian Church. He was doing a Bible class for the villagers.

We did not have a farm, as we lived in the village, which was more like a little town, not real countryside. Yes, that's where we all lived, Vyura. I remember the place.

My parents had six children, including me. I have two sisters, two older brothers, and one younger brother. The little brother—I always called him, "Little Brother" because he was much younger than my other siblings. So, we were three and three, three boys and three girls. Now, the eldest brother lives in Rwanda in Kiziba refugee camp. The other older brother, he and his family live in Uvira city in Congo. But my little brother lives with my parents in Rwanda. My parents are in Rwanda now, and my mom has a store there. She does dressmaking just like she did in Vyura, and my dad teaches in church. He is teaching Bible study. The church pays him a little money, and my mother makes some money with her store.

We lived in Vyura for a long time until the war started around 1998. Yes. Other people started killing our Banyamulenge people, so we had to move. We moved to Uvira city for safety. We went to Uvira first, but then things got bad there, so we went on to Rwanda, and my parents still live in Rwanda with my little brother.

In Vyura, I met my boyfriend, and we started going out together. I think that if not for the war, we would have gotten married and had a family together. But at that time, we both were very young, maybe eighteen or nineteen years old or so. Then, our daughter was born, and we named her Angelique. She was just a toddler when the war got so bad that we had to run. My parents had already left the area, heading to Rwanda, but I was living with my boyfriend's family at that time. I had to follow my parents, and I did not know how it would go; it was a very dangerous trip.

My boyfriend's parents offered to keep our daughter, as the place they were going was closer and safer: they planned to go up the Kivu Mountains and stay there with some relatives. The mountain area was better, as not many people lived there and the rebels did not go there too often, as they had nothing there to find. So, I left my baby daughter with her daddy's parents and left for Rwanda to find my parents.

Ever since then, my parents and I have been looking for Angelique and wondering if she might be alive. We were able to find out that my boyfriend was killed in the war, but his parents and my baby girl had disappeared. So, we thought that she was killed, too, but kept looking, just in case. We could not find my boyfriend's family anywhere. It was as if they had disappeared without a trace. They were not in the mountain area anymore, and nobody knew where they had gone. It was the time of war, and everybody was fleeing somewhere, away from the country.

I found my parents in Rwanda, and we settled to live in a border town called Cyangugu. This town is across the border from Bukavu, which is on the Congo side. We stayed in Cyangugu for a while, and then I went to Kigali and started working in an orphanage.

It was a job I had through a church mission, and it was in Kigali. You know, Kigali is the capital city of Rwanda. I liked this job a lot; it was an exciting thing to do. We helped street children: we had food for them, and they could stay in our mission for the night and get new clothes. But the main thing was that the church would pay their school fees, so they could go back to school. You know that in Africa people have to pay for school. And many children at that time did not have their parents or they did not know where they were. We did not know if it was just for a while or if the parents had been killed. It was the time of the war. Many families got separated as they may have fled without their children or some of their children. Many were killed by shooting, and for some, nobody knew for sure—the parents were just missing.

This job let me help those children and get them away from the streets and allowed them to go to school. I went to training for six months at first, and after that, I was working in the orphanage. Some kids came to stay with us, and we had homes for them. We had people who looked after the children, like house parents. This was all part of the church mission. We went out on the streets to look for these kids and asked them to come to the shelter. In fact, it was not only for street kids; those children that were away from parents but had been taken into a friend's or relative's family could get help, too.

I worked there for two years, but then I moved back to Cyangugu to be with my family. I had to help my mother and father. After a while, I started my own business. I was buying clothes in Congo and selling them in Rwanda, and I made money in that way. I had a friend who lived in Congo, not far from the border, and we worked on it together. The Kigali job was good, but life in Kigali was expensive—that was one thing, but the main reason for moving back was that I had to help my parents in the house and also help my mom with her business. Some years passed like that, and all the time, we were trying to find out about my daughter and my boyfriend's family, but nobody had heard or seen them. No news. I just worked in my business and helped my parents.

Then, my would-be husband, Elias, came from Burundi to us in Rwanda to propose to me. He had a friend who lived in Rwanda, and we lived together with him. I think that this friend had told my husband about me. So, he came to see the friend and also came to me and proposed getting married. At first, I was surprised. I was much younger than he, and he was a widower who had children—daughters, who were almost my age.

So, I told him, "You have children that are almost grown up—they are too big for me." I was hesitant at first. I was thinking it would be hard to be in a family where children are so grown, almost close to my age. I said, "I really have to think about it."

But a friend had told me about the family before we actually met. My would-be husband's wife had been killed in Gatumba, so he was left with a big family, many children, by himself. And people were saying that "the girls from this family, they are nice, quiet; they are doing well."

So, I thought about it, and I talked to my family—my parents—and they said it was okay for me to get married. I gave it a thought and then told him, "It is alright. We can get married." So, after I accepted, I went to Burundi and got married. We had a nice wedding. My parents and siblings came, and friends, too.

The Banyamulenge have a tradition—or you may want to call it a custom—to give cows as a wedding gift. The groom gives cows to his new wife's parents. Here in the US, people give money, but Banyamulenge people give cows instead of money. You can even refer to the money you have as "your cows." That is in our culture. So, when we were about to get married, my husband brought cows to my parents. I think he brought nine cows to my family to get to marry me. When he came, he talked to my parents and gave the cows to them. Then, my parents thought and talked about the wedding costs. How much would the wedding cost to us, and how much would we have to spend on it? You know that when you get married, the family has to sell some of the cows to get money to buy things for the wedding, and some money goes with the bride to start the new life for the new family.

So, my parents sold three cows and bought clothes for me for my wedding and other things that were needed for the wedding, like food and drink. I went to live in Burundi with my new family. On the day I was going, my parents gave me one cow as a gift to start the new family. It was the wedding gift from my parents to us, the new couple. My parents told me, "This cow is a gift for you, as you have a new home, new family, and if you need to have something for the house, you can sell the cow to buy things for the house, or if you want, you can keep it. It is a gift."

That's how we Banyamulenge do it. Elias was pleased with the gift and said, "This cow is a gift from your parents as you enter our family, so let's talk in our family, all of us, what to do." He told the children, "This cow is a wedding gift to my new wife, your new mother. Her parents gave it to her. What should we do with it?"

The children said, "This cow is the first cow, the first gift from our new mom's family, so let's keep it. And then if the time comes when we need money really bad—like we need money to pay for school fees or something—and we have no other way to make it, then we could sell the cow. But for now, let's keep the cow for good luck, since it is a wedding gift." And we kept the cow for several years; it was a very good gift from my parents. But we did not have money in Burundi, so we had to sell the cow to pay for the kids' school. You know that in Burundi, in Africa, we have to pay for school, for education. But that was way after.

Right after the wedding, we started living all together as one family, and it was not easy at the beginning. I did not know how to manage such a big household or how to be a mother to all the children. My husband had nine children then, and the oldest four daughters were almost adults. It was hard the first month after the wedding. But my husband knew how to keep the children together, so everybody was nice. The first time we all met at home, he introduced me to all his children: "This is your new mom, your second mom, and you will be respectful to her, and she will respect you, too. She does not have experience living in a big family, but if you help her and show her respect, she is going to try her best for you, too."

The children helped me live in their house and taught me everything about their family and home, and my husband showed me how they used to do things. We were all mild-natured and respected one another. The children were happy and always talked nicely and were friendly, and we had no arguments or anything bad. You know some of the daughters were almost my age, but we always helped one another, and we got along very well. Their mom had passed away in Gatumba: she got shot and did not survive. It was in 2004. And we got married in 2005, about a year after the Gatumba Massacre.

And we are a good family now. We have had three children in our marriage; the first one is a girl and was born in Burundi. She is eight years old now. Then, we had a boy in the US. He is five now and is going to school already. And then last year, our little one was born. Her name is Joyce, and she will be a one-year-old soon.

When Elias and I got married, he had already started the refugee resettlement application. It was for Gatumba survivors, and his family was one of them. After we became husband and wife, Elias went to ask to the refugee program people what to do to put me on the case with them; he gave them our marriage certificate and explained everything. His old paperwork said that he did not have a wife. Now he had a wife. Immigration in Burundi knew when people got married, it was all in documents, and we had the marriage certificate, too. So, they added me to the case. When we had the interview, we went to it together. They asked me when we got married and where, and they had that information from Burundi, from UNHCR. They asked me some questions like, "When were you married? When were you born? Where were you born?" and they asked about my parents, but they already had all that information as well, so I think they asked just to make sure that what they had was correct.

We were very happy when we heard that we were approved to come to live in the US. When we lived in Burundi, we were refugees, and we did not have anything—no money, nothing. But it was very exciting to be able to come because we knew that we would make a new life. Life is really good right now; everything is going well. We bought a house, and our oldest daughters got married. Several of them are in college, too, and will have good jobs when they graduate.

I have a job at Hendrick Hospital. When we came, you and the IRC took really good care of us, especially you. We liked how you treated us. We always talked in the family about how much you helped us personally. We knew that we could rely on your advice and if we had any problem, we could go to you for help. We could get answers to all our questions. And we always enjoyed it and felt good and safe. We knew that the IRC would help take care of different issues. And you may think it was not true, but you did a lot; it was very important. We always enjoyed your advice—look ahead, be prepared. We did not know what we would have to do, but you told us, "You may want to become the US citizens, and if you wish, you can come to the class." We all went, and now we are all US citizens, which is very important. And everybody is doing very well now.

I thank Berthe for her kind words and then ask if she could share her own future plans.

You know that three of our eldest daughters got married and have children. One of them graduated from a nursing school and moved to Iowa to live. The next one graduated from high school last year, and she is away at Ranger College now. I think she will be there for two years. Then, it will be time for the next child to graduate from high school. So, life goes on.

I have my own plans, but I have to wait a while. I think that when my youngest, my baby girl, starts going to school, I will go to English classes to learn English very well so I can go on to college. Right now, my English is not too good; I need to improve. I want to get my GED. That's why I need to start with English first. I cannot do it right now because I have little kids and I am working, but when they get bigger, I will do that. I want to have a good job in the future. I do not know exactly what right now, but I will see and decide as time goes on. I think I may want to do computers—IT—but that is down the road.

December 2013

A View from the Office

"My Agent Brought Me"

Yaram was a refugee woman from Liberia. I think she was in her late forties or early fifties when she came to live in the US. Yaram was usually dressed in colorful traditional African clothes that attracted everyone's attention. She was strong and outspoken, never too shy to express her opinion or demand things to be set straight.

Yaram lived in Fairmont Apartments with her two school-aged children who were about to start school in a month or so, and I was looking for a job for her. We had agreed that Yaram would really need to work in the morning shift so she could be home when the children came back from school. Since the family did not have any other relatives in the US, Yaram had to rely on herself for everything in the household.

At that time, jobs in the morning were hard to find, as that was when many mothers with children wanted to be at work. I called many companies, but nothing came up. The day when Yaram's financial assistance for her family would end was looming over my shoulder. I called the cookie factory, where I had found jobs for several refugees in the past—they could offer only a night shift, which would not suit Yaram because nobody would be willing to take care of her children at night. So far, the only morning option I had found for her was in hotel housekeeping, but it would not suit Yaram, either, since it would not give her enough hours and money to pay all her household bills.

Finally, I called a friendly HR officer at Hendrick Hospital who often tried to help me with refugee job placements. She had an opening for a housekeeping job and was willing to interview Yaram. Of course, she had to make sure the candidate was a good fit, but if Yaram could pass the interview, the job would be exactly what she needed. It would be for the morning shift and offered a fixed schedule of forty hours per week along with a nice benefit package. Yaram would have time to get both of her kids off to school before going to work. Although it was not yet a done deal, it sounded exactly like what Yaram needed. Things were finally looking up bit.

I called Yaram the day before the interview. "Yaram, you have a job interview for the hospital tomorrow. It is for a housekeeping job. Please be ready at 2:00 p.m. I will come and get you. It is for the morning shift—exactly what we were looking for!"

Yaram did not sound very enthusiastic on the phone, but she promised to be home and ready for me. We had talked many times before about the job search and how to prepare for an interview.

The next day, I went to pick up Yaram for her interview, which I had confirmed with the Hendrick HR officer, so I just had to get Yaram and go. I arrived at her apartment building early, parked, and walked over. I knocked on the door, and the eldest daughter answered the door. It was still summer, so the children were at home; no school yet.

"Hi there, is Yaram at home?" I asked.

"No," she told me. "She went somewhere."

"Oh... Do you by chance happen to know where your mom went?" I asked.

"I think she went to Walmart or something," the daughter said.

"Oh, my, we have to be at a job interview in forty minutes," I told her. "And it is on the other side of town!" I don't even know why I said that; I knew that the daughter could not do anything about it, anyway. I just stood there, trying to figure out what to do and how to find Yaram. Should I go to Walmart and look for her? I still had forty minutes... But what if I missed her and she came back in the meantime?

"What time did your mom leave?" I finally asked.

"Well, it has been a while. She may be home soon," the daughter assured me.

I decided to wait a little longer, hoping that Yaram would appear. And if she did not, I would call the woman at Hendrick and plead for her to reschedule us. I was pacing back and forth in front of the apartment building, too worried to be able to sit still and wait for Yaram inside. After about fifteen minutes of pacing, I was about to call Hendrick when, all of a sudden, an old grey Camaro drove up. Yaram emerged from it, loudly thanking the driver—another refugee from Liberia. She hardly noticed me as she started walking to her apartment, carrying several cases of water and sodas. I caught up with her and offered to help with the packages, *as we were both on the way to her apartment: Yaram ready to rest after shopping and me ready to get her to the interview. I was relieved that she had finally come, but I was also upset because we were running late.*

"Yaram, remember—you had to be at home and waiting for me, ready for the interview," I said. "But I came and you were not there! Do you know how hard it is to find a job like that?"

Yaram dumped the packages on the living room table and retorted, "I had to go to Walmart to buy water. I was out of water, so how could I wait on you if I didn't have water to drink?"

"Yaram, you have all the other hours of the day to go shopping, and on top of that, tap water is safe here."

At least, she was in her best "outdoor" clothes, so there was no need to get ready. I told her, "Hey, Yaram, let's not waste any time. Please, take your bag, and let's get going!"

We were halfway to Hendrick when Yaram suddenly said, "I don't want to work in a hospital. I don't like hospitals."

"I told you about this hospital job yesterday when we talked on the phone, Yaram," I reminded her. "You did not say anything then." I did not want to get into a debate about jobs and program rules right before the interview, so I went on, "Let's just go and see; everything has been arranged for the lady to talk to you. And you may like it after you go and see."

So, we got there a few minutes late, but the HR officer was still waiting. I was allowed to sit in during the interview if I did not interfere or talk for Yaram.

The interview started, and I could tell that the lady had some doubts about Yaram. I knew she had hired refugees before and wanted to help. On the other hand, candidates had to have some basic qualifications, and Yaram could not read—nor write much—and did not know how to use a computer. Also, her English was more Creole than standard English, so that was making it all the harder. I realized it would be a fifty-fifty chance.

Finally, the HR officer asked Yaram, "Why did you come to apply for a job in our hospital?"

It was Yaram's "moment to shine" and tell how much she wanted the job and how hard she would work if given the opportunity. Instead, she promptly pointed to me and responded, "I came because my agent brought me!"

The interview was over. The next day, the HR officer called to tell me that she could not offer the job to Yaram. It was only later that Yaram told me that hospitals made her apprehensive because her dad had passed away in a hospital. But we kept looking for employment, and eventually, Yaram was hired for a food service job.

A face of Rwanda: After turbulent events in Rwanda, storyteller Herman Kalinijabo has found peace in Abilene, Texas. He loves to spend time with his children and has a full-time job he enjoys.

150

CHAPTER 8

Stories from Rwanda

W HAT CAN I SAY ABOUT Rwanda as an introduction? The whole world has heard about Rwandan genocide, and historians are still puzzling over different interpretations of the factors that contributed to it. To refresh your memory, it was a mass killing

From Herman's personal photo album

Herman's uncle on his mother's side (above) and his uncles on his father's side (opposite), before Rwandan genocide. Three men in their late teens or early twenties are looking at us from yellowed family snapshots. Herman's paternal uncles seem cautious and a little guarded as they look into the camera, while the boy on the motorbike can hardly wait for the photographer to snap the picture so he can rush off on his Suzuki. The upper side of each photo is marked by hand with the year of their deaths, and a cross has been drawn on each of them. Their lives were suddenly taken from them in the spring of 1994, like those of a million others. When I look in their unsuspecting eyes, I feel immense sadness. How can we all be human and still have the Rwandan genocide?

amidst the economic and political crisis and civil war in Rwanda in the spring of 1994 when the Hutu ethnic majority killed about one million Tutsis, around three-quarters of the total Tutsi population.[11] Scholars agree that old slights and offenses between the ethnic groups played a role, but most importantly, a big part of the Hutu population was manipulated by political and militant extremist groups to participate in the killings. Radio and other

From Herman's personal photo album

media broadcasts urged all Hutu civilians daily "to do their duty to their homeland" and clean out the Tutsi "vermin." As a result, around 200,000 Hutu civilians participated in the genocide, and within three short months, almost a million Tutsis were killed.

Part of the blame goes to the international community, including Europe and the US, who heard the Tutsis' cries for help and knew about the devious extermination plans but chose to do nothing.

The genocide was ended by the Rwandan Patriotic Front, which liberated areas of Rwanda as the front moved forward and saved those Tutsis who were still alive. On the other hand, the military forces retaliated harshly against all Hutu civilians, even those who were not involved in killing Tutsis. As a result, millions of Hutu people fled Rwanda. Now, twenty years have passed since the genocide, and the Rwandan government has called all Rwandese to forgive one another and seek reconciliation in order for the country to move forward from this terrible moment. Every one of the Rwandan storytellers provides insights into the infamous events of those days in Rwanda, since each of them was directly affected.

Herman: "We Live in Peace Here"

Herman calls me one day to ask whether his children can apply for green cards. He says he would like to visit me in my new office, and I explain how he can find me. I do not know Herman too well. He was not resettled by our organization but came to the US through a different agency and to a different town. I know he is a refugee from Rwanda, is in his midthirties, and moved to Abilene in 2010. I first met Herman when he came to the IRC to get help with petitions for his minor children, who at that time were still in Rwanda. Now, both his daughter, Christa, and son, Confiance, live with him in Abilene.

When Herman arrives, our conversation naturally revolves around his children. I ask how they are coping with all the new things in their lives: new family, new friends, and new school. Herman says that it was not easy for them, but now a year has passed since they came, and both of them have found friends and are doing really well at school. Herman has a full-time job and has started pharmacy school.

I ask Herman to share his story, and he agrees. We schedule a time when he will come for a storytelling session. He notes that he prefers not to be recorded, so I will take notes.

MY NAME IS HERMAN, and I am from Rwanda. I was born in Kinazi, Ntongwe, and I was a student at Gashike School. I had four sisters and three brothers, so we were a large family. I was the second eldest of the siblings. My father worked in a Catholic church called Central de Gashike. He was a catechist. He helped the priest during the service and did other different things in the church. My mother stayed at home, taking care of the children and the house.

My parents had two houses where our family lived: Father and Mother were in one house with the younger children, and we—the older siblings—lived in the other. I had a cousin who was twenty years old at that time, and he lived in our house, too. The houses were next to each other. We had barns and cattle sheds because we had cattle—cows and calves to take care of. We had three farms, three plots of land. One was around our houses, but the other lands were some distance away. Our lands were really big.

We children went to school, and we also had different responsibilities in the household. My sisters worked inside the house, helping with cooking and cleaning, and we boys worked with the cows and calves and helped in the fields and yard. In our culture, men do not go in the kitchen, even to get their food. They wait until somebody brings the food to them outside. Here, it is different, but in our tradition, men take on the physical work, like the fields and cattle, but do not do the housework. That is left for women.

We Tutsis like cattle; we have always been called "the cattle people." When I was a teenager, maybe twelve or thirteen years old, it was my duty to take our cows out to pasture for grazing. We do not feed cows in the barn like it is done here but take them outside to the pasture. Also, I had to bring the cows back to the barn in the evening, and I had to attend to the calves, too. It was my duty, and I had to tell my dad right away if I spotted something wrong with any of the farm animals. My dad was very strict, and I would get a good spanking if I missed something with the cows or calves, like if one of them was not looking good or had developed a skin rash or something like that. I had to tell my dad right away. So, it was a serious job.

Also, it was my job to fetch bananas; I did not have to do it every day but maybe once a week or once in two weeks. It may sound easy, but it was not. I had to walk a long way to the fields where we used to have bananas. It was far away from our home. First, I had to walk a long way, and then I had to cut down a banana tree—that's how you get bananas—and then cut them off the tree and put them all in a basket and carry them home. And they were quite heavy. We all had our duties in the household.

When I was a child and went to primary school, I used to play with other kids in the village. They were all children of our neighbors. We all lived in peace and got along very well. Even the adults were all friends and good neighbors. None of the kids paid any attention to ethnicity. I think none of us even knew to give it a thought. I did not know anything about "Tutsi" and "Hutu." We never discussed it at home. My parents never mentioned it, either. I am sure adults knew which ethnic group they belonged to, but we never talked about it.

I knew that my dad was born in a different place in Rwanda and had moved to Ntongwe later in life. But I did not ask him questions about why he had done that. When I grew older, I found out that my dad had moved to Ntongwe after the 1959 Hutu revolution. Before the revolution, Tutsis were in power and the king was the head of the country, but in 1959, there was the Hutu revolution, and the Hutus took over the power. Many Tutsis left the country then, and many others were forced to move to less desirable areas of the country, like to places where nobody had lived before or to areas with lots of tsetse flies. Those flies are really bad and can attack people and cattle. I found out that's why my father had moved to Ntongwe.

I remember my childhood as a time of peace. I was not even thinking about the Tutsis and the Hutus when I was a child. I played with my neighbors' kids, and we did the things all kids do. As I said, nobody was paying attention to ethnicity. I remember when I started primary school, our teachers carried out the so-called census every two months. It was a roll call of the students in the class, and we had to stand up by our ethnicity. The first time when it happened, I stood up with Hutus, but the teacher then told me, "No, no, you are not Hutu, you are Tutsi," and then I thought, *Oh, then I must be a Tutsi.* Those words did not have any meaning for me at the time. I wondered about that roll call and asked my parents why the teachers were doing that. My dad told me that teachers had orders from the education administration to find out how many students of each ethnicity were attending school.

But we never discussed other people's ethnic groups at home. It was not important. We had our own large family and had many neighbors, and we treated everybody the same: good people were good and bad were bad. My family, especially my mom, helped everybody who needed help and were less fortunate. We lived in an area that was mostly Hutu, but the majority of teachers were Tutsis. A teaching job was not well paid and thus not considered desirable, but Tutsis had traditionally been teachers and liked to stick to this profession.

When I think about my family, I always remember my mom. She was the most important person in my life. She raised me, took care of me from the time I was born. My dad was a great man and he taught me many things: how to be strong and fair and how to deal with the outside world and with society, but my mom is the one I remember most. My dad was often busy working, and he was quite strict with all of us kids. So, I was a little scared of my dad when I was growing up.

I had one best friend, Jean De Dieu Kagabo, and his father was my teacher. His mother was also a teacher, but she did not teach my class. My friend and all his family died in the genocide. They were Tutsis, and nobody from Jean De Dieu's household survived. When I think about them, I feel bad in my heart. I have just one teacher who survived: she was a Hutu and taught me in the fifth grade. All the other school teachers were Tutsis, and they died in the killings. Even Hutus died, so no one from my old school is left who I used to know.

But in the days before the genocide, life was peaceful. We tended to our fields and farm animals. It was mostly adults, but we children had to help as well. Sometimes, when we had to do the planting, we had people who helped us. Two workers would come to work in the fields. But sometimes, my parents would invite all the neighbors, make beer, and cook food, and then everyone would come together and help with planting. All the people would turn out to participate, to do the planting together, and to sing songs while working. Then, we planted cassava, beans, potatoes, sweet potatoes, different vegetables, corn, and greens. About fifty people would gather to help and then stay on to celebrate. People would eat and drink and enjoy themselves, dance, and sing. It was called *obudehe*, and it was only for the planting of new crops.

I enjoyed this celebration. We kids did not take part in the planting because it was a hard job, digging the soil and putting the crops in, but we could help here and there and then participate in the celebration. I was excited and waited for this day to come, and then we could dance and sing with everybody else. And we could get all the good food that was prepared for the planting fest.

But now everything has changed. The land belongs to the government, and nobody celebrates like that anymore. My old house is gone, burned down during the genocide, and no one lives there.

Both of my parents died in the Rwandan genocide in 1994. Only three of us eight children survived: my sisters and me. I do not know how the genocide came about since I was young then, but my dad was killed on the first day.

It was April 16, 1994. We were all together with our neighbors, and the adults were talking about defending themselves and all of us. I remember that our family was in another neighbor's house, and we knew that the killers might come. And my dad and our neighbors' men were planning to stand together to defend themselves, but we were expecting the killers to just carry machetes, not real weapons. The adults thought they could stand up to them.

But when the Hutu extremists came, they were armed with serious weapons, like guns, rifles, and grenades. The government had armed them like that. The government propaganda at that time proclaimed, "If you kill Tutsis, you get their property for yourself, houses and cattle, everything," so many people did kill for material benefit.

Thus, my dad was killed on that first day. We buried him on Sunday, just a couple of days later. At that time, our Hutu neighbors told us how very sorry they all were for what had happened to our dad. They wanted us to know that they were not part of this. The neighbors advised us to go to Ntongwe Town Center to tell the authorities about the killings and that the people at the center would help us stay safe. I guess the neighbors were not expecting things to get much worse.

We went to the town center, but it turned out that the chief of Ntongwe town was on the side of the killers. He did not tell us that openly, so we did not know it then. He assured us that things would be alright, he would take care of everything, that we did not need to worry. He advised us to make a list of all our family members, to make sure that everybody was accounted for. But in fact, he wanted this list for the killers, so nobody would escape and every single one would be killed. So, when the list was ready, he secretly passed it on to the killers.

We could not stay in the town center, but we could not find a safe place to go. All over the area, things were only getting worse. Tutsi homes were burning—everything around us was burning, smoke and fire wherever we went. We knew that we could not escape.

Two of my sisters were with Hutu neighbors, and that's how they survived—the neighbors hid them. But my mom and the rest of the kids, we were together. We decided that we would go home because there was no place to run. So, we were walking home from town center. On the way, we saw a group of six or seven men coming toward us, and from the way they were dressed and what they were carrying, we knew that they were the killers. It was already getting dark. It was after sunset. I climbed up in a tall tree, but everyone else stayed on the ground. It was too late for them all to hide. My mom cautioned my little sisters and brothers not to tell anybody that I was up in the tree.

The killers were close and had seen our group, but they did not know exactly how many we were. One of the killers was a young man who was our neighbor. I think he was just twenty years old, and my mom had helped him many times. She had fed him, we had meals together, and we had given clothes to him because his family was poor. I went to school with him. But now, he was with the killers, and my mom could not believe her eyes.

She asked him, "How can you do this? You are like a son to me."

But he shouted, "Stop talking!"

I think my mom did not think that he would kill her. And he might have let her live, but the other men, whom we did not know, were rushing him. "Let's be done here quick, we have more things to do!"

And he did not help her. After the killers butchered my mom and my siblings with machetes, they threw them in a latrine and just went on. They killed all my siblings at once, but my mom was still alive when they left. I could see and hear everything from my hiding place up in the tree, so I saw how my family was killed. I got down from the tree when the killers left, but it was too late—my mom and brothers and sisters were dead. The last words my mom said were the words of a prayer to God. Then, I ran away and hid in the Catholic church, and that's where I stayed for two months.

The church was full of people because everybody was seeking refuge there. Killers came every day and attacked that church; they captured people and took them away to shoot or kill with machetes. It was a terrible time. Every morning, we were trying to hide somewhere so that when the attack came, we would not be close to that side of the church grounds. Like, if the killers had attacked from the south one day, we would go to the north side of the churchyard and hide out of the way, so we could survive another day. The killers got some people every day, and for me, it was like waiting for the day of my death, daily.

Then on June 2, Kagame's front came in and liberated all of us, and it was over. Many Hutus had fled when they saw the front approaching. It was not just extremists who fled, but many others as well. The front was coming from Kigali side and was retaliating for the Tutsi killings. So, many Hutus were scared that they would be killed along with the extremists, and thus, thousands of them fled to Democratic Republic of Congo or Tanzania. Kagame sent military forces after the Hutus in Democratic Republic of Congo, and that's how war started there. Not everybody who fled to Congo was guilty, but the actual killers were among them, too.

I forgive Hutu extremists, although they killed most of my family. I think it is all in God's hands and that I have to forgive. I think it was all politics, and the politicians who wanted power agitated among the common people who did not know better. Government propaganda on the radio was so powerful that even our Hutu neighbors who had always been friends were affected. But before that, all the people lived peacefully side by side and helped each other. If a Tutsi got sick, a Hutu neighbor would take him to hospital. And if the Hutu needed something, the Tutsi would come to help.

And I truly believe I will see my mother and other family again one day. My mother prepared me to be a good person, to be forgiving and good, and I know I will see them again.

Here in Abilene, we are a mixed community—Tutsis and Hutus, but mostly Hutus. We live in peace here, we acknowledge each other, and we are friendly. And I know that the ones who are here did not kill my family. Those people who now live in Abilene, I did not know them when we all lived in Rwanda, so I do not know what they did or did not do. So, I can regard them as friends, like our neighbors in those days when I was a child and life was different.

But we do not talk about specific things, those things that relate to the genocide.

I have another young Tutsi man here in town, and he used to live in the neighboring district in Rwanda, about fifteen miles away from Ntongwe. He is younger than I am. I think I was in middle school when he started primary school. All his family was killed in the genocide; he is the only one who survived. So, here in Abilene, he is the only one to whom I can talk about these things—the suffering—and we can remember our families together.

I think when I become a US citizen, I will be able to go back to Rwanda to put up a tombstone for my mom and all my family members who were killed, and we will commemorate them. I hope I can get it done by this coming May. One of my surviving sisters lives in Ntongwe, so we talk about how things are there now. She has her own business, and I try to help her a little from here. The other surviving sister came to the US, but then got married and now lives in Australia. Both of my sisters were saved by Hutu neighbors who hid them during the genocide. We all need to get together in Rwanda and commemorate our parents and family.

I have forgiven in my heart, but I cannot forget those days and my family. And I will see them all one day.

December 20, 2013

Angela and Ellie, Mother and Daughter: "War Followed Us Everywhere"

Angela and Ellie have agreed to share their stories. They are mother and daughter, and both arrived in Abilene in the summer of 2004 as one of our first Rwandese refugees. They came as a family of four: two parents and two daughters, although Angela and her husband have more children who live in France.

Angela and Ellie are well educated, and both had good careers in Rwanda before the Rwandan Civil War started. Angela was very involved with different women's programs and projects and worked for the Rwandan government. Ellie had graduated from a nursing school and used to be a practicing nurse. Now, I am in my office with Angela and Ellie. They share their memories and take turns in storytelling, adding their own impressions to the other's story, so it becomes a true "family story." They agree to have their stories recorded.

ANGELA: For me, my "good days" were from about 1977 until we had to leave our country in 1994. I had all our five children in school already then, and it was good for me because I was working with women in those days and was extremely busy. I did a lot of program work, and my experience with rural women was truly rewarding. You know, people are not rich in Rwanda, and they are not educated. So, we really had to do something for them, especially for women, in the areas of education and rural development. It was my job, and I loved it. It was the best time for me.

Now, life is a bit hard, but the real problem is not life here; it is communication. If you want to do something good for people, to get involved, you have to talk. And if you cannot talk, you cannot do much good. So, I cannot get involved because of my limited English. But I like it here because we are safe, and we are free to do things and to talk, and it feels good to be free. But the most important thing here is safety and security. You know that we had to leave our country, Rwanda, and then we lived in Congo, and then in Ivory Coast. Wherever we went, there was war and fighting, and we were so tired of fighting. It was so stressful. I could not sleep at night because of the war, and I did not know if we would be alive next day—really, it was an awful feeling. Now, I go to work, I come home, I eat, I sleep quietly. It is very important.

I had started college here in Abilene, but I had to give up school because I did not qualify for financial aid and had to pay for everything myself. Then, I realized that I would reach retirement age in two years. I had to decide whether to continue with school and leave my job with benefits, or stay on the job and give up school. I decided to keep my job. Because what would I do after I graduate in my age? Go back to my old job? I already have it now. So, I decided to give up school but take some classes sometimes, just to keep my mind busy.

ELLIE: I used to be a nurse. When the war started, I was done with my nursing school and had just started public health studies at the university. I was in my first year. But we had to get out of the country and go to Congo DR and live in a refugee camp, so I had to stop my studies. I worked as a nurse in the camp with Red Cross for about two years. I was taking care of kids who had lost their parents or just had gotten lost in the war. And after we went to Ivory Coast, I worked as a nurse again. We lived in Ivory Coast for eight years, and six of those years, we were really active. I could not go to school anymore because we were in a new country and money was tight, but I enjoyed my job as a nurse. Then, in 2002, the war broke out in Ivory Coast, and we had to leave Buake, the town where we lived then, and move to Abidjan, the capital city. Our town was not safe anymore. While in Abidjan, I worked a little bit here and there, helping with refugees, too. These last two years, we could not do as much because of the war. But then, we came here, and I had to change my career, and this change was very difficult.

Remember when we met last week in the post office, I told you that I was selling books on Amazon now. And I enjoy selling on Amazon, but I would also like to do medical billing. I started medical billing once, but then I got married and moved to Weatherford. Then, my husband got sick, and I was very busy taking care of him. My husband passed away in March of 2012, and I came back to Abilene to my parents' house. So, I am back here now, and I have medical billing on my mind again, but I have to put it off for later, since I would need quite a bit of money to start it again. But I have not given it up entirely.

ANGELA: How was everything here at the start? When I just came to the US, I felt bad. I had to start with a dishwashing job in Hardin-Simmons University (HSU), and I took the bus to get there. It was my first day at work, and it was really hard. But I told myself over and over again, *You have to do it, you have to do it, we have to pay the bills, pay the rent, buy food, everything, and we have to have that money.*

Still, it was very hard. But then, I started to like my job, and I did it very well. I remember that I started at $5.50 per hour, but I worked well, and then after a couple of months, my manager raised my salary a little bit, to $6.00 per hour or so. When I was leaving the job almost a year later, my pay was $7.50 per hour already because the manager noticed that I knew what I was doing. I was responsible for dishwashing, but later, they let me serve students in the dining room, so I started to like it.

But as Ellie had a job with Abilene State School then, she told me one day to try to apply there. She said, "Mom, just try, and maybe they can hire you for something here with your little English."

At Hardin-Simmons University, we started at 11:00 a.m. and worked until 2:00 p.m., and then we had a break until 5:00 p.m., and after that, we worked again from 5:00 p.m. till 8:00 p.m. It was called "the split shift." So, I had several hours between the work hours to work on my English. I would bring my books with me and learn to read and write in English from books, but I could not speak well. So, when I had to say something to my manager, I used to write it on a piece of paper for her. Then, she would read it and respond; that's how we communicated. So, when I did the interview at State School, I got all the papers right for that, but when they wanted to speak to me, I said, "Oh, no, please don't ask me. I cannot speak English."

But the interview went alright, and I got hired for the job. Now, it has been almost nine years in State School for me. I like my job; we work with people who are in wheelchairs and who are mentally handicapped, and we do everything for them. When I started, it seemed a little hard, but with the years, it has become better, and

I know my job well. We make good money and have benefits, and that is good, too.

ELLIE: We arrived in Abilene in July of 2004, and it seemed a strange place, so unfamiliar and flat. And it was so very hot—now I know what July in Abilene means, but I did not know then. It was difficult to start living here, and the English language was the main challenge then. Even the local manners, culture—it was so different. And if you work with other people, you have to understand one another to work together. It was hard sometimes because I was a foreigner, and they were Americans. But I think I coped with time, got to know people better, and everything got easier.

How did I get adjusted? I was reading a lot, and that helped. I had graduated from college before, so I was used to reading and studying. We had to discover things on our own because we did not have a big refugee community here yet who could help us. Mister Gary and his wife, Tracy, helped us a lot. They came to us on Sundays to take us to Walmart, and they helped me learn how to drive. That's how I could pass driving and get my driver's license. And they helped my sister with schoolwork.

ANGELA: I think the IRC helped us, too. You know how it is in Africa: when you have a problem, you go to your family to get help to solve the problem. Here, we went to the IRC when we had a problem, like we would go to our family. And we got advice from you, and even when the IRC could not help, you could tell us where to go. As the first refugees here, it was very important.

ELLIE: What I am seeing in this country is that people take care of themselves; Americans are really independent. The IRC was training us in that spirit, too. Because here, people have to get the jobs for themselves, and if they want to go to school, they do it on their own. You have to save some money, and then you have to enroll in college and study. And we can have the same life as American people do. But when we just got here, it was difficult to do because we did not know the language and we did not know the country. But I do not see anything else that could have been done; people had to learn. The IRC got our first jobs for us, but then we were on our own.

Even if it was difficult sometimes, it was the first job. When I lost my job in the cookie factory, I got help from you. Do you remember? You found me a job in a medical facility, and I went for an interview. Then, I applied for a job in a hospital, and I gave your name as a reference. It was not easy for me, but I was educated and knew some English, so it was easier to learn and become independent.

It was much harder for older people who had never been to school before coming here. They had a hard time keeping their jobs and understanding what was going on; they really needed more help from case workers. This is just my opinion. I remember my first day on the job in the cookie factory; the job was pretty simple, and I learned everything very quickly. The job was not hard. But some things were hard, especially the attitude of the people around me at work.

I ask Angela and Ellie about the time the war started and how they became refugees.

ANGELA: The war started in the capital city, Kigali, and we lived in a suburb about fourteen miles from Kigali. We used to work in Kigali and then come home to our town in the evenings. But when the war started, we were just looking from our home to Kigali, and we could not get anywhere. We had no money because all the banks were in Kigali, and we could not go there. We spent about two weeks like that, watching and feeling that the war was coming closer. At least we lived out in the country and had fields around us where we used to grow vegetables, so we had something to eat. But when you are worried, you do not even think about food, you do not feel hungry or anything.

We constantly heard shooting, but we thought that everything would calm down, and we would be alright. But the shooting was getting worse, and the front kept coming closer and closer to us. Then, they started shooting with big mortars and hitting people's houses. Houses were burning; smoke and noise of explosions were close-by. It was very scary.

Then, we fled on foot. We could not take our car; we had to leave it behind because if you took your car, they would see you and shoot at you. So, we went through fields and forests. It was very hard. We went as a family all together; we went to Congo.

ELLIE: I was in the bathroom all the time—not to hide, but it was so scary that my stomach got upset, and I had to run all the time. But when the time came, we felt we had to leave home, and we could not take anything with us. We left home and went through woods and fields on foot. It was not just us; we walked with a big group of people for many hours and without any food or water. All our neighbors were leaving their homes—everybody fled—and we went with everybody else. It was a steady stream of people going to the border.

When the night came, we slept on the ground. And we got shot at, and some of the people died that night. I think three hundred people died that night. You may have seen it on TV when they showed the Rwandan War: thousands of people walking, carrying things, parcels on their heads and backs, families with kids, kids crying, and that's truly how it was, everybody fleeing.

ANGELA: That's how it was, it's true.

ELLIE: And when bombs started falling down and explosions were all around us, things got very chaotic. People were wounded, crying, dying, and everybody else was trying to run and hide. Many parents lost their kids in this way, and kids lost their parents. So later, when I worked in the refugee camp with kids—their parents had disappeared in attacks like this. The Red Cross kept searching for them, and some would turn out to be alive later, but many would be gone. Dead and never found. I worked with kids of all ages in the camp, and the youngest one was a seven-month-old baby. And the oldest was seventeen or eighteen years of age.

ANGELA: We left Kigali in May, and we went to my husband's countryside place first, which was at the Kivu lake, close to the border with Congo. We stayed in his country place for about two months, and the war came close again, and then we left for Congo in July. We went across the border and stayed in Bukavu. For the first two months, there was no refugee camp, there was nothing: no water, no food. We slept on the ground, and people just slept everywhere and anywhere. There was no help at first because the international opinion was that "the people who fled Rwanda were the killers, so no help was needed."

Even the babies and kids were the killers! How you can say that?

We did not know what would happen. It was good that Congolese people sometimes helped us a little—made food and brought it to us—or we went to ask for food from them, and they would feed us. But some days, we did not eat all day. And we could not wash, could not take a shower for three or four days at a time. Personally, I was very sick at that time, and I thought I would die. Because we even did not have a way to wash our hands. But then, in September, they started building refugee camps, and we moved to a camp then.

ELLIE: There was an epidemic of dysentery and cholera at that time. But before long, I had found a job with the Red Cross. They had their own camps inside of the country, and I was working there.

ANGELA: When in a refugee camp, I got busy, too: with some teachers from different schools from our country, we created an education center for young people. We worked with UNICEF and had five hundred students, all young people, and the teachers were volunteers. Our thinking was, "When we have peace in Rwanda again, we will all go back home, and at this time, children go to school in Rwanda. So, why should we leave our young people behind?"

We had one hundred volunteer teachers, and we had a high school and elementary school. UNICEF and UNHCR helped us with resources and other things. It was from 1994 until February of 1996. But in February, HCR in Kigali said that people should not have social activities in the camp because these activities would make people stay in Congo, but Rwanda wanted their people back. So, we were not allowed to teach anymore because it was considered a "social activity." Camp management said, "If you continue school, you will go to jail."

We were afraid they would want us to go back to Rwanda when they stopped school, but they did not; they kept the camps open. And we knew that something may be coming.

ELLIE: It was an ethnic conflict. The politicians wanted to use ethnic groups to make war, and then, the rebels did the same. Because in Rwanda, Tutsi and Hutus were together in the same villages until the conflicts were started. Tutsis came to take power with war, and the others did the same, and it was even worse. And innocent people died who had nothing to do with politics. Why? There was no reason. Our history is very complicated.

While in the camp, I was busy with my nurse's job. We had three camps, and we had kids between two years of age up to fourteen years of age, about three hundred children in total. In the first camp, I worked with children of ages between seven and fourteen. The Red Cross provided clothes and place to sleep for them, and the Red Cross had staff to watch over the children and stay with them day and night, feed them, and attend to them. They needed nurses, too. It was like an orphanage, but we had just tents on the ground, and we had ten children in each tent. It was an okay job, although it was emotionally hard because all these children had lost their parents. Some of the children suffered from post-traumatic stress disorder: they would have seizures, would fall down and cry. But all we were allowed to do was give them Valium to calm them down. That was all. And there were many diseases, too, because they lived in cramped conditions.

Most of the children had come to the camp in the same way as we did—walking down the road from Rwanda—but some were brought over by the Red Cross; they would pick up lost children on the road on their way to Congo. Children were found in places where their parents had died or where they had been lost. I worked with many of those children. Now, when we came to Abilene, I met one of these children here in town. He is a young adult now and came on the refugee program. I did not recognize him initially, but he was looking at me, and then he said, "I think I know you from somewhere." And then we recognized each other. He was very young when I worked in the camp, one of the youngest. It was good to see him again now.

ANGELA: Our family, we were lucky to survive. But we lost a lot of people in our extended family. Also, many friends, coworkers, they all are gone now. Some of them died in Rwanda, and some others in Congo. Many of them were educated and involved in politics. I think many of them were specially sought out and killed; they were not just casualties of war. It is very sad. Four of my youngest sister's children were killed, just like almost all on my husband's side of the family.

ELLIE: Yes, one of my dad's sisters got shot in the woods, both her and her husband. She was my aunt. It was some time after the war already. We had lost contact with other relatives when the war broke out and found out about them only later. We tried to look for them while in the refugee camp. There was a service in the camp, an agency—I do not remember its name, but if you wanted to find a family member, you could fill out a piece of paper, and they limited how many words you could write, and you put down also where you thought the person could be. Then, the agency would send that piece of paper to different refugee camps, and it would be posted in a public place there so everybody could read it. And people would come to look at those postings to see if they had anything from their missing relatives. The paper was sent from place to place, and if they found the person you were look-ing for, he or she would write you something back on the same sheet. And the paper would come back to you after some time. That was how we found my mom's family when we were in Congo. But about my father's family, we did not have any news until we came to the USA.

After living about two years in a refugee camp in Congo DR, Angela and Ellie's family moved on to Ivory Coast. War reached Congo DR from Rwanda shortly after. I ask them both how the family knew that it was time to get out of the Democratic Republic of Congo and go on.

ANGELA: It was suspicious when the camp management stopped school but did not close the camp. At that time, we felt something ominous was coming. That's why my husband and I arranged for Ellie and her sister to go to Ivory Coast. It was in February of 1996. We had a big family and did not have much money, so we could not go all at once. Our son and another daughter left some months after. Then, my husband and I left as the last ones from our family. It was in September, just one week before the war broke out in Congo, so we were really lucky to get out on time. But after we left, many people were killed in Congo—among them, many of our good friends.

On the whole, Ivory Coast was a very good country; people were nice to us, people helped us, and we helped each other. But after six years, a war broke out in Ivory Coast, too. It was not the same war; it was their own. Too many wars! And when a war starts, it seems never to end.

But before this war, we had very good jobs in Ivory Coast, and life was good. I was the director of a college, and I did follow-ups on teachers and dealt with students and prepared tests and examinations. I did all kinds of things, and my salary was good. My husband was an instructor in a different college; he was in agriculture and agronomy, and it was a good place, too. Ellie worked as a nurse, and my second daughter worked in my college as an information secretary, and the youngest went to school. So, life was good there, and I thought that we would stay there if we could not go back to Rwanda. But the war came again.

ELLIE: Yes, the war came again. You know, wars in Africa usually start in capital cities, but this time, I don't know how or why, the war started in the city we lived in, in Buake. The war started very close to us. It happened all of a sudden, overnight: everything just went silent, no cars in the streets anymore, nothing. We were trapped in the house until we got evacuated. That night, it was just me and my sisters at home—nobody else. My mom had to go to the capital city, Abidjan, the night before to get money for her college examiners, and she was going to stay overnight in the capital. My brother needed a new refugee ID, so he also went with her. But my dad had to go to the western part of Ivory Coast because they had to establish an agronomy school there, and they had invited him to share his experience. So, he was not at home, either. My mom and dad and my brother—oh, my God, they all went on a trip the evening before, and I was at home just with my sisters. And the war broke out exactly that night while my parents were traveling to the capital!

The rebels came into our town that night, and everything was off—the phones, television, radio, everything! The country was split in two. The people who wanted to take over the power started with our town and took it over that night. So, we did not know what to do or how to get out of this. We were together with another Rwandese family and some other refugees. Later, we called our families, and they notified the United Nations in the capital, and the United Nations talked to the consulate of France in our town, and the consulate organized to take out those people who were not from Ivory Coast. So, we had to get our luggage and everything together in just three days. My parents did not have any clothes with them, and they could not come back to town, so it was just a crazy time for all of us. We did not live in a refugee camp when we got evacuated; we lived like immigrants. But we had to go to the UN again when we came to the capital city to get help from them to find a place to live. So, we became refugees again. We all were in low spirits then.

ANGELA: When we moved from Buake, my college moved to the capital, too. I was still working but did not get paid anymore. They said, "We get money from the government. Now, the government is at war, so we have no money for you."

But we still continued working. You know, students still came, and we thought that if they saw that nobody was in school, it would be hard on them, heartbreaking. So, we all instructors agreed that we should keep teaching, and that maybe next month, some money would come. But when we left for the US, it was still like that. Yeah.

ELLIE: The UN finally rented a community house for us. Each family had a dorm, so we started living there, just sitting, eating, and waiting on what would happen next.

ANGELA: We wrote numerous petitions and letters, and many refugees went to fight and signed petitions asking for help and saying that the government of Ivory Coast did not take care of refugees.

ELLIE: The United Nations came under pressure and started looking for countries for us to go to and selecting people for resettlement. We lived in the capital for about two years, and when the resettlement offer came, we did not have any choice—it was the orders.

ANGELA: While we were waiting, some of my children had a chance to go to France. Two daughters and my son went to France because our friends helped them. They left before us, and that's why we have three children over there now and four grandchildren. The United States program came later, and we are now separated. But we talked with our friends in France and said that it was okay because it would have been very expensive for all the family to go to France. That's how it all happened.

November 2013

Today, it is June 26, 2015, and I have just visited Angela at her home. The family has a nice house in a quiet neighborhood in Abilene. Angela takes me for a little tour of their backyard where tomatoes are ripening and eggplants are blooming. Everything looks wonderful, big and lush. I joke with Angela that I can tell that her husband has a degree in agriculture.

Afterward, we settle down at the breakfast table and talk about the book. Angela reads through her own story and says, "Yes, that's true, that's how it was." Then, we catch up on each other's lives, what has happened since we met last year. Angela looks content with her life and says that she will reach retirement age next year but will keep working. She is a career woman, whatever changes life brings and wherever she is.

A View from the Office

"The Rainy Day, or Paul's Job"

Very soon after the first refugees started arriving, the time came to find jobs for them. When the office opened, we did not have any refugees for the first two months. I used that time to meet with managers of larger companies to explain the refugee program and what they would gain by hiring the newcomers. Several company HR managers or supervisors were quite interested and said they would be willing to try as soon as we had any refugees looking for jobs. It was good that I had made these connections first; when the stream of people started flowing in, it would have been difficult to find jobs for all of them as fast as was needed.

Finding a decent job with full-time hours and somewhat decent pay is a crucial part of the rocky road to self-sufficiency, and my role as an employment coordinator ("job finder" and "career counselor") was very important. My first job placement was for Paul, a man in his thirties from Liberia who used to be a farmer in his country. The job opening I found for him was in a hotel. It was a housekeeping position. The old housekeeper had unexpectedly quit, and the manager was desperate to bring a new worker in as soon as possible. No health insurance was available, and the work hours were uncertain and probably not full-time.

I should have known better than to send Paul to take this job, but at that time, it seemed like a good idea. I was thinking, *Let him start here, and if something more solid comes up in the meantime, I can always get a new person to replace Paul and get him a better job.* Paul still had at least two more months on the financial assistance program, so we had more time for additional job searching if necessary.

I see now that this job was not a good fit for Paul, and Paul's skills were far from ideal for it. He was a farmer and used to living in a village. The housekeeping chores had most probably been in the hands of women in his house. But here we were, in the hotel manager's office on a Friday morning, and Paul passed the job interview. Around noon, the manager called me to offer the position to Paul on the condition that he would start on Monday morning. This was good news—my first successful job placement—and I was excited. And not just me: I told Paul the news, and he was eager to start.

I tried my best to make sure Paul's attendance and job performance would be perfect. He had been through our Job Readiness Training already, so we briefly went over the main points again—how important it was to be on time, to learn while training, and to work hard. Since it was essential for him to find his way to work, I went to his apartment that Friday afternoon. We walked to the bus stop together, rode the bus to his workplace, got off, and walked over to the hotel where Paul would be working. Then, we circled around the neighborhood and walked to another bus stop, the one where Paul would have to wait on the bus after his workday was over. I showed Paul the bus schedule and explained how to read it to tell the time buses would arrive and leave. Everything seemed to be good, so we parted for the weekend.

Paul's first day of work was on Monday, and he had to start at 8:00 a.m. That Monday morning came with pouring rain. Low grey clouds were pushing across the skies, and it seemed like the middle of the night to me when I entered my office. Hardly had I settled in at my computer when Paul's hotel manager called.

He sounded quite sour. "Hey, you gave me that sales pitch about refugees, how good they are and all. Now, where is that guy, Paul? It is almost nine now, and he is a no-show!"

"Good morning," I responded with a sigh. "I am so sorry to hear it, and I really do not know what may have happened. Paul was ready to go when I left him Friday. Just give me a few minutes, and I will call him real quick and call you back. I don't know what happened. Maybe he got lost on the way; it is his first time. Just let me try."

The manager calmed down a bit. "Alright, then. Today, we'll manage; the hotel is not too booked today with all this rain. But that guy, he has to be here tomorrow at eight a.m. promptly if he wants to keep his job. It's business, not some children's games."

And he hung up before I could say more.

I dialed Paul's number, dreading that he would not answer, which would have meant he was somewhere in town, maybe lost on his way, and I would have to go look for him in this weather.

But Paul picked up on the second ring. "Yeah?"

"Hey, Paul, remember you had to be at work today at 8:00 in the morning? It's after 9:00 now. What happened? Why are you at home?"

Although I tried to sound strict on the phone, I felt quite relieved that Paul was at home, safe and secure. Thank goodness, he was not lost in the rain in some strange location. And rain was still coming down quite hard and I had so many things to do in the office; it was a Monday morning, after all.

"But it is raining outside. How can I go when it is raining?" Paul answered.

I was left totally speechless. It seemed the most unbelievable answer I could ever imagine. I was ready for all kinds of explanations—feeling bad, having a headache, missing the bus, having overslept, not being able to find the place. The list could go on. But *rain*?

It was only later that I found out that rains in many African countries are so hard and torrential that when they start, all activities come to a stop. People usually stay at home and wait for the downpour to be over. I imagined it as somewhat like monsoons in India. So, Paul's claim about rain was not as insane as it seemed to me that Monday morning.

Then and there, I told Paul that rain does not stop business from going on in this part of the world. I advised him to go to Walmart, get an umbrella, and report promptly to his boss at the hotel next morning. Then, I called the manager back, but it seemed too unbelievable to tell him that Paul did not come in because of the rain. So, I made something up—I forget exactly what. Maybe I said that Paul had an upset stomach, but would be good to go next morning.

Another little crisis solved and a job saved.

Photo from Patrick's personal photo album

Nick Kloster

Faces of 1972 Burundians: Storyteller Patrick (top), after his 2014 grad-
uation from Abilene Christian University, with his good friend Etaslon
Kabura, visiting for the big occasion. Jeremie Sindayihebura and his wife,
Sophia (bottom), came to the US in 2007. Jeremie works a custodial job
and is a part-time pastor; Sophia is a homemaker.

CHAPTER 9

Stories of "1972 Burundians"

THE NAME "1972 BURUNDIANS" is used to describe the Burundians (and now, their offspring as well) who fled their country in or shortly after the 1972 massacre in Burundi and spent the rest of their lives in exile afterwards. Right after the

massacre, the majority of them settled temporarily in the neighboring Democratic Republic of Congo and lived there for more than a decade. Then, in mid-90s, a new war in Burundi spilled over the border to Congo, and the refugees fled to Tanzania. A new exile period followed as the group settled into Tanzanian refugee camps. A third country resettlement was offered to them only after more than ten years in Tanzania. The arrival of the "1972 Burundians" in the US started in the spring of 2007 and continued until the end of 2008.

Despite the long absence from Burundi—or perhaps exactly because of it—this group has been able to keep their Burundian cultural identity alive, although Burundians from Burundi often say that Tanzania group "is different" in their traditions and ways of life because the culture in Burundi continued to develop after they left, while for the "1972 Burundians," it remained more static. But it also changed because the group quite naturally adopted some local traits while in Tanzania.

The older generation would have their memories about Burundi, but their children and grandchildren growing up in the refugee camps would call Tanzania their home. Because of their life in exile, very few from the older generation had a chance to attend school or have any profession except small farming or fishing. The younger generation was a little better off. They had schooling opportunities in the camp, but other than that, their lives were very much constrained within the borders of the refugee camp. Entry and exit from the camp was with authorization only, and refugees could venture only about five miles from the camp to work the land and grow vegetables for themselves. Moreover, Tanzania camps were notorious for their meager food rations, harsh living conditions, and limited medical assistance.

It is hard to imagine growing up in conditions like these, without being able to experience the outside world and explore beyond that five-mile limit and then, after having lived in the confined world of a refugee camp, to be released all of a sudden into the free world with all its wonders, from television and airplanes to running water in one's own apartment.

Patrick: "I Felt Like I Could Fly"

Patrick is a young Burundian man in his midtwenties. He belongs to the "1972 Burundian" group, or as he himself says, "1972 People." He came to Abilene at the beginning of 2008, when the largest numbers of the "1972 People" were being resettled to different parts of the United States. Although the change from living in a refugee camp in Tanzania to the prosperous life in the US has been dramatic and sometimes challenging, Patrick has wisely used the opportunities the new life has given him.

I have known Patrick since he arrived in the US, and he has a bubbly, friendly personality and is always ready to share a laugh or a funny story about his adventures in the new country. He is one of those people who can make friends instantly wherever he goes. Patrick is living his "American dream" right now and is a political science student at Abilene Christian University. He will soon graduate. He works part-time at the local HEB grocery to support himself and pay some of his tuition.

Patrick lives in Abilene with his parents and younger siblings. His older brother, Max, is away at college, and his younger brothers and sisters are still in school. I think the youngsters are as "education-minded" as they are because their parents have laid a good foundation, always encouraging and supporting their schooling, even during the hard years in the refugee camp in Tanzania. Patrick agrees to have his story recorded.

MY NAME IS PATRICK. I can say that I was born a refugee, as I am a Burundian by nationality, but I was born in Democratic Republic of Congo, or as I say, Congo-Kinshasa. My parents could not go back home to Burundi because their parents—my grandparents—were killed there, so our family lived in Congo-Kinshasa, and that was where I was born. We lived in Congo while I was little.

Then, things got worse in Congo and a war broke out there. I think it was in 1996—the end of the year, maybe November or December. So, our family had to find safety somewhere else, and my parents decided to try Tanzania: it was safe, and they were welcoming refugees there.

But we had to take a boat to get to Tanzania. There is that lake called the Tanganyika Lake, and it divides Congo and Tanzania and Burundi. If you go to Tanzania from Burundi, you can go by bike or drive, but from Congo to Tanzania, you have to take a boat—there is no other way. Our journey was very difficult: it was war time, and the boat was very crowded, as all the people were trying to get out of Congo and get to safety. I do not remember how long the journey was, maybe five or six hours, but it was hard. Imagine all those crowds of people trying to get on the boat to get out of the warzone. Everybody wanted to go to Tanzania.

Then, we arrived in Tanzania and went to a place that was called Kigoma. Refugee workers interviewed us there, asked about all family things—maybe I have to call it "screening." They registered us, gave us pills and vaccinations, and then they had to decide how to divide all the people up, who would be going to which camp. There were thousands of people there, waiting, and not just Burundians. I think they tried to put together people who spoke the same language. Like, we were almost all Burundians in our camp. We spent about a week in that initial place, waiting on their decision. Then, they loaded us in a truck and took us to the actual camp.

It was about a seven-hour journey in the truck, and here we were, in our new home in the camp—a huge camp that was divided into two parts: Mutabila and Muyovozi. It was huge, tens of thousands of people. And that was just one of the fifty or more camps in Tanzania! So, we settled in alright, but with our family, we had a complication.

Our dad had gotten lucky and found a job in Tanzania on the lake, and it had happened before we left from Congo. So, he and my younger brother, Alex, were in Tanzania already when we arrived as a family, and my dad had already registered. So, when we came to Kigoma and got registered, they counted only the people who were there: my mom and all of us, but they could not count my dad and Alex because they were not there. When we got to the camp, my dad and brother joined us. My parents tried to explain to the camp workers that we all were one family, but they said they could not put us together as one case because my parents did not have official documents to prove that they were married. It was because we were refugees already in Congo. So, we were just kept as two separate cases—you know, I guess it was hard to believe that we were all a real family. They just gave us plots of land to build our houses on next to each other, and that's what we did. My parents and girls lived in one house, and we older boys took the other house. But this was a complication that had to be corrected later.

Initially, there was not much to do in the camp until some people started building schools. That was about two months after we got to the camp. The school was built of grass; they cut grass and built walls from grass. The roof of the school was made of a piece of canvas. But before the school building was ready, we had a teacher who was a volunteer, and he was teaching us. The teacher would find a tree somewhere, so he could hang up the board and have a little shade, and gather about thirty or forty kids, and we would get little stones to sit on, and we had classes. "Going to school" like that was really hard, as it was terribly hot in the sun without any shade, and it was hard to see our school papers. But that's how we started.

Then, the government of Tanzania got interested in educating refugees; they thought it was a good project. So, they decided to pay the teachers. And UNHCR found some donations, and the United States was helping, too. Then, we had a school, and compared to how the life in the camp was overall, it was good to have a school building, even though it was made of grass and had a canvas roof. But other than school, there was not much to do in the camp.

We could not go outside of the camp; we had to ask and be given permission. One of the reasons they restricted movement of people was to keep us refugees safe. At that time, war was still going on in Burundi, and some bad people would try to come to the camp and brainwash people to go to fight in the war. So, for our own safety, we had to stay inside the camp, and the guards would check who was coming into the camp. We could get kidnapped and taken to fight, and we could also get robbed. Tanzanian security did not let anyone from Burundi come into the camp, as they could be killers, bad people, and also the camp guards did not want anyone to come and do political campaigns or try to get money from refugees and take food from the camp to Burundi. We were getting food from UNHCR, and the camp guards did not want that food to end up feeding military in Burundi.

But sometimes, the camp security did things in an aggressive manner. If they suspected somebody of some criminal stuff, they would take that person to jail without any trial. That was one thing we did not like. If they suspected you, you would have no rights, no way to defend yourself. We refugees were "the minority;" we had "nothing to say." It was really tough that we could not do anything and we had no way to complain.

I remember that once one man stood up for our rights and told the Tanzanians, "What you guys are doing is not right because you take innocent people, people we know. We live here, we know more about people because they live with us, but you guys don't. You just come here and take people to jail!"

And the camp police beat him up so badly that he died the next day. Took him to jail, and he died there. He had a lot of injuries from the beating and did not make it. It was pretty bad. I was there when he talked to them, and other people were there, too, but we could not do anything. We were powerless in the camp.

But other than that, our family was doing okay. Except that officially, in their books, we were not one family. I think UNHCR was in charge of this, and they could have put us together easily, but it would have been a long process. But for us then, it was not a big deal; we just built houses close to each other, and we lived like that for more than ten years. But later, when we needed to prove for resettlement that my mom and my dad were really married, it took us a long time to get us all in one case. We really did not have any documents because of the war. You know, when the war broke out in Congo, we did not think about getting our documents or other stuff from the house—we just ran to save our lives. It was hard for the interviewers to accept that my parents were really married.

My dad used to go back to Kigoma and do fishing. It was a hard job as he had to be on the lake all the time and work with Tanzanians, but it brought us a little money. So, he would be gone for a month or two and then come back home, and then go again. We kids just went to school, and my mom would go a few miles away from home. We had a limit on how far one could go from the camp—it was five miles—and she would work the land, plant vegetables, crops, you know. We had like a little farm. We all used to go there on weekends and help her; we had corn, beans, and yucca. Those were the main crops, and sometimes we had potatoes. We could eat the vegetables or sell them for a little money. Most of the time, we ate them, as the food we were getting in the camp was not enough: we never ate breakfast, and sometimes, we had to skip other meals, too. We really had to manage very carefully not to run out of food before the next food allowance became available. They gave us a food allowance every two weeks, and the food was the same all the time: it was just corn or beans. Oh, I was so tired of it! We all were. So, when we had our own produce, we could have a little variety. But when our dad got home from the lake and brought some fish, we were like, "Yay! We have fish!"

It was like a party, a celebration, when we had fish at home. Fish was one of the biggest "luxury" meals we ate, and fish was really expensive. We could not afford to buy fish; we could only eat it when Dad brought it home from the lake. You know, people could go and buy more food, like meat or rice if they had money. But we did not have any money because all our money went to pay our school fees.

The best thing in the camp was that we had the opportunity to go to school. Not many could afford it because high school in the camp was expensive; you had to pay for it. But my dad had a job; he would go fishing and come back home with some money, so my parents could pay for my school, and for my older brother, younger brother, and sister. That was the best thing.

The second best thing was that I really learned to live in misery. I learned what it was to be a brother to someone you did not know, to share with others, and how to handle life in tough situations. This has helped me to get where I am today. I can easily put myself in somebody else's shoes and understand another person's suffering. I really understand it, and I would not ignore anyone who needs help. These were the things I went through myself; I learned from my experience while living in the camp.

But my best day in the camp was when we found out that we were approved for resettlement and that we would be going to the US to live. That was so exciting! But I have to tell you how it all started.

You know that we are called "1972 People" (Burundians). Resettlement workers gave us this name. They said, "Maybe we need to take those '1972 Burundians' and let them go to another country to live."

But it started with a census. They would come to your house and ask you questions, and you would tell your story, and they would listen and write things down. They would go from one house to another, see everybody, and quietly ask questions: "Where are you from?" "When did you leave your country?" "Where did you live before, and when did you leave?" Questions like that.

They took down each family's case numbers when they were doing the census. These were the numbers the camp used in food distribution. The workers were looking for those "1972 People," but nobody knew about it at that time; they did not tell anyone and just did it their own way. Then three years later, they said, "Okay, we have 15,000 '1972 Burundian' families from this camp."

Three years later! And they said, "Those are their case numbers—they are the ones."

After the census was over, they posted those numbers, and people could go and check if their family was included in the group that would be interviewed further for resettlement.

The case numbers were given to each family at the very beginning, during the screening in Kigoma. They were like your social security number; they never changed. And we got our food distributed by those numbers. When you go for your family's food allowance, you show the card with that case number, and they punch the card. And it means that you have got your food for the next two weeks.

But remember, my mom had a separate case from our dad; we were in two separate cases. My dad and my younger brother were together, and the rest of the family was separate. And my dad and my younger brother's case came up, but ours did not! It was crazy.

After the numbers came up, we had to go for an interview, and we tried to put our cases together during the interviews. But it took about two years to get it done. It was a long process because they had to make sure that they really had the right people in the family and that we deserved what they called a "third country resettlement." We had to go to questioning, and we had to answer all the questions so they could make sure we were really one family.

They would call us randomly, like, "Patrick, here we go: What's your dad's name?"

"Joseph."

"What's your mom's name?"

"Maria."

"How many goats did your family own back in Congo?"

"Four."

"Okay, then."

Then, they would call my younger brother, Alex, and ask him: "How many goats did your family have in Congo?"

"Four."

And they asked us a lot more questions, and our answers did match, so they thought, okay, they are really related. They asked my dad random questions and my mom random questions, and all our answers had to match. If they did not match, then we were not one family. It was like that; that's what they did. Then, we were all put in one case. The funny thing is I am still dreaming about the process.

I was so happy when we were approved. Imagine that someone came to you and said, "Hey, I am going to give you ten million dollars."

You would just get excited, right? And you would think, wow, it is so great. It is a lot of money, right? For me, it was way more than that!

I had always felt I could do so much with my life if I were given the opportunity. But to get that opportunity, I had to be free. And this country grants freedom. On the top of that, all my life since I remember myself, I always wanted to live in America. I always wanted to be American, to serve in the army, to be called American. Even when I was shopping for clothes in the camp, I bought a US army shirt. I still have it; I brought it with me, although it is too small now, as I was way younger and smaller back then. These are my memories. It was so very super exciting!

All my family were so happy. We felt like we were going to start a real life, with freedom. One of the things we all craved was freedom. We would be like all other people. Now, I was going to be free.

I would be going to school, I would work, I would have an opportunity to do things I did not have a chance to do in the camp. And my brothers and sisters would have the same opportunities, too. For me, it was a blast. I was so excited that I felt I could fly.

I still remember the day when we got the letter that said that we were approved for resettlement to the US. The aid workers had told us in advance what day and time the results would be announced. We would get our letter that day. One of our family members would have to go to a place in the camp, and they would give us a letter. They told us to open the letter, and although we could not read English, they showed us what to look for: there would be a mark on it if we were accepted, and the letter would say "welcome."

I spent all morning of that day away in the mountains with the goats because I did not want to be disappointed. I was thinking, *I don't wanna know, I don't wanna know...cross my fingers.*

Time was going on, and around one o'clock, I decided to go back to our house and see what was going on. My brother brought the letter home, and we looked inside; I saw my dad's name in the letter. And there was the welcome mark, and the letter said, "Your family has been approved."

Oh, my God, we were approved! I was jumping up in the air: "Finally! I'm gonna be free! I'm gonna be free!" It was a big day.

Many other people had also passed their interviews and were approved, and we all were excited. People were hugging each other. "Bye-bye, goodbye, take care. We are going. We are leaving in two weeks."

A few weeks after that, it was time to leave the camp. So, we just had everything packed up and left the next day. Oh, my gosh, it was so very exciting! It was like the luckiest day of my life. That is something I will never forget.

Then, we came to the US and settled in Abilene. Everything was really different from the camp here. For me, one of the hardest things was school during the first months. When I started high school here—I will be honest with you, the first months, I was so dumb, and I did not understand the system. I had to get used to the whole school system. It was all totally new for me, and it took me a while to learn it. Like, they gave me a Scantron—you know a Scantron test, where you have to answer by shading bubbles—and I was like, "What is this? What do I do with it?"

It was my first time, and yes, it was pretty bad. And the language, of course! So, at first, I could not make good grades at all. There was only one class, only one class I could make decent grades, and it was math. The way they solve math problems here was different, but I could use my understanding and the ways I was taught and come to the same result, the same answer. That was the only class I felt I could pass.

But for the rest, I had to retake the classes the next year. Then, I was really understanding more, gaining more English. The first semester, I went to school and spent all my days in ESL classes, reading, writing, spelling, things like that. Later, when we started our regular classes and when I had difficulties, I would go back to our ESL teachers and ask, "Hey, what is this? How do we do that?"

And the teachers would help me with the problems that had to be solved. That was the biggest challenge. The following year, I started spending much more time with Americans, learning, reading, listening to radio, to music. Also, I was watching a lot of cartoons. I always asked about things that other students were talking about and just learned from them quickly. I wanted to go on to college, and I only went to high school here for two years, so I needed a good GPA, good grades for college. So, I really had to work hard. With hard work, I came from not understanding anything to doing well, and I could graduate. It was awesome! And it was a huge challenge for me. At the beginning, I had no idea if I would ever graduate from high school at all.

Then, the time came for me to find a college and be admitted, and it was not easy. You know, I had to go for tests and stuff. All I could do was to study hard. Really, really hard! I was admitted as an international student to Abilene Christian University, and I had to start with the basics of academic English. College classes are more challenging; they are not like high school.

So, I had to start with English basics for the higher academic level for one semester, and it was extremely helpful. I got to understand what it was to research a paper. You know what I mean? We didn't do those things back home or in high school. I learned how to do research, I learned how to write a paper, how to search for information—many things. It brought my English up to the college level, and then I did not have to struggle when I was in college. From that time, I have really been doing very well in most of my English classes, better than any other class. As I had so low a level at first, all that learning helped me very much. But I am in my senior year now in political science.

After I graduate, I want to go to graduate school. I want to pursue politics and do grad school, yes. And then, go to work with the United Nations, if I can get a job with them, in New York City or Washington, DC. And from there, I would want to go overseas because I love to travel, and I love working in different places. I even don't know why I love it, but I feel like I could be good at it. I feel I could do it. That is one of my main focuses.

I do want to do school as much as I can. As I am the first generation in my family to go to college, I just want to do as much as I can and be happy. And work for United Nations. But when I turn forty, I want to come back to politics and work for the government.

But with the United Nations, I could do any job that they would offer. But if I had a choice—if I can dream—I would be a UN observer. You know, those people who go to the countries where conflicts are going on. They go there and watch what is going on there and then report back to the organization. They check if everything is handled in the right way, and they give the information to the UN, so they know that everything is going according the rules. I would love to do that.

But if this does not work out, I would take anything, in the office or outside. That's what I have been dreaming about: I want to work with the United Nations. I feel I have experience with different cultures and that I can represent the country. I could work in Kenya because they have large UN office in Kenya somewhere, and I could represent the country. These are big plans, but I am on my way. My parents and siblings are excited for me; they are very supportive. They know that I am not going to school just for my own benefit, but that other people will benefit from it as well. And you know all my family members are trying to get education; even my dad is picking up more English.

But these were serious stories, about my life in the camp and the start in the US, and my future plans. But let me share some funny stories about my first experiences in the US—mostly, they are about language. This one is really funny: how I got my name, "Number 4."

Well, a few months after we came, I got a job in Zoltek. It was pretty soon after our arrival, and I did not have a car or driver's license yet, so my supervisor used to come and pick me up for work. And we would always get food before we went to work. My supervisor would take me to McDonald's on South Fourteenth Street. As I had never ordered any food and did not know how to drive, I did not know how ordering food at McDonald's worked. My supervisor would always order "Number 4": it was a double cheeseburger meal, and it came with a drink and fries. As he knew that I did not know how to order, he would get me the same thing, "Number 4," and I would pay him back in cash. We did it several times like that, and then he said, "When you are hungry and I am not around, you can come here and tell them that you want Number 4."

He explained it all to me, but he spoke so fast and his American English was so hard to understand that I was having a hard time getting it.

Anyway, a few months later, I got a car and a driver's license. And I thought, *Yes, now I am going to order my food on my way to work and have my lunch.* Oh no, it was not a good idea. No, it was not a good idea at all!

So here's what happened: I drove up to McDonald's, to the order window. A lady's voice greeted me, "Welcome to McDonald's. How can I help you?"

I remembered what my supervisor told me, and I said, "Yes, can I have Number 4?"

"Sure. Do you want the meal?"

And what I really wanted was the meal because that was what we always got, but I did not know it then. That name did not sound familiar to me, so I said, "No."

"Okay, you just want a cheeseburger then. Do you want cheese on it?"

"Yes."

"Pickles on it?"

"No."

"Sir, do you want the meal?"

"No. Just Number 4."

"Do you want fries with it?"

Hmm...what's "fries"? What's "fries"? I asked myself. She was waiting on my answer, so I said, "No."

"Okay. So, you want a meal without fries?"

"No."

"Sir, could you please drive up to the window?"

And I thought, *Oh, my God. Oh, my God.*

I looked in the rearview mirror and saw a long line behind me with people waiting...I drove up to the window.

"Sir, you said Number 4. Do you want to do a meal?"

"No."

"Okay, sir, here is your Number 4. Cheeseburger, no fries. Do you want a drink?"

"No."

"Do you want pickles on it?"

"No."

"Do you want ketchup?"

"No."

"Oh, my," she said. "Who is this guy?"

She went away for a minute and came back with the manager, another lady. She said to the manager, "I cannot help him. I don't know what to do."

People behind me were honking, and I shouted back to them, "Hey, easy, easy!"

That was what I knew to say. I really did not know what I was doing. I wanted a burger, I wanted fries, and I wanted a drink, but I did not know how to get it all. When they were asking if I wanted those things, I did not understand what they were saying, so I answered "no" all the time.

So, the manager asked me, "What do you want, sir?"

"I want Number 4, a double cheeseburger."

"Okay. Do you want anything else?"

"No."

Then, they gave me my Number 4, the cheeseburger—just plain cheeseburger. And I was shocked. "And that's it? What about a drink?"

"Oh, my God, but you *did not* order a drink!" The manager was so frustrated, and the people behind me were so frustrated. And I just wanted my burger with fries and a drink, and I had no way of getting them! I was getting mad, too. I wanted my fries and drink!

The manager and the other lady were just looking at me, so upset. "Okay, sir, just tell me what you want. Tell me what you want."

Then, I pointed at the things with my finger. "Hey, I want this drink over there, and those fries."

And you know what they did? They gave me another burger, with a drink and fries. For free. Then, I drove off. "Thank you!"

I went on to work and told my supervisor what had happened. He listened to me and said, "Man, you just messed everything up. You just messed the whole thing."

So, we went back the next morning. We went in and apologized, and my supervisor explained everything to them. He told them, "This is the guy I was coming here with every day. I was trying to teach him how to order his food. And I am really sorry. I told him to try to buy his own food, but he was not ready yet."

Then they said, "Oh, it was you!"

It was embarrassing when I was learning English and how things worked. I told them, "Guys, I really want to apologize. I was trying to blend in the culture."

They said, "No offense, sir, but you were really frustrating. But it's okay. We'd love to have you back anytime."

And you know what else they said? "Now, come to us, and when you come up, just order your Number 4, and we will know you. And we'll know what to give to you."

So, I spent the whole next year driving up to McDonald's and saying, "Hi, it is me, Number 4, please."

They started calling me "Number 4." People who worked there used to call me "Number 4" after this incident. Most of them do not work there anymore, but some still call me "Number 4" when they see me around. It is quite embarrassing, you know. But now I tell them, "No, now I know what I want. I am fluent now."

But it was most embarrassing back then, you know.

Another thing that was pretty funny happened in the mall. Do you know Kabura, Emmanuel's son? Yes? Okay, this happened when we were both together.

We went to the mall one day, right, to look around and do some shopping. Some American friends had told us, "When you need to attract a person's attention, say, 'Excuse me, sir.' Or say, 'Excuse me, ma'am.' It is the polite way. Okay? Say, 'sir' or 'ma'am.'"

So, we went to the mall and went to Best Buy, I think. We needed some help, so we went to one shop assistant, a young lady. Kabura said, "Excuse me, *sir*?"

She asked him, "What?"

Kabura repeated louder, "Excuse me, *sirr*."

You know, it is the polite way. But the shop assistant asked him, "Hey, do I look like a man?"

"No, you look like a lady."

"Then, why do you say 'sir'?"

We started thinking, *Wait, what's wrong here?*

"Well, because it is the polite way!"

The friends had told us that we could either say "sir" or "ma'am," but we did not know that a woman has to be addressed as "ma'am" and a man should be addressed as "sir." We thought we could use either one of these words.

So, the shop assistant said, "Do I *look* like a man?"

But when we explained, she was really friendly. She said, "Okay, guys, look: if you see a woman, you say 'ma'am.' And if it's a man, you say 'sir,' okay?"

"Oh, yes, okay."

"Now, go practice!" And she wrote down these words for us. "Next time you come here, practice, 'Excuse me, ma'am,' or, 'Excuse me, sir.'"

We were so embarrassed when we walked out. After that mistake, we decided not to say a single word at all. But it did not last very long. And now it all seems so funny. But it is still embarrassing if you meet those people you offended like that.

When I came, I hardly spoke any English. My brother, Max, was better. But now, we are all fluent, but I could not picture this day would ever come. It was not really that easy to accomplish. So many things have happened along the way, so many funny stories. But what is good about Americans is that they will take at least a couple of minutes to explain your mistakes to you, explain what you said wrong, and they will tell you an appropriate way to say it. That's what I love about people here. They will just say, "Hey, don't say that anymore, don't say that anymore. Say it this way."

Seriously, Americans are good people. They would not take offense; instead, they would say, "Don't say that anymore. That is so bad."

And I would say, "Okay, no more!" That's how I learned.

November 20, 2013

Edward: "How Could I Know?"

Edward is a Burundian refugee in his late thirties. He was born in a small town in Burundi but had to flee while still a teenager when the civil war in Burundi broke out. He was almost killed just because his parents had different ethnic origins.

Edward came to the USA in May of 2007 with his wife Elivania and a baby named Lucky.

What I remember about Edward's arrival: I was the IRC Abilene site manager then and out of town for training in San Diego. One early morning before the training sessions started, our case manager called me. "Oh, we have a problem here. One family's paperwork does not match."

It was about Edward and his family. They had just arrived, and when the case worker checked their documents, she noticed that the paperwork listed the family baby as a girl when, in reality, it was a boy. Some other documentation stated so as well. By resettlement rules, such situations had to be reported to the manager, who passed it up the management chain. It could have been a case of babies having been switched, and the wrong person being brought into the United States.

While the "reporting" was going "up" and reaching the "top level," the family had to wait with the applications for the social security cards and for public assistance—food stamps and Medicaid—since their documents did not match. It was quite frustrating for them, but things eventually got sorted out. The baby boy had been named Lucky Nelson because he had been born on the day the family received the resettlement approval letter. Edward had reported the new family member to the agency in charge of refugee resettlement in Tanzania, which was standard protocol. Obviously, somebody from the agency staff had made a mistake and listed the newborn as a girl. Maybe it was the name, Lucky, which easily could have been a name for a girl or a boy. Some other documents that had been completed when the baby was present, like medical check-ups, listed Lucky correctly as a boy. So, all the paperwork had to be redone and corrected, but apparently, no crime was involved, just an error, and we could go on with services as planned.

Now, we sometimes remember this difficult start, and I joke with Edward about his son Lucky who "was a girl." Lucky is a big boy now and attends school, and the family now really does have two girls who were born here in the US.

Edward came to the US with minimal English skills, but he tried really hard to master English and used every opportunity to learn. Case workers had seen him in Walmart several times, just walking around and talking to other people for English practice. He was riding our local public bus for hours, engaging in conversations with other passengers to learn English. When he started his job in Aramark Food Services, a company that serves food in Hardin-Simmons University's cafeteria in town, he practiced English with university students and professors and anybody else who was ready to talk to him. Everybody loved Edward at work because he was always smiling and ready to test his English skills.

Now, Edward speaks English fluently, and we can talk easily about his past and present life. You could not really guess that he did not know any English when he came to the US. Edward wants to continue his education, and we talk about his options for obtaining his GED certificate. Adult Education school in town offers GED classes, and I encourage him to start. Although Edward says that he "has never been to school," he has a gift for languages and is quite smart, so I am sure he will do well in GED. Edward would rather not record his story, so I will take notes.

MY NAME IS EDWARD. I was fourteen years old when the civil war started in Burundi, the country where I was born. As a child, I lived with my mother and grandmother, but my father did not live with us—he was not married to my mother. He did not have any other woman, but somehow—I don't know why—he had not married my mom. Maybe it was because my parents were from two different tribes—my mom was Hutu, but my dad was Tutsi. Or maybe because he was a military man and he served in the army.

He did not care much for me, although he was aware I was his son. He never came to visit me nor gave any money to support us. My dearest person was my grandma. She was always happy and upbeat, although we were very poor, and some days, we did not have anything to eat at all. We could not afford to buy a house for ourselves, but we rented a little place so we had somewhere to live.

My mom was running a vegetable store in the village, like a little stall, and selling homegrown veggies, tomatoes and corn, so she often left me with her mother, my grandma, when she went to the market to sell. After all, she was the only one to bring money home, in other words, "to put food on the table."

Although we had nothing and lived in extreme poverty, I felt happy because I knew my mom and my grandma loved me. My family would not have been able to send me to school if not for a volunteer who offered to pay my school fees. Thus, I went to school, and my mom bought me a school uniform. Uniforms were mandatory in schools, so I could not go without, but I had no shoes. My family did not have the money to buy both uniform and shoes, and shoes were not the main necessity. So I had a uniform, but no shoes. I went barefoot like that from the first grade to the fifth grade. Other kids were laughing at me, teasing me that I had no shoes. But then one day, I was in town with a group of other students. We were in the fifth grade then. A woman saw me with the other kids, and I was the only one without shoes. Then, she came up to us and asked, "Are you the only one without shoes? Why don't you have shoes?"

I said, "My family is very poor, ma'am. I have only my mother and grandmother and no father, so we don't have money for shoes."

She said, "Let's go to get you shoes."

We went and she bought me a pair of shoes, right there, and I put them on right away. I was so happy, I was shouting, "I have shoes! I have shoes!"

It was the happiest day of my childhood.

But then, the days of war came. I was about fourteen years old then. We were in that house we were renting when some people came to kill us. They were our family, so they knew we were all at home. They killed my mom and my grandma, but I escaped; I climbed up on the roof and went off, and they could not find me. They kept looking for me because they knew that I lived there, but I did not return home. That day I fled. I left the country and went to Tanzania instead. I have never been back to Burundi to this day. I lived in a refugee camp in Tanzania. It was some time in 1994, at the end of the year.

My life in the camp was very hard. I had no family, no mother, no father, or anybody else, so I was just a teenager without anybody there. I don't know if you can imagine how it was, but the camp had over 43,000 people, all in one camp and all trying to get something. It was called Lukole refugee camp. Everybody had family or friends, except me; I was all by myself.

At that time, the camp had a school. UNHCR had set up a school, but I could not go to school. It was because of food. The camp gave us some food, but it was rationed by the number of people in a household. They gave only eight pounds of *fufu* (maize or cassava flour) and four pounds of beans per person, and I had to survive on this food for two weeks. People tried to eat only one time a day or one time in two days, and many went out of the camp to look for food or to work for Tanzanian people who would give them food for work. Then, you could eat.

But officially, we were not allowed to go outside the camp, not more than four kilometers away from the camp. But we had to! People were sneaking out in the middle of the night—we just *had* to! Otherwise, you would die. No food inside. People from outside of the camp, the Tanzanian people, were bringing food to sell. They knew that some people in the camp worked for the UN and that the UN gave them some money to buy more food. Yes, they were bringing food, but we did not have jobs, so we had to go outside the camp to find jobs to get some money.

Overall, it was easier for people with bigger families. They could take turns to go search for food and put their food together. If you had adults in the family, they went in search for jobs and food, but children could go to school and help with house chores. Some adults even stayed away for months, earning some money. But I was about fifteen years old then and was all by myself, so it was extremely difficult to survive.

I really wanted to go back to school, but I was so hungry that I went out of the camp to work for food. And then I came back, but I had to go again, so going back to school did not work for me. Imagine if you had to choose to eat or go to school totally hungry— you would go for food, believe me. So, in this way, I just had my primary school, and that was all.

Then, a terrible thing happened to me in the camp. The people who had killed my mom and grandma and were looking to kill me had also fled Burundi and were right here in the same camp in Tanzania. They were together, like a gang, and they recognized me. They had also fled because they had lost power in the government, and they were afraid that the Burundian military would come and kill them for what they had done. So, they saw me and thought, *Oh, no, he is not one of us; he must be here trying to spy for his dad.*

And they tried to kill me. We had been neighbors, and they used to know my mother and father. But I had no connection to my father. He did not live with our family; he was in the military. I was afraid they would try to kill me again, so I jumped the fence and fled from the camp.

I went to live with a Tanzanian farmer for about two years. I lived in Biharamuro, in Kagera province. I lived with that family as a hired hand: I was working for food, not even money. I was just working all day, from seven in the morning till seven in the evening, and they would feed me for that, that was all. No wages, no money, just food. I planted their fields, peanuts, beans, and corn.

I broke my hip while working on that farm, and it has never been the same ever since. But it happened like this. One day, I went to get water. You know, in Africa, many people do not have water in the house, so they go to a lake or a river to get the water and bring it home. So, I went to a little creek that was down the hill from that farm I was working on. At the creek, I got the water, but when I leaned over to pick up the container, I slipped, fell on my side, and I broke my hip. I was in pain and could not walk anymore.

But the people I was living with did not care about me enough to take me to a doctor and pay for it. The family was very well off. They had the money, but no, they did not want to spend it on me. After all, I was not their child; I was just a worker boy, so they said they could not pay for a doctor for me. A doctor would have to do surgery, and it would cost a lot of money in Tanzania. So, I was there on the farm, and they helped me to bandage the hip up, and that was all. After some time, I recovered enough to walk, but I have been limping since that time.

So, one day, I went to the nearby village market. The farmer's family had sent me to get some things from the market for them. In the market, I met with a UN worker from Lukole camp, and he recognized me. He said, "I think I know you from the camp."

And I said, "Yeah."

He asked, "Can I take you back to the camp?"

I said, "No, I really cannot go back." I told him my story, how I had to run away because of those guys in the camp.

The worker told me, "Believe me, we will protect you. We know what happened in the camp, and we protect people like you. And we are sending some people to live in other countries, and we help some others to go back to their countries. But also, we have different protections we can use to help you."

When I heard that, I said, "Wow, in that case, let us go back to the camp."

We went back to the camp together, and the UN people told me to live right behind the police house. We had police in the camp who protected everybody, and my house was right there with people who helped kids with no families. So, I stayed there, and I told my story to the UNHCR people. They wrote it down, and they were preparing people to go live in other countries—Australia, the US, Norway, wherever they accepted refugees. So, they sent my case to many countries, including the US. I went to that UNHCR worker to talk about my case. His name was Olivier, and he was from California. I was still young, and he gave me advice as if I were his child.

He said, "Edward, believe me, life in the US would be very difficult if you went all by yourself. You have no parents, no brothers or sisters, so find yourself a wife, or a fiancée, and we will put her on your case, and then you can go with her. Or better, marry, and then you could go together."

I said, "Let me think. But that is a good idea."

Olivier told me, "Listen, Edward, I know that our government will send JVA workers to select people from the camp for resettlement to the US. They will come next year, I think in January, but will start interviews next March. But you can go and get married while we are working on your case, and then we will put your wife on your case."

I had not thought about getting married, being all by myself and having that problem with my hip. But after talking to Olivier, I went to see my friends at church. It was in 2003 when I started thinking about it. I used to go to church a lot. I was in the church choir, and I spent a lot of time in prayer. You know, when you live in a hard situation like I did, you pray a lot to God.

So, I looked around in church for a future wife. You know, some girls may not want you because you are poor or you have no family. And with all the troubles I had had in the past, I had not even thought about finding a wife. But Elivania was in the church choir with me, and I usually was very quiet, did not talk much. But then I started talking to her. At first, she was surprised and asked, "Why are you talking like that? Are you thinking about getting married?"

And I said, "Yes."

Initially, she did not want to marry me, but I tried and tried, and then she said, "Yes, we can get married, and I will go with you."

I had not told anyone yet that we would go through resettlement together or that we would go to another country. But after she said "yes," I told her about resettlement. She did not want to go as a fiancée though. She said, "Then, let's get married, and I will go as your wife. If I go as a fiancée, you can find somebody else in America."

So, I got married to Elivania. We did not have a big wedding because we were poor. I did not have a job, and Elivania did not have much, either. She used to live with relatives—not parents, but an uncle and his family—so they gave us their blessings. Her uncle said, "It is your decision. If you want to get married, do, and if you want to go live in the US, we will not make it hard for you."

Her uncle's family was poor, too, so they could not help us with anything. But the church was good to us. They gave us dishes and some things for the house, and we got married and went home. Then, I reported to the UNHCR about my marriage, and they put Elivania on my case. After four months, the US government sent JVA people to our camp, and I told them my story, and then I had my case. And then, we passed the interview with the US immigration, and they said that we had to wait on the answer. Both interviews were the same year: JVA came in March, and immigration came in May. So, we had to wait until we got an official answer from US immigration, and it took time.

It was in 2006, and at that time Elivania was pregnant. Then on July 26, I received a letter from IOM asking if we were ready to go to the US. And exactly the same day, Elivania was in the maternity ward and gave birth to our first child! That's why we called him "Lucky." He was born on the day we received a letter of approval for resettlement to America.

We had been waiting for a long time! Now, we had another person to add to my case, so I went back to JVA, and they asked: "Why do you have another person? We have to add him to the papers, and you have to wait now."

So, we had to wait for another nine months to add Lucky to our case.

About six months after I got married, I found a job as a social worker in the camp. I was making eighteen dollars per month. It was not good money, but it was better than nothing. We could buy some food now. I enjoyed that kind of work. Every day, I went to visit disabled people in the village inside the camp. I asked them what they needed and made a report to my supervisor. People got sick sometimes, and then they could not get out of the house, or something else had happened. I had to write all that in my report and submit it. Or, people needed help to get to a hospital, things like that. It was an easy job, like a desk job. I had to go and talk and make a report in Swahili and then send it to my supervisor, and that was all. Those were my job duties, and I enjoyed that job.

Then, the time came when we had to travel. I remember that the first place we came to in the United States was Chicago. We stayed overnight in Chicago in a hotel. They gave us food, but we did not want to eat that food because we did not know what it was. It was chicken and salad, and we ate the chicken, but we did not like that green stuff, so we did not eat it. They brought us some sodas and juice, and we drank those. We were happy to be coming to America and thought that life here would be without problems. You know, the US, the richest country in the world. But no! It was terrible how I got in trouble here without even knowing it.

I ask Edward to tell me more about what kind of "trouble" he had, and he goes on.

To understand what I am talking about, I have to explain everything. You know, in Tanzania, we lived in the camp, and we did not have any bank accounts, checkbooks, nothing like that. Even if you had a job, they would pay you in cash, and you would go shopping with your cash. And when the money was gone, it was gone. But when we came here, people around us thought that we were like everybody else, that we went to school and could read English, understand things. It was a big problem for many refugees in the US.

When we came, nobody asked us if we could understand or read English, no. So, I did not really know anything about banks and checks. It was different here. But this trouble, it started in 2008. I had bought a car. You know you have to have some transportation here. I went to the bank to see if I had money in my account. I saw my balance and thought, yes, I had money. But I had forgotten that I had written a check to pay for electricity. At that time, I was thinking that if I wrote a check, the money would go out of my account immediately. So one day, I needed gas for my car, and I went to get gas at the gas station, and I paid with a check. It was $30.00. And I thought that was it, and I forgot about it. At that time, I did not know how to balance a checkbook or how to follow what I had paid for. So, some time passed. It was 2010 already. I was helping friends to go to Lubbock for green card fingerprints, and I got a flat tire on the road. I called roadside assistance, and they sent the police to help me. The police came, and they checked my driving license and told me, "You have a crime on your record."

I was shocked. "What crime?" It was a surprise for me. The policeman told me that I had written a bad check, and I asked him, "What bad check?"

And he said, "Back in 2008."

It turned out that it was that check I had written for a gas station. The check I had written for the electricity payment had cleared before I wrote the gas check, and I had no money in the bank, so my gas check had bounced. But I did not know about it. Then, the court had issued a warrant for my arrest, but they had sent the warrant notice to a wrong address, so I did not get that, either. All this time, I had just lived without any knowledge about it.

So, the policeman took me in custody, put me in jail. But I did not know I was going to jail. I asked the police, "Are you going to put me in jail?"

But the policeman said, "You are already in jail." I did not know what a jail in the US was like. They told me, "You know, you had a bad check, and you have to pay. You cannot get out of jail if you don't pay that money."

I said, "I know I have money in my account. Can I pay now?"

But the police said, "No, you have to wait, as we have other people who came before you."

So, I waited four hours. Then, the police gave me a phone to make a phone call. I called my bank, and I had at least four thousand dollars in my account. I had to pay five hundred dollars. The policemen explained that it was thirty dollars for that gas check, and then the rest was other charges, court fees and stuff—I did not know what else. The only thing I knew was that I wanted to get out of that jail. I was ready to pay anything. So, I paid, and they let me go. Just then, I was thinking and thinking and could not understand how it had happened.

Even now, I do not understand why they had waited those years, from 2008 till 2010—more than two years. In the past, I had been driving, and the police had stopped me for speeding, but they never said anything about a bad check. I don't know. Even now, I don't have peace because I don't know if there may be something else on my record. Maybe I have done something I don't know. Yeah. I just went to apply for US citizenship, and you know, they denied my application because of this bad check issue. It makes me sad.

I would like to investigate this old thing, how it could have happened, but I don't think I can find any lawyer who could help for free. So, I have to wait until 2015 to reapply for citizenship. This has made Elivania scared of life in the US, too. She does not think too much of it, I am telling you.

Another issue Edward has had since his Tanzania days is the problem with his hip.

Like I told you, I broke my hip in 1998 when I worked on that farm in Tanzania. When I had just come to the US, I saw a doctor, and even in Africa, I went for check-ups, and they wrote down on my medical record that "this person has a hip problem and may need to get it fixed." When I saw a doctor here, he told me, "I cannot do a surgery on you because it has been too long a time. This bone has already grown. Let's see if we can fix it with wearing one shoe with a thicker sole, and then the shorter leg will be on the same level as the other."

I agreed with him, and I got the special shoe. It was working fine for a while. But in January of 2013, I was getting pain when I was working eight hours on my feet, and the pain was getting worse. So, I was not able to work full-time hours anymore. I would work a few hours and then sit down to rest my leg, and sometimes the manager would tell me go home. I saw another doctor, and he said, "You have been working too much, and your hip is getting worse. I think you may need surgery to fix it. We will take the bone out and put it back in the hip, and then in three months, you would be back to work."

They would put some screws and a metal rod in my hip to hold it better. The doctor did the surgery, but the surgery did not come out good. He put the screws in, but the screw came out in May 2013, so he had to open it up again and put something in it and put the screw in again. The hole he made in the bone was too big, and the screw kept moving, so it would not heal. And the bone could break again. I saw a different doctor for a second opinion. The second doctor did an X-ray and said, "You will never heal if you don't do another surgery."

He said he could put in a longer metal rod to keep it all together and cover up the hole. But he said that this surgery would be very difficult because it would be to correct the first one. I went back to the doctor who did the first surgery, and then he told me that the other doctor had already called and talked to him. He said, "Okay, go ahead and let the other doctor try to fix it."

But my Medicaid had ended by then, and the second doctor could not do anything without insurance. And I needed Medicaid for at least three months after the surgery as well. So, I went to see

Medicaid office, and they said that in Texas, Medicaid had changed and that they could not give me Medicaid anymore.

So, I am just sending letters to our elected representatives and senators asking to help me. I find their websites and send emails and letters. I write it in Swahili first and then translate into English and send them. I wrote to Randy Neugebauer, to Susan King, and to our governor Rick Perry. Their office staff told me they were going to see what they could do. They have sent letters to the social security office to speed up my case, to see if I qualify for disability. And if I do, then I would get Medicaid and could do that surgery. But right now, I am just waiting. I will try to get that surgery and then go back to work, but I don't think I will be able to go back to work full-time, like forty hours.

Although life has been a little challenging, I do not think I will ever go back to live in Africa. I like the United States; it is a great country for education, both for kids and for adults. Here, the education is free or at a low cost, and many people can go back to school. But in Africa, it is very difficult. Many people cannot afford going to school because they do not have money for school fees. I want my kids to grow up here and get an education here, and they could work for the US. But my wife, Elivania, is thinking of going back to live in Burundi one day. She loves Burundi more than I do. So, she is considering it, but she is not ready yet. She misses the friends and family, and they are all in Burundi now, and they talk on the phone often. Yes.

But I do not need my kids to go back to Africa because they are not going to get an education there. They are doing well now. My son Lucky is seven years old and will be eight on July 16. He is in second grade and is doing very well in school, passing all the tests with 100 percent. He has never gone under 85 percent. He wants to play football, American football. He says, "I want three things: I want to play American football, and I want to play soccer, and I want to be a doctor." He says that he wants to be "a doctor," but he really means "a dentist." That is because he has had trouble with his teeth.

And I have a little girl, Rachella, and she is in pre-K. She is four years old now. And she says she wants to be a doctor, too, but that is because she wants to help me with my hip. She says, "Daddy, when I am a doctor, you can come to me, and I will fix you." They are good kids and love school.

But about myself, I think while I am waiting on my surgery to happen, I could go to GED class. I don't think I could become a nurse, with my leg and everything. But I could learn something else to have a better job. I have a good friend, Juvenal, and he is in medical school right now. We talk often, and he is pushing me to go back to school. And I think that's what I will do. I want to go to school to learn more English, pass that GED test first, and then I could get a profession, like medical billing or accounting. And then, I could get a better job, where I could be sitting. Like a desk job. But now, my big problem is education. I have not graduated from high school, and I cannot get an office job. Even now, I could do something while sitting, just a few hours. So, I will go to GED class.

Since we talked, several good things have happened in Edward's life: he has finished the GED class and passed his test, so he has a high school degree equivalent that allows him to go to college. He plans to start college in the fall of 2015. Also, his "bad check" issue has been resolved with the help of a church member who happens to be a lawyer. Edward's case was reopened, and the court cleared him of all wrongdoing. He has become an American citizen as well. Edward says he feels much more content with life now and confident that he is on the right track.

I have to add that many refugees initially struggle with the financial system here because they use checks, debit cards, and credit cards for the first time.

December 11, 2013

A View from the Office

"Neleh's Job, or the Social Workers' Struggle for Refugee Self-Sufficiency"

In early 2004, Bouake was our first refugee who came to Abilene. He was a married man from Liberia, but his wife and three little children had been separated from him when they all were fleeing the Liberian Civil War. So, Bouake came first and had to wait for his family to come later. I have noticed that it happens fairly often in war-torn countries.

I am not exactly sure how they got separated, but when unexpected fighting breaks out in your hometown or village, it's not easy to keep track. Imagine coming home from a seemingly peaceful day in the farm fields and seeing that all the houses in your neighborhood are on fire. You run for your life and just hope your spouse and children are doing the same. It's only when you are safe again that you start looking and asking about your loved ones. The search may take a long time—sometimes, even years. If you are in a place where resettlement is offered, your own interviews may have started by the time your family is found. Including them in your case could involve long delays, so refugee workers often advise those with lost relatives to go on with their own process, leaving spouses and children to follow in due course. In immigration legal terms, it is called "follow-to-join" process. I think this happened to Bouake as well; he was here, but his family was not.

Bouake lived in a two-bedroom apartment with his roommate, Lionel, who was another refugee from Liberia and had arrived on the same day as Bouake. He was also married but had been separated from his wife during the war. Both men used to visit our office daily, although we really did not need them there and had no news for them.

I asked them, "What can I help you with? Why are you here?"

Lionel said, "What else can we do? We just came here to have something to do!"

I asked, "Don't you have anyone to visit, like neighbors or friends?"

Lionel said, "We do not know anybody. There are no other refugees around. And we do not know the town, so we have nowhere to go."

And he was right: they were the first refugees and did not know anyone to talk to except our office staff. I assured them that they would have jobs soon. I had talked to a few managers who were willing to interview them and hoped that both men would find some friends at work. At the moment, though, we were waiting on their employment documents and social security cards to come in the mail.

So, we were their "friends" and case workers at the same time, trying our best to answer all of their questions and dispel their concerns. Without fail, their daily question was, "When is my family coming?" And a close runner-up was, "When can I get a job?"

Soon, their documents arrived, and both men started working. I found a job for Lionel at the hospital laundry and Bouake was hired at a hotel. Bouake's job was not a perfect match, but both men got busier and did not come to the office as often as before.

Time went on, but there was still no word about their families. Bouake was a calm man and took it well, but Lionel grew more and more impatient. He started coming into our office during late afternoons after his shift, and instead of going to the visitors' counter, he took to sneaking into the staff's back rooms. There, he would pop up in front of the manager's desk.

"Hey, when is my wife coming? What are you doing to speed it up?"

It felt a little spooky, and our manager started locking the office door when she was there by herself. It was unfortunate, but we really could not do anything to speed up the men's family cases. Then, one day, the big news came by fax from headquarters: Bouake's wife and children were coming in two weeks!

That was a big relief, although Lionel felt slighted. "Why not mine?"

There was no explanation or reason; it was "just life." It seemed Bouake got rewarded for his patience. We were happy for him, and soon, the day came when his wife, Neleh, and their three children arrived. I met them a day later when Neleh had to come to the office for her initial visit. Neleh turned out to be in her late twenties, a slender young woman in a winter coat too large for her and a red woolen hat. It was winter in Abilene, and I think the clothes were from a donation closet.

Her children came with her. While Neleh looked exhausted, the two older kids, Prince and Princess, watched everything with big brown eyes, lively and inquisitive. Jet lag and long travel did not have any effect on them. Prince was about six at that time and Princess was four. I am not sure if they understood they would be living in the US. The youngest one, Nelson, was around eighteen months old, and all I remember about him was that he was constantly crying if not asleep or feeding. The family took him to a doctor soon after, and I think Nelson became happier with time, but at first, crying seemed to be his natural state. We just had to deal with it because he had to go wherever Neleh went.

I was in charge of finding jobs for refugees, so my challenge was to find a job for Neleh and do it soon. I would have to work around the children's school schedules, Bouake's work hours, and always crying Nelson. How could I fit in a job for Neleh with all of this? It seemed almost like *Mission: Impossible.*

All refugees have initial work and financial assistance programs, but they have to have at least one household member looking for a job to receive it. It was different in the past when I had to find a job for each family adult, and in this case, it included Neleh. How to make it work? What could she do? We sat down to talk with Neleh and Bouake.

I asked, "What can you do? Have you had a job before?"

Neleh shook her head. "No, I don't know. I have never had a job."

She had never been to school and had never worked outside her home. The idea of going to work at a certain hour daily was a totally new concept for Neleh. While Bouake had finished primary school and could read and write, Neleh could not do any of these things.

What to do? I had a few ideas; in some jobs, you don't really need much literacy. Still, how to make things work with all the crazy schedules, the children's comings and goings, and Bouake's own work? And on top of that, they needed to be able to get around town. The family did not have a car and were not about to get one soon or even close to passing the driving test. Abilene had (and still has) a public transportation system but not for every hour and place. It was like a puzzle with a thousand pieces.

Okay, I thought. *Let's start. What do we know?*

Bouake said, "Prince will go to school—to elementary school—and Princess will go to Head Start. But we don't know how it will be."

Head Start, a federally funded preschool program for low-income families, used to send a school bus to pick up children from their homes. So, it would be easy to send Princess off to school each morning; one of her parents would just have to walk her to the bus and then be out there when the bus brought her home in the afternoon. This seemed alright; we just needed to know what time.

Then, another problem surfaced: one day, the school district said that Bouake and Neleh lived too close to the school for Prince to take the school bus. If a family lived within two miles of the school, the parents had to take the child to school. Bouake or Neleh would either have to walk six-year-old Prince to school or they would have to go by city bus, drop Prince off, and then come back. While it would be only about a fifteen-minute walk, it did not fit into Bouake's schedule. He had to board the bus in the morning at 8:15 or he would be late for work. But if Neleh took Prince, how could she see Princess off to Head Start? And what about little Nelson?

An average American family would have a car or two, and an "American Bouake" would drop the child off on the way to work or an "American Neleh" would load all the kids in her car, strap them in car seats, drive over to school to drop off first-grader Prince, go to Head Start with little Princess, and then back home or on to other things. Or, she would ask a friend or a good neighbor to watch the other two kids for a few minutes while she dropped Prince off at school.

But the situation was much more complicated. Bouake and Neleh had no friends yet, no car, and no knowledge of how to manage it all. In the US, child-rearing was so different from what they were used to in Liberia and Ivory Coast.

How would things have been resolved in their home village in Liberia? Very easily! Prince would walk to school with other kids, slowly moving through the village, kicking along stones and cans, and all the neighbors would be watching over them. If the kids got distracted and started playing instead of going to school, one or another neighbor "Mama" or "Baba" would come up to them and say, "Hey, boys, go on, school is starting!" Or, the teacher would teach them a lesson about being on time, probably with a stick or a switch. No highways and busy roads to cross. No child abductors lurking in the shadows. *Just walk all together, and don't be late.* Little Princess would be in the house, following in Mama's footsteps, or Grandma would help take care of her. Baby Nelson would be content in a piece of cloth on his mommy's back, going everywhere she went. Neleh would do some laundry, hang it to dry, walk over to the vegetable stand, chat with the other women, and then go home and start fixing supper. Bouake would work in the fields, take a break to chat with other villagers about the crops and rain, and then he would come home to eat. Prince would appear after school and quickly run out to play with other kids. Here, life was totally different and not as simple to manage.

Then, some good news came: a student volunteer could take Prince to school every morning and pick him up after school. That left Princess and Nelson to worry about.

More good news: the HR manager from Fehr Foods called me one day.

"I need three people for job interviews. When can you bring them?"

Fehr Foods was a local factory that made cookies, and they sometimes offered production jobs. Neleh was number one on my list. I called her that afternoon.

"Could you be ready to go to a job interview tomorrow at nine a.m.?"

Neleh said, "Sure, but I will have to take Nelson with me. Bouake will be at work, and I do not have anyone else to leave him with."

Well, how would an interview work with a baby in your hands? That would not look professional at all!

I told her, "Let's find a way. Be ready with Nelson tomorrow morning, and one of us will pick you up."

As soon as I was off the phone, I went to the assistant case manager, Peter, to talk.

I asked, "Could you help me with transporting people to the cookie factory for job interviews?"

Thank goodness, his schedule was not too busy for the next day, so he agreed to help. We asked the agency's manager for her permission, and she said, "Okay." After all, the result would be three more jobs for refugees, and jobs were hard to find!

On the way to the interview, I asked Neleh, "Which shift do you want to have, if they give you a choice?"

She said, "I am not sure, but I think morning shift would be best."

We had talked about it in the past and had agreed to try for the morning shift. Then, she would be home for the kids in the afternoons and evenings. Morning shift started very early at 7:00 a.m., but she could not make it by city bus. Bouake was at home until eight in the mornings, so he could see Prince off with the volunteer and make sure Princess was picked up for Head Start before leaving.

I asked Neleh, "But what about Nelson? He would have to go to daycare. Is that alright with you?"

Neleh agreed; we had talked about this option before. Nelson was signed up for daycare, but Neleh had to have a job offer before he could start attending because it was a special program run by the county. I signed Neleh up for a special transport program with CityLink, Abilene's public transportation system. This program helped low-income adults who needed to take kids to daycare and go on to work. So, CityLink would send a van for Neleh at her apartment and take her and Nelson to daycare and then go on to drop her off at work. After the shift, the same would happen, but in reverse order. Everything was all set and waiting for Neleh to start.

When we got to the factory, I asked if Peter could watch Nelson while we went in for the interview.

He shrugged and said, "Alright, what else can we do?"

I went in with Neleh and the other two job candidates we had brought, but Peter stayed outside with Nelson. From the interview room window, I could see Peter and Nelson pacing back and forth in front of the factory, Peter holding Nelson's little hand like an attentive daddy. The sight made me laugh. The things you do in a resettlement office to land jobs for your clients!

At the interview, the manager asked Neleh a few questions and then asked, "Can you count cookies?"

Neleh said, "Yes."

We came out with excellent news. Neleh got a job! She would have to count cookies in trays, and she could do that. She did not need to read or write, just make sure the number was right. All three candidates got hired.

Now, my next worry was to make sure the CityLink van came for her at the right time and that she found the van. I reminded her, "Don't forget the car seat!" She had to have a car seat for Nelson to be able to ride the van.

The evening before Neleh's first day at work, I felt anxious. What if she did not have a good alarm clock? And what if the van did not come? I decided to go out to the apartment complex early and see for myself if everything went well. I was afraid that if something went wrong, she might lose the job before even starting. So, the next morning, I got up early and went out to the apartment complex. I was ready for the worst and had decided that if the van did not come, I would take Neleh and Nelson to daycare and work myself. I almost fell asleep waiting, and then, yes! The CityLink van rolled into the parking lot right on time, Neleh and Nelson boarded, and the van disappeared from my sight. I felt relieved and went on to the office where a lot of things were waiting to be done. I had not been in the office that early before. Yes, Neleh really had a job! All the pieces of the puzzle were in the right place.

Faces of Bhutanese-Nepali: Storyteller Roji Rai, photographed in 2017 (top) arrived in Abilene in 2008 with her parents and younger brother. She has chosen studies in the medical field and is currently in college. Roji's father, Mon Bahadur Rai, at his nephew's wedding with his brothers Yam and Harka (below), Abilene, Texas 2013.

Nick Kloster

From Roji's personal photo album

CHAPTER 10

Bhutanese-Nepali Stories

T HIS IS THE OFFICIAL flag of Nepal. But for the Bhutanese-Nepali refugees, which flag represents them? Are they Bhutanese or Nepali or both? History is complicated as always, and ethnicity has been a major player in the developments that affected the Bhutanese-Nepali, who first lived in Bhutan and then, after the early 1990s, in refugee camps in Nepal.

The Bhutanese-Nepali ethnic group was forced to leave Bhutan when the Bhutanese government started repressions against them. Since then, over 100,000 refugees were confined to seven refugee camps

in Nepal. Many years ago, people from Nepal gradually migrated to southern Bhutan, settling in the empty lands near the Bhutan's side of the border. They lived there for many years, working the land and keeping cattle. The Bhutanese government was aware of them and some even became citizens of Bhutan.

Then, in late 1980s, Bhutan's policies changed, and the government launched a campaign claiming that the southern settlers were "not true Bhutanese." They had a different religion and spoke a different language and were jeopardizing Bhutanese national unity. Since the Bhutanese-Nepali had lost ties with their old homeland they had left a generation or two ago, repatriation to Nepal was not an acceptable solution to the settlers. Bhutan's officials made their life intolerable because they were "not Bhutanese," while Nepal did not want them because they were "from Bhutan." Even after Bhutanese-Nepalis had fled from Bhutan and settled in refugee camps in Nepal, several attempts were made to restore the group's rights to return to Bhutan, although without success. The ethnic group was left in limbo, "between the countries," since they could neither return to Bhutan nor were they allowed to integrate into Nepali society.

In late 2007, several countries involved in refugee issues proposed a joint offer to resettle the Bhutanese-Nepali ethnic group. The United States pledged to resettle 60,000 people, while Australia, Denmark, Canada, New Zealand, and the United Kingdom agreed to smaller numbers each. As of 2015, about 84,800 Bhutanese-Nepali have been accepted in the US, and this number should slightly increase in the years to come.[12] a few Bhutanese-Nepali live in neighboring India, and some have managed to stay in Bhutan or obtain citizenship in Nepal, mostly by marrying a native citizen.

When I started interviewing Bhutanese-Nepali refugees, I asked everyone what they regarded as the correct name and ethnicity for the group. Each one gave me a slightly different answer. Some said they liked to be called "Nepalis" or "Nepali-Bhutanese," since they had lived in Nepal most of their lives. Others preferred "Bhutanese-Nepalis" or just "Bhutanese," in order to emphasize that Bhutan was their homeland before they were forced to leave.

Roji: "And I Thought: It Is Beautiful—This Is America"

Roji and her father, mother, and younger brother were resettled through the US refugee resettlement program and came to Abilene in March of 2008. They were one of the first refugees from the Bhutanese-Nepali group to arrive and may even have been the very first. I remember that their family attracted quite a bit of publicity in the refugee resettlement field as "one of the first Bhutanese cases," at least for our agency. They were met by a reporter in New York upon arrival, and the story made the national news. Bhutanese resettlement from Nepal had started!

Since those days, many members of Roji's extended family have come to the US, and she has plenty of aunts, uncles, and cousins around her. Roji's maternal grandmother lives in Australia now with two of Roji's maternal uncles.

Roji is twenty years old now. Her actual name was Rosi, but during the resettlement interviews, her name was misspelled because the two are pronounced similarly. I ask her if she would like to change her name back to what it was before, but she says, "No, I am fine as it is. It is pronounced the same way, so no need to change."

More than five years have passed since her initial days in the United States. Roji has graduated high school and is now in college. She has also become a US citizen. She does well in school and is very serious about her studies. She is good at painting and arts, both of which she says she has always liked, but she did especially well in her arts class in high school in Abilene. Roji shows me several of her paintings. They are very attractive, and I ask her if she is studying art. She says, "No, nursing." All her family wants her to do nursing and she likes it, too. It is a good profession, and she could make good money. Her mom's brothers have always encouraged her to study medicine. Roji says that she is not sure if she could really make it to medical school, but nursing would be the next best option.

Before Roji starts her story, I ask her what she thinks would be the right name for her ethnic group. Roji answers, "I like being called 'Bhutanese,' although all my life was spent in Nepal. That's why I sometimes say that I am from Nepal when people ask me where I am from. That's what I said in college; I said that I was from Nepal. And I speak Nepali. But still, I think we should keep the name 'Bhutanese' also because we are Bhutanese."

Roji would rather not get recorded, so I will take notes.

I AM ROJI. I DO not remember how we started living in the refugee camp, since I was very little when we came to Nepal. I know I was born in India, and we came to live in the camp in Nepal when I was three months old. My family had to leave Bhutan because it was not safe, and we could be put in jail just for wearing our traditional clothes—that's what my dad had told me. So, my parents first went to India from Bhutan, and I was born there. But soon after I was born, we moved to Nepal, and all other relatives soon followed. So I have not even seen Bhutan. I do not know much about those days, just what my family has told me.

I became a refugee because of my parents and my ethnic group. My dad told me that the government had changed in Bhutan and that everybody had to speak Bhutanese, which is different from our language, and that schools would close, and we had to change our religion. Many of our people went to protest, and then there were shootings and arrests. My family did not go to protest, but they left because they were afraid that they could be beaten up or even shot or put in jail.

In Nepal, we lived in one of the biggest camps. It was called Beldangi-II. Altogether, there were seven camps, and ours was the biggest. We had a small house or, as we called it, a "hut," and I lived in it with my parents. Then later, my brother was born. My dad's family lived close-by, too. His brothers and parents were in neighboring huts, so we were all in the same block. My mother's brothers lived in a different camp, and that camp was called Sanischare.

They live in Australia now, where they were sent to Australia to live. Also, my mom's mother, my grandmother, went to Australia. They like it there, and we often talk on the phone. So now, I have uncles in Australia. They always tell me, "Roji, you have to go to school and become a doctor." But I don't know about being a doctor right now. I am studying to become a nurse. Maybe I will go visit them with my mom next summer. I miss them and my grandmother, too.

But the camp was and still is, by the way, very big. A lot of people are living in one big place. There is a Nepali village not far from it. It is like this: the Nepali village, then empty fields, and then the refugee camp in the middle of those fields. The camp has streets and lots of small houses on each side of these streets. The camp is divided into "sectors" and blocks of streets and huts. Across the field, we can see the village of the Nepalese people. Some of them have set up little shops closer to the camp, and that's where the Bhutanese people would go to shop and make phone calls. But camp area is big, and we had a school in our camp and a camp center and a distribution center where people got their food supplies.

When we lived in the camp, school was very important, and our family was better off than many other refugee families, so I could go to school. My dad was a school principal in the camp when the schools started. He worked in that school in the camp that I attended.

Later, when my brother was born, our family needed more money, so my dad took a job outside the camp because it paid more. For that job, he had to go outside of the camp, which was a little risky, but we needed the money. He was a teacher in a boarding school, teaching fifth grade. He used to come home on the weekends and then go back to work during the week. When I graduated from camp school, I went to that same boarding school where my dad was a teacher. He was not my teacher because I was in a different grade, but when our teacher did not come, was sick, or something else, my dad taught me. It happened only once or twice, but I remember it was very embarrassing for me. I did not know how to act or what to say, like how to address him: "Dad" or "Mister" or "Teacher"?

My mom was a childcare teacher in the camp. Thus, my parents were able to earn money. It was good for me, and I always had what I needed for school and for life. I felt protected. And my family could afford to send me to school. Normally, people could work in the camp, but it was very low pay. You could get more money if you worked outside the camp. I am not sure if people were allowed to go outside to find work, but I know that you would not be hired if the employer knew you were from the camp, so you got the job only if you really were the best candidate or there were no other Nepalese candidates.

How did your resettlement process start?

I ask this question, and then I remember how we were told at the IRC that many Bhutanese-Nepalis initially opposed the idea of a "third country resettlement," since all they wanted was to return to Bhutan and their previous life. And truly, many people had left a good life behind—houses, farms, land, cattle, and many other familiar things—and hoped to return. Thus, the offer to resettle in another country did not sound enticing, and the overseas agencies that had to process paperwork for resettlement to the US were struggling at first.

The Bhutanese-Nepali people were invited to fill out forms and apply for resettlement, but nobody was doing so. Agency staff did not know what to do: time was ticking away, government funds had been allocated, but there was no interest. This reaction contrasted sharply with staff experience with those from many other countries. Usually agencies could hardly deal with the crowds there, since everyone wanted to go. So, the agency began to go from house to house to explain the program and the benefits of living in the United States in more detail. According to "agency lore," they succeeded in recruiting a few families to start the preparations for resettlement only after several attempts to reach out, and that's how the whole process started. This is not "official" but is our "agency lore."

You know, initially, there were just rumors going around. People were talking about different countries, speculating what to do if your family was given a choice where to go or where not to go. When we found out that this may be a real opportunity, all our family got together in my grandparents' house to discuss it. Our family, dad's brothers and sisters and cousins, we all had a meeting. Many people, the whole extended family together. That was when my grandfather was still alive. My grandparents did not want to go, but the younger generation all said that they wanted to go. My grandparents said they did not want to go because English would be very difficult for them, and they were afraid they would lose their camp friends and community. You know, in old age, it would be very difficult. But the younger ones were all excited to go. Our family was happy, too, and I was happy. We had heard people describe America as "a big thing, a positive change, where you can work and make money," and we had heard that "people are helpful in America." After that family meeting, America was on our minds, and we talked about it a lot.

When the time came, my mom filled out all the applications for the four of us because she was the one who lived in the camp with my brother. I was at boarding school with my dad at that time. So, some time passed, and then we were called for an interview. On that day, Mom called us at the boarding school to tell us to come home as soon as possible. We had to go for the interview. So, we came back, and my dad told me, "When they ask you, tell them that you live in the camp. You cannot say that you are in boarding school." We were afraid that our family may not be selected if we said that two of us lived in the boarding school. The officer asked me if I was from the camp, and I said, "Yes." After all, my mom and brother were there, and we used to come home for weekends.

Then, we had to go for a second interview and then go to medical checks and take pills, and it all went pretty fast. In about four or five months, it was all done. I remember it started around the time of the Diwali festival, and that is at the beginning of November, and then we were ready and got our travel date for March of the following year.

And then, the time came for us to go. It was a long journey, and I remember it very well. I liked the trip, but the beginning was hard. We had to travel in a small plane from Beldangi to Kathmandu. The small plane was packed with people, no air, and the ride was very bumpy, ups and downs as we flew over high mountains. The weather was really bad, clouds and rain, and I got sick on that small plane. It was bad. But from Kathmandu, we went to Abu Dhabi, and that plane was big. It felt like I was in a house, like in my room. Then, we went on to New York, and then to Dallas, and from Dallas, to Abilene.

On the planes, I was watching movies, and time was passing quite quickly. I was very tired in the end, and all I wanted was to sleep. I remember how we were landing in Abilene: it was dark already, and from above, I could see all the lights of the city, and it was beautiful. And I thought: this is America!

The next couple of months were a little hard: I did not know anybody in Abilene, and I was scared to leave the apartment. We were the first Bhutanese family to arrive, and nobody from our community was around yet. I did not have any friends, so I just stayed indoors with my parents and younger brother. I did not know where to go. I started school soon after, but as soon as school was out, I was just by myself. It was like that for about two months. The only place I went beside school was to do shopping at Walmart with my parents.

Then, after a month or two, my cousins arrived from Nepal— Saran and Baskar—and we could visit one another and do things together. So, life got easier for me. Also, more Bhutanese people were arriving. We used to go out to Red Bud Park with my cousins and play ball games and sit in the swing. We just got together, walked, talked, and sometimes my cousins would play soccer. Sometimes, we would play a singing game together. That is a game where you have to sing.

Or, we would go out to eat with our families; we really liked that Chinese place not far from Fairmont Apartments. I think it is closed now. Sometimes, we went to eat pizza at Mr. Gatti's. It is across the street from here, and I used to work there some time ago. At first, I did not like the taste of pizza, but now I like it. And I got to like some other American foods, too. I still like the spicy Bhutanese food, but sometimes, I do not mind a pizza or a burger. But at the beginning, it was, "Oh, my, no." The taste seemed so terrible.

Now, I do not have much time to go out because I have to do my schoolwork, and I also work part-time at Walmart. But I still like to listen to music and watch movies. I know it is a little difficult right now, but I think it is very important to be able to support myself and be able to help my parents. I will stay and live with my parents until I graduate or even longer. I know that here people leave their parents as soon as they turn eighteen, but for us, it is different. You have to stay and help them and be with them. I will stay with my parents. It is especially important for sons to stay; women sometimes leave when they get married. But I think I will stay to help them, at least for a while.

Camp life has really changed since the resettlement started. You know, when our people first started coming to the United States, very few people in the camp had cell phones, or any kind of phones.

If somebody called from the US, like we used to call our relatives, we called a little shop in that Nepali village that was next to the camp. We told the shop assistants who we were calling for, gave the address, street, and hut number, and told them what time we would call the second time, in twenty minutes or in one hour. The shop owner or assistant would go and find that person, and tell him to come to the shop and wait for the call. Our relatives from the camp would have to pay the shop owner money for this service, for coming to find them and for letting them use the phone. Now, people do not call that way anymore. They use cell phones, and the shop does not have this business anymore.

Also, everything has become very expensive in the camp. Many people send money back from the US and Australia, so prices have gone up. Now, people can afford to buy things they could not before; now, a pair of jeans costs 1,000 to 1,500 rupees, and in the past, it was almost half that price. But now, all our relatives are either here or in Australia; nobody is left in Nepal. I have a few friends there, but we do not talk often.

What I want to mention is that people here often ask us about the castes in Bhutanese-Nepali culture. I think that the caste system in our culture is a thing of the past. I know the same caste system exists in Nepal and it is practiced more, but in the camp, we were not too much affected by it. I think that older people would know more about it. And in the United States, it is even less acknowledged. But that is what I think.

My family has always been open-minded, and my parents themselves are from two different castes. You can tell castes by family names. For example, my dad's last name is "Rai," but my mother was "Chettri" before she got married and changed to dad's last name. She was from a different caste, a higher one. My mom's parents were from two different castes, too. So, we have been mixed for several generations. "Rais" are in the middle of the caste system, not at the very bottom and not at the very top.

The top is supposed to be Brahmins, who do not eat meat or eggs, and they wear those things around their chests—I mean, their boys, men, not girls. And the adults have those special clothes. We have one family here in Abilene that is part of that upper caste. Some of them moved, but some are still here. And when their grandson reached a certain age, they had a special ceremony for him. His grandmother came to our house and invited us, but we did not have time to go. I had to be in school. But the ceremonies are still held. Those in the upper caste are the ones who serve in temples.

Our middle caste includes last names like Mongars, Rais, Subbas, just to mention a few. And then there are last names that belong to the lower caste, and people with those names were considered the "untouchables." It meant that other people could not even eat the food or drink the drinks they had touched or prepared. I am sorry to say that because I have nothing against them. I think in the past, it may have mattered to some people, but not anymore. But you know, there are always people who hold onto an "old mentality," old ways of thinking.

In our family, we do not think about the castes. The main thing is the person. Maybe those in the upper caste hold onto their status more than anyone else, but we do not. And I did not feel the caste system in our camp, either. But when I was in boarding school, I had a teacher who was from the upper caste. I could tell from what he was wearing and how he behaved. He paid more attention to teaching boys; girls were second-class. We had fewer girls in my class, maybe ten boys and five girls. That teacher's family lived in the same apartment building that we lived in, and I visited them sometimes. He had a wife and two kids, a boy and a girl. I noticed that he always ate first with his son, but his wife and daughter had food only after the men were done. I did not like it. *Why do things like that?* I thought. *In my family, my mom eats with everybody else, and sometimes, she even eats first!*

But let me tell you about Diwali. It is our traditional festival, and it is always in November, but the exact dates change each year. I think that has something to do with the Bhutanese calendar, but I am not sure. It is for family, for brothers and sisters especially, and on those days, you give gifts and sweets to your brothers and cousins, and they give you money. It lasts for several days. The first day, we decorate the house with candles and flower garlands, and we cook a lot of food. The first day is also the day of prayer, and we decorate a statue of Lakshmi Puja and then spend time in prayer in the apartment. We have to put money around the statue so we will have money in future. We always pray for peace and happiness.

It is a day for family. Everyone gathers for prayer, but we do not have a formal prayer; each person worships silently. After the prayers are done, the festivities can start. The first evening, friends and family start visiting each other, but the young people go from house to house and play music and dance. The third day is the main day. That's when all the relatives gather for a big meal, all the sisters and brothers and parents.

Last Diwali, all the family came to our apartment: my grandma came, and Dad's sisters and brother came, and his cousin, all of them with their families and children. Normally, we would just make rice and soup and some meat, but for the Diwali meal, we cooked rice, curry, soups, a special bread, eggs, potatoes, everything. And other people brought food with them also when they came. Then, all the brothers and sisters exchanged gifts. That is an important part of the festivities. And when people perform, you have to give them gifts and food or money.

This last Diwali, my cousins and my brother went around to different families to play and dance. They did well. My brother danced really funny, and people liked him and gave him money. They brought home $80.00, so each of them made $20.00. Girls can go also, not just the boys, but I did not go last time. When we were in the camp, I used to go with my cousins, but I could not dance. I am not good at it. I went to sing, and we all sang different songs. It is somewhat like Halloween here, only here, it is small kids who go for treats, but in the Diwali festival, young people perform; it can be anyone, teenagers or twenty-year-olds. You sing and dance in front of somebody's house or in the house until the people feed you or give you money. In the camp, people paid us with food. Here, they like to give cans of beer or a little money. And at the end of the third day, the festival wraps up and is over.

I recently became a US citizen, and I really feel good about that. I lived in Nepal for sixteen years, and they never gave me a chance to become a citizen. But here, I got my citizenship in five years. I really appreciate that. Now, I can travel to all the countries I want, and that also feels good. I passed the test, and everything went well.

I am in college now, and I want to do the LVN program and, when I finish, get a job in nursing. The LVN program is for twelve months, but I have to finish this year first. It is like pre-nursing. And after that, I will study to be an RN.

I have made friends with other students at college—not just Bhutanese, but other refugees as well. They are all my friends. But not many young Bhutanese attend college. Bakhti and Yam are attending, and maybe five more. I think it is because many young people have families with children and work two jobs to have more money for the family. I am really lucky that my parents can help me with college, and I have financial aid, too. I also work part-time, you know. I think it is important to have my own pocket money and to help pay bills while I am in school.

I am sure that at some time in the future, I will get married, but not now. I am not thinking about it right now. It is more important to do well in school. Studies are not easy; I have to spend a lot of time on all the schoolwork. But in the future, I would like to work with poor people who need help. Not in the United States, because life is good here, but maybe in Nepal—wherever people need help. You know, in Nepal, people are doing well in big cities, but people in small villages are very poor. They do not have good doctors or education. I have wanted to help ever since I was very young because we did not have good doctors or good medical care in the camp. So, I know how it is when doctors are not available. I always admired Mother Theresa, how she went everywhere in the world and helped the poor. I want to do the same, but first, I need to have an education, finish school, so I can help.

November 5, 2013 and December 16, 2013

Purna: "We Came Here for Our Children"

It is a Saturday morning, but I am in my office, waiting on Purna to come to share his story. Purna is one of the Bhutanese-Nepali refugees who came to the US in 2009 and was resettled by the IRC in Abilene. He works every day during the week, so we have agreed to meet here on a Saturday.

The Bhutanese-Nepali resettlement started in the spring of 2008 and reached its peak quickly in 2009. At that time, it seemed as if all the refugees we were resettling came from Nepal. Purna was one of them. He is in his late thirties now, and he came with his wife and three children. Around the same time, one of Purna's brothers arrived with his family, and several months later, still more brothers with their families had followed. Purna and his brothers were concerned about their elderly parents who were still in Nepal and had to go through resettlement interviews by themselves, but not too long after, the parents joined them, along with their unmarried daughter. So, little by little, the whole extended family had resettled in a new homeland.

The only siblings to come after Purna were his brothers until the arrival of the unmarried sister. I did not give much thought to it then but assumed that his family consisted of many brothers and just one sister. Then one day, Purna came to the office to talk with me about one thing or another, and he mentioned his married sisters. I asked him why his sisters were not coming.

Purna answered, "They are in the US already, just in a different state!" He explained that they had been resettled in several other states with their husbands and extended families. I was surprised. Then, I found out that Bhutanese-Nepali refugees were resettled along paternal lines, which meant that the adult brothers of one family were resettled to the same location and elderly parents followed their adult male children. Married sisters would go to a different resettlement location since they would resettle with their husbands' families. In that way, some siblings got separated, but it gave some structure to the resettlement process, since all the siblings could not go to the same place.

But now, Purna is here and starts his story. He would rather not get recorded, so I will take notes.

I AM PURNA KAMI, AND I am thirty-seven years old. In fact, my last name was "Lamgadey," but when we went to interview, they wrote it down as "Kami." My parents lived in Bhutan, in a place called Tsirang, which was in the south. Our area was on the mountain slopes, and the climate was cooler than in lowlands. I was born in Tsirang, Bhutan, just like most of my siblings. Our life in Bhutan was good. My parents owned a house and a large plot of land; we had cattle, cows, and our family farmed. My father was also a knife-maker, and he taught us boys this trade, so we know how to make knives.

My grandmother, my mom's mother, was born in Nepal. She was first married to a man who had seven wives, and my mom was born during that marriage. When my mom was about five, my grandmother was married away to a new husband. My grandma then went to live in Bhutan with her new husband and her daughter. That's how my mom happened to live in Bhutan, but she was born in Nepal, just like my grandmother.

My mother, Phul Maya, got married very young: she was just ten years old when she married my father, Maha Shwor. Marrying so young was a custom of the old days; now, it is not practiced anymore because everybody knows that it is not good to marry at such a young age. But my mom stayed together with my dad, and they had twelve children during their years together. Three of them died while still in Bhutan because there was no doctor where we lived. So, we are nine brothers and sisters now.

In Bhutan, life was quite peaceful. Then, in the mid-80s, the government of Bhutan changed, and the new rulers started to enforce new laws that were against our Nepali people who had come to live in southern Bhutan years ago. The land that had previously been empty was now turned into cultivated fields tended by people of Nepali origins. Maybe the government was afraid that too many Nepali people had come or they resented the land use. It was hard to tell.

All of a sudden, Nepali people were forbidden to speak their own language, and if somebody heard them doing it, the offender would have to pay a fine or even go to jail. Nepali schools were closed, and the military came to the schools and burned the books. Nepali people used to wear their own traditional clothing, but that was not allowed anymore. Only Bhutanese traditional clothes had to be worn, called *baku* for men and *kira* for women. This clothing was very uncomfortable for working the fields and for doing other things. The army came to Nepali houses and threatened people. Men and women were taken to labor camps, where people had to work as slaves for several months without any pay, and if you said anything against it, you would be killed. Girls could be taken from schools and raped by the military men.

So, Nepali people were very upset and scared, and that's why people went to protest and claim their rights. In 1989, the revolution took place in Bhutan, and many people who had come to Bhutan from Nepal—just like my parents and grandparents—turned out in the streets, asking for their rights to obtain citizenship and be treated in a fair way, like everybody else in the country.

I was about thirteen when we left Bhutan and went to Nepal. I do not remember much about what had happened before, but my dad told me a lot. I remember very well that the school in our village closed, and after that, there was no school for three years. I finished second grade, and after that, no school. My dad and my elder brother, Santa, were taken from the house by the army to a place where they had to make knives for the Bhutanese military. They were kept there for two or three months, working without any pay, and then released.

Then one day, our *mandal* (that's what we called the head of the village), Fuktenzi Drukpa, called a meeting of all the villagers. Everyone went to that meeting. In the meeting, the *mandal* pulled a plant out of the ground, held it up high for everyone to see, and then asked, "Do you think this plant will grow if I put it back in soil?"

And the people said, "Yes, it may grow. It still has soil on the roots."

Then, the village head shook the plant so that all soil broke loose and fell to the ground.

"And how about now?" he asked again.

And the people answered, "No, it will not grow anymore."

Then, the *mandal* said, "That's what we are trying to do with you, Nepali people. We cannot let you put down roots and grow here."

The message was clear: the government had decided that the Nepali people could not be left in peace to live and put down roots. The government thought that if the Nepali people were left in peace, then one day, too many would be here, in their land.

After that meeting, the villagers understood that better times were not coming for them in Bhutan and that the government would not leave them in peace. And the villagers started preparing to leave.

It was at the beginning of 1992. We left in March of 1992, and our neighbors were leaving around that time, too. Some of them had left first, and our dad and mom were getting ready to leave. We had had a good life in Bhutan before it all happened. We had nine acres of land, houses, cows, and other farm animals, and we had to leave all that behind. Also, we had enjoyed the climate: the weather was not too hot because we lived at a higher elevation. It never got really hot like it was in Nepal.

Since we were living higher up in the mountains, there was no road to take. We had to walk for five hours just to get to a real road. And we could take with us only what we could carry, and it was very little: some food, some little things. We went with many neighbors, thousands of people. When we reached the road, we all went by trucks to India first. We stayed there for about a week and then rode in trucks again onto Nepal.

In Nepal, there were only dirt roads, and the weather was very hot because we were in the lowlands. When we reached Nepal, there was really nowhere to go. At first, we were in the Maidar camp for about two months, and it was very hot, humid, and dirty. There was no clean water, no bathrooms, nothing. It was just a temporary settlement made by the arriving refugees. Many people died in this first camp in Nepal: many got diarrhea from the dirty water, since we had to use water from the nearby river, and some people got other diseases there. Sadly, many died. We all lived in tents and waited to move on because there was no room to settle down in this area. I think it was close to the town of Maidar (that's why it had this name). More and more people were arriving every day.

Then, we were moved to Beldangi-I refugee camp. There were seven refugee camps in Nepal for people who had fled from Bhutan, and Beldangi-I camp was the biggest. I know that some other people moved to a camp called Goldhap, some went to Pathri camp, and some to Sanischare. We had three Beldangi camps: Beldangi-I, Beldangi-II, and Beldangi-Extension. I have been to six of the camps, but I have never been to Timai. I have heard that it is a smaller camp, and I think I would have liked it better if we had been in a smaller camp. Beldangi-I seemed too big and too crowded for me, so I think maybe Timai would have been better. But I have not seen it with my own eyes.

So, our life as camp refugees started. And all I can say is that our life there was really terrible. We did not have any electricity, so the only way to cook was on an open fire, and the cooking fuel was always an issue. There was never enough. Everything was organized. We were given rice and beans, but it was never enough to live on. We could buy more food if we had the money, so we had to go outside to work and to earn money, even to get firewood from the forest. But we were not allowed to go outside the camp. So, we had to work, but where to get a job if not outside the camp? There were very few opportunities in the camp. But some guards were nicer than others, and they would let us go if we needed to.

We had to live in a hut built out of bamboo, and houses like that could catch fire very easily. For example, when we had a big fire in 2001, 107 houses burned down, and one little girl died in this fire. She was just four years old.

When we moved to Beldangi, school soon started, but it was not in a building. We did not have any school building at first. The school children were gathered in an open space. We all were sitting on the ground. The school house was built only after one or two years. It was made of bamboo and bricks, and our education improved when we had a school house. The school was free until you got your certificate. The certificate was called SLC, and you got it when you had reached the tenth grade.

After the tenth grade, I started to attend Campus College in Damak, and it cost money. Damak was the nearby city, and it was about thirty-five minutes by bicycle. I sometimes stayed on campus, and sometimes I came home. I liked to go to school. After graduation, I applied for a teaching job in the camp and got that job. I was teaching little kids, second and third grades, for two years. After that, we came to America. I liked that job, working as a teacher, but it did not pay much. I was paid 937 rupees a month.

Since we didn't have enough food, we had to buy it, and so our family started farming. We rented land and planted vegetables, and we were raising pigs. We paid fifty rupees per month for land rent. A good one-year-old pig would sell for 8,000 rupees, so it was a good supplement to the family income. If it was not such a good a pig, then we could get around 5,000 rupees.

Besides that, my father and elder brothers made and repaired knives. That has been our family trade for a long time. They knew how to do it and had done it in Bhutan as well. I can make knives also, although I am more interested in making jewelry, working with silver and gold. (*Purna shows me photos of his jewelry, which looks really good.*) I am not sure how to get tools for that here in the United States, but I would like to continue with jewelry-making. Learn how to do it the American way. I don't know how to sell it after I am done, but I would like to find out more. I enjoy that kind of work.

My parents, Phul Maya and Maha Shwor, have nine children. My eldest brother is Nar, and then follows Hem Lal, then Dhan, Santa, and myself. I am the youngest of the brothers. I have two sisters in Georgia who were resettled there with their families. The youngest of all the children is my sister, Ran Maya, who came with us to Abilene because she was not married yet. You may have heard that she recently got married and moved to Washington state. And I have another sister who lives in Bhutan. She was married to a Bhutanese man, but he passed away. She has a nineteen-year-old son, and I don't know if she could come to live here or not, but she is in Bhutan. She is not a refugee and may not be able to come as did other people from the Nepal refugee camps.

I came with my wife, Lachi Maya, and our three children. I was just seventeen when my parents told me that I had to get married. But I said, "No, I am not ready." But my parents insisted that they wanted me to get married. My brothers had gotten married and moved out of our parents' house, so it was my turn. I wanted to go to school. I was in the third grade (*grades are different*) at the Green Vale Academy, and Lachi was in the second grade then. My parents went to her parents and made all the arrangements.

I had not seen her before the wedding. I saw her for the first time on our wedding day. I liked her, and I think she liked me, too. So, we got married and started living together. When we came to the US, we had three children: our son, Dipendra, and our daughters, Puja and Dibya. Now, we have another daughter who was born just a few months ago.

When the time came to travel, we did not know exactly what to expect from the US. When we arrived, we were met by the IRC case workers at the Abilene airport, and they took us to our new apartment. Soon, we met with an American lady named Pat Cranfield, and we are still in touch with her. She helped us a lot at the very beginning, like taking us grocery shopping or to the market and showing us how to get to places in town. We had other volunteers who helped us, too. For the first ninety days, we went to different orientations at the IRC, like housing and job orientations, and then my brother, Santa, and I got jobs at the Abilene Christian University cafeteria. We worked there for two months, but when the summer break came, we had no job anymore because the school closed for summer. I was worried because we had bills to pay, and I thought, *How am I going to pay the rent?*

Pat Cranfield invited us to her house for dinner, and we went and met her son, David, there. He owns a wholesale shop, called CCC Supply, where they sell paint and other supplies. So, I told him that I was looking for a job and that I really needed a job, that I was worried about paying my rent. And David offered me a job, and I was very happy. I told him that I did not know any computers, but he said that it was okay, that I would be doing other types of work. So, I got the job in the warehouse.

At that time, I could not drive either, but David sent me to Coach Miller's driving school. He even paid for it! Now, I can drive and operate a forklift. I still work in CCC Supply warehouse, operate a forklift, and do deliveries several times a week. David has several warehouses in other cities in Texas, so I go to Odessa or to the Salado-Belton area to deliver supplies to those warehouses. It is about three-and-a-half hours from here. I like driving now; the school taught me well. I really like my job.

You know, compared to life in a refugee camp in Nepal, Bhutan was much better. But life in the US is like heaven. In Nepal, if I worked all day, I could not make enough money to buy food for one meal for the family. Here, we can work and make enough money to live. But the best thing is that in the US, you have hospitals and doctors if you need them. In Nepal, nobody would see you if you could not pay up front. We had a doctor in the camp, but he was there for minor emergencies only—like, you cut a finger, then you would go. That was free. But if you had something more serious, there was no help at all. And if you went outside the camp, then you had to pay big money to see a doctor. But here, if you get sick, you will be seen by a doctor, and then you can pay the bills later, or insurance will cover it. And old people have medical insurance from the government, like my mom and dad.

When I came to America, I learned a lot from the church where we went for English classes, and now, I have become a Christian. About thirty or forty people from the Bhutanese-Nepali community have become Christians. Some of our family members have also converted: my brother, Hem Lal, and sister, Ran Maya, and other sisters, too.

Do you know how it started? I was reading our religious books and did not find the answers. In our holy books, like Mahabharata and Vedas, there were many things that did not make sense to me. It was even before we started with the American church. Like, if somebody passes away, you have to stay home and fast for thirteen days. How could we stay home for thirteen days? I would lose my job if I did it. And also, how could we fast so long if we had to work? So, I found our religious books too regimented. The Bible does not say that. It teaches the main principles. So, I found answers to my questions in the Bible, and I think that Jesus is our Savior.

One challenge we all have in the US is the English language. If I had more time, I would go to Adult Ed, but I am at work all the time. I speak some at work and have to read and write, too. And on

Wednesday nights, we go to the Southern Hills Church of Christ. We have English classes there. I have my own teacher; we work one-on-one, and that helps a lot.

We came to the US mostly for the children, so they would have a better future and do well and go to college. I have heard that you can get a scholarship if you do well in sports. And I am really proud that our children are doing well here. My daughter Puja is playing volleyball and basketball. My son Dipendra is good at tennis. He is also attending the First Serve, a tennis school through the IRC. I am hoping they will get sports scholarships and will be able to go to college with that. It is too early to make plans for our little ones.

And I am thinking, well, I am thirty-seven now. When my wife starts working again (she is at home now with our new baby girl), then we will buy a house. I think when we live in an apartment, it is not ours; we pay rent and waste money. We could have a yard and grow vegetables, and I could make jewelry, because in a house I could do many things, not like in apartment where there is no room. I have to save a lot to have enough for a down payment.

I am thinking about that jewelry business. I just have to find the time to get more information. Also, it is time to apply for my citizenship, and I want to change my family name when I do the application. When we went for the refugee interviews, they did not put our family name down, but just wrote "Kami," which is more like the trade we do—it means "a knife-maker," not a family name. Our family name was "Lamgadey," so I want to have my name changed to Lamgadey. All the people whose family names are "Lamgadey" or "Rasaily" or "Gazmer" are knife-makers, so they are all "Kamis" in a sense. For other families, they put their family names on the applications, but for us, they did not. So, I want to correct it. But overall, life has been good in America, and I am happy about it.

February 16, 2014

Since Purna and I talked, almost a year has gone by, and he has become a US citizen and has bought a nice house. He also has corrected his name and is now called Purna Lamgadey, instead of "Kami, the knife-maker."

A View from the Office

"Meskhetian Turks and the Vase"

Summer 2005

This happened in the summer of 2005, and more than ten years have passed since then. It was one of the many little things that made resettlement work fun, and that's how I remember it.

We had just started resettling Meskhetian Turkish refugees, and we were really busy with them. Their resettlement program went on for about a year and a half, and when it was over, about one hundred or so Meskhetian Turks had settled in Abilene. Most of them had cousins, sisters, uncles, and aunts in one or another city in the US, but the largest Meskhetian Turkish group lived in Pennsylvania. We used to hear from other resettlement agencies that their workers sometimes would go to the airport to pick up the newly arrived family only to find the airport empty and the new refugees already loaded into their relatives' vans headed for Pennsylvania. It was one of our worst fears, too, because we would have to undo all the preparations for the new arrivals. How could we explain to the apartment managers that the apartment we had booked would not be needed anymore? What were we supposed to do with the household things and food we had bought? Thank goodness, our fears did not come true, and our Meskhetian Turkish refugee families arrived here safely—maybe because Abilene is just too far from the "mysterious" Pennsylvania that attracted everyone like a big magnet.

For a while, all the Meskhetian Turks were quite content to live in Abilene; they had jobs, their children went to school, and life just went on. Then, one family inadvertently upset the balance: they *had* to move to a larger city because they had a very sick daughter who needed specialized medical care. That was their doctor's advice. They took their daughter to a specialist in Austin and checked out the city at the same time. No, they did not feel Austin was the right place. Then, they traveled to Boise, Idaho, and came back with another "no." Boise was too small and, as they put it, "had no style." Then, they decided to have a look at Richmond, Virginia, where they had relatives. They returned all excited and started packing right away.

The news that "Zeina's family is moving" spread like wildfire within the Meskhetian Turkish community and alerted everyone. Now, every Meskhetian Turkish family started counting their relatives in other states and tried to figure out the best place to go. Time to move! One large clan moved to Lexington, Kentucky; another big family went to live in Indiana; some chose that same "mysterious" Pennsylvania and Idaho "with no style." It happened really fast; Turks are dynamic people, and once things are decided, they do not want to waste any time. By the end of 2006, just two small families were left in town. I do not even know why they decided to stay.

While the Meskhetian Turks were in Abilene, I got to know them quite well, since at the beginning, I was the only one in the office who could speak Russian fluently. All of them knew Russian well as a second language, except for a few truly elderly refugees who had not gone to school during the Soviet times. They spoke only Turkish. The newly arrived families visited our office quite often, and they always came to me after they had talked with the case manager, since they wanted to "verify" everything. We would go over all the new information again, this time in plain Russian, to ensure that they had grasped all the details correctly.

And there was a lot to learn. I think they sought me out partly because I had lived under the Soviet system just like they had, so I could help them make sense of things that were so different here. I am not sure how most of them looked upon the Soviet days— whether they had regretted or enjoyed those times—but they had come to the US fresh out of Russia and, thus, tended to keep up many of the common practices from Soviet life.

One of them was the "gifting" system, which was very common in Soviet times. In essence, if you wanted to get anything done—especially when dealing with government clerks, doctors, or office workers (and in the Soviet Union, this covered almost all the official business because even hospitals were government-run)—you had to give people little gifts or tokens of appreciation. They were not truly *bribes*, since one usually did not give money, but gifts that "smoothed the way" or worked as "one good turn deserves another." Such a system could flourish only in a Soviet-style economy, where the constant shortages of consumer goods and groceries in stores made people develop "inside connections" in order to obtain coveted items or essential services. They would present "appreciation gifts" to those from whom they wanted something in return. Since wages were so low, those gifts were like "hard currency" that was traded on or used to supplement the pay.

If you are not familiar with the culture, let me explain. First of all, if you needed services from any city office (for a document or form or information), you would bring a box of chocolates or a can of instant coffee, just to make sure you got what you came for. If you came empty-handed, you would be told, "Oh, the clerk is out until next week" or, "Go to Room 25, and the other lady will help you." And so you went, but Room 25 was locked.

Second, you could not simply buy these gifts in a grocery store because the shelves were usually empty or at most offered only a few "du jour" items that nobody would want to buy anyway. So, you would have to befriend a sales assistant who would put these gifts aside for you when they were delivered from a manufacturing plant. And if that friendly salesperson saved something for you "under the counter," you had to gift her something in return, something also coveted and hard to find in the empty Soviet shops. For example, if you "got" three boxes of chocolates from her (you had to pay for them, of course, but money usually was not the issue; the lack of goods was), you "gave" the salesperson, let's say, a pack of imported hand soap or a nice bottle of shampoo in return. So equipped, you were ready to handle your official business with doctors, city officials, office clerks, and so on. I have a family friend who happens to be a doctor, and he used to remark, "If I ate all the chocolates my patients brought, I would be size twenty-four now, and if I drank all that alcohol they gifted me with, I would have ended up in a rehab center a long time ago."

So, Meskhetian Turkish refugees arrived with the same idea: they had to give gifts to people if they wanted to get their attention, be well treated, and help solve their problems. The first people they met were the IRC staff. When you think about it, we were "the important people" for all refugees, although I had never thought about it that way before. After all, who would take care of the newly arrived and find jobs for all of them if not the agency worker? Or, who would make sure they get their doctor appointments scheduled promptly? Even small things, like which apartment they would live in or who would be paired up with a volunteer or mentor first depended on the agency worker.

Thus, many families tried to give me gifts, too, just as they had done in Soviet times at home. I don't know how it was with other agency staff, but the Turkish refugees may have tried harder with me because they thought I had first-hand experience with the practice. The first surprise for me came when, after a home visit, one family man presented me with a specialty brandy they had brought from Russia.

"Here, a special present for you."

I declined, although it was not easy to take a stand. "Sorry, I really cannot accept gifts. And I do not drink, either, so I'm really sorry."

He said, "No, don't worry, nobody will know. And if you don't drink, it is not a problem. Please take it for your husband, then. I am sure he will appreciate!"

I repeated, "No, sorry," although I could see that the family was disappointed. They may have been thinking, *No guarantee that we will receive good treatment since she refused to take the gift.* It was quite embarrassing on both sides: I could not accept the gift and really did not expect it, but it was hard to say "no" because I did not want to offend them. On their part, it was equally hard to be rejected, especially since it had been the practice that had worked for them until coming to the US. Was it really different here?

A few other families also tried to "gift" me, but gradually we managed to limit the gifting to "wonderful Turkish bread." When they offered a gift, I would decline and say, "I'd rather have a slice of your bread." Turkish refugee women used to bake their bread at home daily and were very proud of it, and it truly tasted very good and fresh. So, asking for a piece of bread after refusing the gift came as a peace offering and helped to soften their disappointment.

A few weeks passed by. One day, I went to visit another Turkish family for three of whom I had to find jobs. We talked over our plans, and as I was about to leave, the head of the family presented me with a nice glass vase.

"I want you to have it because you have done so much for us," he said.

I could not accept it and I said, "I really cannot take it. We are not allowed to take gifts. It is against our agency policy, and I may lose my job if I take it. But thank you for the thought."

After a short while, I went back to the office. When I parked the car, something clinked in the back seat, which I knew should be empty. I opened the rear door of my car, and voilà! Here was the vase I had not taken from the family. It was right there, wrapped nicely in a newspaper. I took it into the office and when I saw the family again, I gave the vase back to them. This time, I tried to put a positive spin on my refusal by saying, "You know, I have to give it back. But in a year, you will be finished with all the refugee programs and we will not have a professional relationship anymore. So, if you still want to give me the vase then, I will accept your gift." I said this because the family was really disappointed by my refusal. I knew that one year is a long time in refugee resettlement, and I was thinking, *They may not even be living in Abilene then. Who knows what will happen?* It just felt like a nicer way to give the vase back.

This family had come to the US in March, and after they started working, I did not see them as often. We were busy in the office, as always, and soon summer was over. Then, fall and winter arrived. My birthday is in December. Imagine my surprise when the family came into the office on my birthday and presented me with the vase I had returned to them.

"Happy birthday!"

I don't know how they had found out about my birthday, but this time, I just gave in and took the vase and thanked them. As I write this, the vase still decorates my coffee table. The family has long since moved to that "mysterious" Pennsylvania, along with their many sisters, brothers, and aunties. I hope they are doing well. When I see the vase, I think about them.

Faces of Iraq: Storyteller RSA's mother and sister in a children's party in Iraq in early seventies.

CHAPTER 11

A Story from Iraq

W̲E STARTED RESETTLING REFUGEES from Iraq in late 2008 or early 2009, and their resettlement came as a direct result of the war in Iraq. The people who had worked with Americans and supported the US troops were the first ones who needed to get out of the country when the situation there became worse. Some of these Iraqis had been interpreters for the US military, while others had helped the troops as mechanics and engineers or had done some other contract work. The chaos and deteriorating situation in Iraq soon created a steady stream of civilians leaving the country as well. For the most part, people sought refuge in Jordan, Syria, or

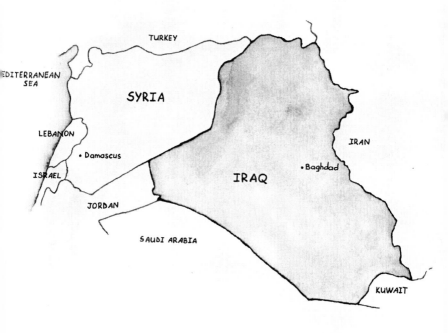

Egypt. At that time, every group and faction in Iraq tried to seize power and benefit from the void that Saddam Hussein's demise had created. An ordinary person could be in danger because of ethnicity or not belonging to the right religious group or even for not showing enough support to one or another political faction. New conservative religious laws set in place by the new power structures directly affected the lives of many, especially women. The secular tradition was forgotten, dress codes changed, and a neighbor might well report you to the authorities as "the enemy of the new government" simply out of envy for your spacious house.

Our first Iraqi refugees seemed to be well-educated professionals who had left a good life in Iraq. After several years in exile in one or another country, they had come to the US with a desire to live as comfortably as they had lived before as soon as possible. Several had savings and bought houses soon after their arrival. Members of this group could be quite demanding because of their drive to succeed, and the slow pace of the refugee resettlement process did not suit their goals. Quite a few did not want to accept entry-level jobs simply in order to pay their bills. They wanted to find employment in their professional fields. Not everyone managed to do so right away, but some did, especially those with mechanical skills or other professions in high demand in the US. Sometimes, the high expectations of these Iraqi refugees put them at odds with agency staff, who could not fulfill all of their wishes right away. As a whole, Iraqis were a dynamic and hard-working refugee group to resettle.

RSA: "Lucky to Get Out"

RSA is a well-educated Iraqi woman in her late thirties who came to the US in 2012. She lives in Abilene with her family and is an engineer by profession. She notes that a good education for women was not uncommon in "the old Iraq." RSA has done very well here and is one of those rare refugees who was able to find a professional job soon after arrival. She is very motivated and seems to realize that she needs to keep studying in order to stay competitive in the job market. RSA is a very conscientious person and has always complied with every resettlement program requirement. She has attended orientations, accepted job offers, and followed refugee handbook instructions. She is adjusting well to the new cultural and social environment and enjoys learning more and more about "American living." RSA has agreed to share her story but would rather not have it recorded, so I will take notes.

MY NAME IS RSA, and I am from Iraq. Before all the troubles started in our country, I just lived a very normal life. I lived with my parents, sister, and brother in a quiet neighborhood in Baghdad. My father had our house built when he married my mom, and they both lived there from 1971 until the end of their lives. And we all lived in our parents' house back then. I lost my parents early: my mother suffered from cancer for about four years before she passed away, and my dad followed her two years later. I was still a student in college when it happened.

I was attending a high school for girls that offered a good education. The school used to be affiliated with a church until sometime in the 1970s, but then it became independent. What stayed on from the past was a good education, discipline, and the headmistress who watched our every step. I remember that our teachers really did their best to teach us, and I never needed any private tutors or private lessons while I was in high school. We had to wear a uniform at school, and neither makeup nor jewelry was allowed, even in the senior grades. The school was free; in fact, all schooling was free in our country. Even higher education was free of charge, provided you received a high enough score on high school graduation exams for college. The school would tell you in advance what specialties you were allowed to apply for, and it was based on your high school graduation score. Like, if your score was from eighty to ninety out of one hundred, you could go to a college of science, and if you had from ninety to ninety-five, you could go to dental school, and if you got from ninety-five to one hundred, then you could apply to medical college. They grouped high school graduates by their scores like that. But of course, we could choose any specialty at a college that accepted lower scores; we just could not go to one that required a higher one. For example, I had a high school friend who got ninety-seven on her final exams, but she did not want to go to medical college, although she could. Instead, she went to a college of arts to study English.

As for me, I was a good student, but when I was in my senior year, I had just found out that my mom had cancer, and I did not do that well on my tests. I was not happy with my score when the results came out. I had wanted to study medicine, but I did not get a high enough score. So, in my frustration, I told my parents to decide for me what to study. I knew that I could not get what I really wanted, so I said to them, "Oh, whatever, I don't care. Just pick me something."

And they discussed it and then said to me, "We want you to become an engineer."

Frankly, I did not enjoy the college specialty that my parents had chosen for me. In Iraq, if you failed your freshman year's final exams, you could transfer to a lower college, so I could have transferred if I had failed my first year's final tests. I was thinking about changing to a lower college to do my MBA and then go on to get my PhD, so I tried to be careless about my tests, hoping I would fail them, but honestly, I could not do it. It just was not me, not my character, you know. So, I passed my freshman year's tests, but I could not transfer; I had to continue with engineering.

Now, when I am working as an engineer, I quite like it, but when I had to study for it in college, I did not like it too well. And in my country, I did not have the opportunity to work in my specialty, mostly because of the situation there: we had an embargo at that time, and the overall situation in Iraq was pretty difficult.

Everything was very expensive, and people did not get paid enough to live. And nobody knew what might happen next. So, it was a very challenging time for me and my family.

In 1999, I graduated and was about to start working. In our country, college graduates did not need to look for a job after graduation; instead, they were "distributed" or "assigned" to work under one or another government ministry, which is like government departments here. In Iraq, they are called "ministries." So, when I graduated, I was assigned to work at the Baghdad airport under the Ministry of Transportation, but I did not start that job. I knew that a job at the airport would be considered a highly sensitive position, and I would have to have all kinds of security clearances for it. I would also need to be a member of the Arab Baath Socialist Party, which was the ruling party at that time. I just told myself, *No, I am a peaceful person, and I do not want to get involved in anything like that and get in trouble later.*

So, I transferred myself to another ministry. I went from the Ministry of Transportation to the Ministry of Industry. It was 2001 when my transfer went through, and by that time, the situation in the country had become critical. We all were watching the news on TV, and we knew that something was coming, so my family advised me not to start this job, either. And I myself was hesitant, too, because if we decided to leave the country, I would not be able to get out because of my job. With an engineering degree, it would be almost impossible. That's how things were in Iraq: education was for free, but I would not be allowed to leave because of the education I had received and the job I had. Thus, I did not accept that job then but worked as a tutor from home. I was trying to talk my brother and sister into selling the house and leaving Iraq, but they did not want to do it, hoping that things would get better with time.

In July of 2003, I felt that I could not stay in the house any longer; I wanted to go to work. At that time, many people were leaving Iraq. I went to the Ministry of Industry to ask about the job I had not accepted earlier. They had already transferred me to a state company of tobacco and cigarettes, but I could not work there because of my health. I have had asthma since I was a teenager, and I told that to the company managers, but they did not care. They only needed people to work in production with the tobacco. I tried to transfer myself away from there, but they refused to let me go. I fought with them a lot, and finally, they assigned me to their printing department, away from the tobacco, and I started going to work every day, although there was nothing to do. The printing department had very little work in general, and all the machines were in good condition, so for an engineer like me, there was absolutely nothing to fill the time. I stayed on until mid-2004, when I used the opportunity to get half-pay and stay home.

I was starting to get threats at work because I was not covered—not wearing a veil. That was the beginning of my problems at work. The threats were not coming directly from the management but from my coworkers, who talked loudly about women who did not cover themselves and how badly it ended for these women. They made sure I could hear them. Religious posters supplied by my coworkers started appearing on the walls in our printing office. One of them said, "Be innocent like Holy Mary or Fatima—cover yourself," and it depicted both women wearing head scarves. The message was clear: "Start wearing a veil, or...you know. It may not end so innocently for you."

The change was related to the new people in the Iraqi government who were not tolerant of different ethnic and religious beliefs. It was quite a shocking change because Iraq used to be a secular state in the past. Women could wear regular clothes—maybe not really short skirts or shorts, but just "normal" clothes were fine, just like we wear here now. And nobody expected you to cover yourself, nothing like that. I wish I could show you my family photos when my mom was wearing a miniskirt in the seventies. But things had changed a lot during the last few years we lived in Iraq, and not for the better.

Then, our new neighbor started threatening us at home. It was some time at the end of 2003. He was a neighbor who had recently moved to our street from a different, very cheap neighborhood. That neighbor had made a lot of money from stealing during the 2003 chaos, so he could afford to live in our neighborhood. I think that he kept coming to us with his "warnings" because he had set his mind on getting our house. He had a nice house himself, but why not get another one if such an opportunity was right there? Our house was really spacious, and it was worth a lot of money. And it was just the three of us living in it.

So, whenever he talked with us, mostly with our brother, he would say, "Oh, it is just the three of you living in this big house, and only one man with two women. Anybody could come into your house and kill you and take your house away from you. Aren't you scared to live like that?" And his wife used to come over quite often to reproach me and my sister: "Why do you refuse to wear veils and cover yourself? Why do you want to wear pants? Don't you respect our religion? You may get hurt on the street because of that."

Our neighbor was from a big family, a big tribe; he had, like, ten cousins from his mother's side and maybe twelve cousins from his father's side. They felt powerful. Their talking scared me and my sister, so we rarely ventured out on the street other than to go to work. Then, we started getting threatening phone calls from strangers. They would call and curse us and threaten us on the phone. We suspected that the callers were related to the neighbors who were coming over and "warning" us. The callers spoke with the same accent as those neighbors. Like here in the US, you can tell from the accent what part of the US a person may be from. And the neighbors were from an area of Iraq where people spoke with a specific accent, and the callers spoke the same way, too.

We took all those threats seriously and moved to my uncle's house, which was empty at that time. My uncle was a college professor, and he had gotten a job offer from a college in a different country and had left Iraq. So, me, my brother, and my sister moved to my uncle's house. In Iraq, each neighborhood has an older man who is entrusted by the government to help people with civil documents, kind of like a notary. We had one in our neighborhood who used to be a good friend of our parents, and he knew us very well, too. So, my brother went to that man and told him that we would be gone from our house for a while. He explained to the man that our neighbor was giving us a hard time, and he asked the old man if he could go and talk to the neighbor for us. You know, in Iraq, you could ask for help in situations like this. It would come across as a more respected action. And the man agreed to talk to the neighbor for us since he was a good friend of our family and we had lived in that neighborhood all our lives. But when the man went and talked, the neighbor acted surprised and denied everything. He was like, "No, I have not done anything wrong. I want to help them."

When we moved to my uncle's house, our friends told us that the UNHCR office in Syria was accepting refugee applications. So, my sister and I traveled to Syria and went to the UNHCR office. We did all the paperwork and applied for the refugee program. The secretary in the refugee office told us that the only thing the refugee document would give us was the protection to stay in Syria as refugees. It would help us get residency in Syria, but no more, no less. When we asked her about chances to emigrate, she said, "No, don't rely on us for that, really."

So, we stayed in Syria until our brother told us on the phone, "I got the old man to talk to our neighbors. I think you can come home now; it's safe." Only then did we go back home. We had stayed in Syria for two and a half months, and then we went back. There was nothing more from our neighbor at that time. He had stopped coming to us, at least for a while. Back in Iraq, we could not say that we went to Syria to apply for a refugee program; we just said that we went to visit old neighbors who had moved to Syria.

After we returned, I went back to work at the same tobacco company. They had started to hand out their party newspaper every morning: a man would stand at the entrance and offer it to you, and if you did not take it, you showed that you were against their party. That was the start. I felt pressured to take that paper; I could not say, "I don't need it."

I couldn't take the paper and trash it right away, either, because other people would see me. I had to take it home and burn it, because if I put it in our household trash can, our trash collectors would find it and say, "Oh, she is against our party, against our religion." So, I had to take it every day, thank the guy who was handing it to me, and pretend to read it.

At the same time, my salary was very low; few people had a salary as low as mine, even those who had just started their jobs. I knew that the main issue in my case was that I refused to wear a veil and I came to work uncovered. And I was wearing pants. Things were changing in Iraq, and these changes were related to each government and their religious preferences and how tough a line they were taking on things.

Before 2004, nobody paid attention what religion you belonged to, whether you were a Christian, an atheist, a Shiite, or Sunni; everything was alright. And if you went to a mosque to pray, it could be a Sunni mosque or Shiite mosque. It was not important. A mosque was a mosque. But then in 2004, only Shiites had a mosque, and the Sunni mosque was not the right one anymore. And now, religion dictated how a woman could act and what she should wear or not wear. As for me, I respect all religions, but I am not going to wear a veil just because one group likes it that way. After I saw people killing one another because of religious beliefs, I no longer wanted to be part of any religious affiliation. I may recover here in the US, but it may take some time.

At that time, in 2004, the whole country was in chaos. That's how it was. What was going on? Let me explain. I did not like our ex-president—I really did not care for him—but he was the one who controlled everybody; all groups and all tribes were under his control, and everybody obeyed him. The president had the power to keep peace among all the different ethnic and religious groups. During his time, if you did not belong to any groups and stayed away from politics, you would be safe forever. But if you were part of a religious group or tried to criticize the government, you would be in trouble. So, if you kept your mouth shut and stayed away from politics—as we used to say, if you "walked beside the wall"—you would be fine. Live your normal life and be safe. You could even have government positions, like my uncle, who was the second man in command in a ministry, even though he had never been part of the ruling party. He got the job because he was really smart and had his PhD from England, so he was highly qualified. There were some exceptions, but not too many.

Then, the 2003 war started, the president got captured, and all the groups and tribes started fighting with one another. Things turned violent as many people tried to seize the moment and benefit from the chaos, either to get easy money or to secure power positions in the new government.

Let me tell you how it played out in our neighborhood. As I mentioned, our family had lived in that neighborhood since 1971, and we had the same neighbors for twenty-five years and longer. During all those years, everybody lived there in peace: Shiites and Sunnis and Christians, and people of different ethnicities, from many tribes. They lived there peacefully and did not have anything to fight about.

But then in 2004, our peaceful neighborhood started to change. It was not as quiet as it used to be. After "Desert Storm" in 1991, good people had started leaving the country, one by one. Most of the educated people felt they were wasting their time in Iraq. And under the embargo, it was a hard life. We really experienced some hard times. So, the majority of the people who could find jobs in other countries left Iraq, and the neighborhood changed; new people moved in. For example, I used to have a friend who is in Belgium now. He went to Europe and got married, and now, they live in Belgium, and he is doing fine. And he never went back to Iraq to visit, all these many years. It would be twenty-four years now since he left. But he left Iraq with just a little money in his pocket, did not have any savings or anything. It just shows how desperate people had become to leave Iraq. But that was just the beginning.

In 2004, some neighbors started fighting among themselves. It was mostly over money, quite silly, and the fights escalated to unthinkable levels. Some of the neighbors were Muslim Shiites, and many others were Sunnites, and now they had to fight, although they had lived peacefully side by side for many years in the past. But now, their relatives belonged to these different groups, like Al Jihaad and Hezbollah, and some belonged to the Al Dawa party.

One family in our neighborhood arranged for some people to kill our other neighbor's son. Then, those neighbors retaliated and sent people to kill the other family's son in return. So, they both lost their sons. It was terrible, especially since they had lived there side by side for many years. But the conflict started just like that: the Sunni neighbor had a mini-market, like a convenience store, and he was making good money. Then, the Shiite neighbor started his own mini-market in his home. The first one got upset that the second had gone into the same business, since that would mean fewer customers for him. The new market was much closer, maybe a five-minute walk away, so people would not want to get in the car and drive to the other market anymore. So, it was a competition, a money issue. The killing of the other family's son was very extreme revenge, but it happened in our neighborhood in those troubled times.

In 2005 and 2006, militias or national guards were often coming to our neighborhood, going into people's homes, and killing the people they found. Like, we woke up one day, and our street was full of police cars. Our street was really long, and we heard gunfire, gunshots at the other end of the street, and we could not go outside until the militias had left. The militias came in, got out of the jeeps; they were all disguised and armed. I remember seeing that house after the guards left: all the windows broken and all the people killed. The police had opened fire from outside and killed everybody in the house. Mostly, the police were looking for men, and if your beliefs were on the wrong side or you went to the wrong mosque to pray, you would get killed. Or, if you had a lot of money, they would want you, too. I remember that one family lost their three sons one day. The guards came and killed them, and their mother was pleading to spare at least one of them, but no. All three young people got killed.

And you might wonder, "How could they know who was who?" But it was easy to figure it out: in 2003, there was no control of government records, so the new government had access to all the documents, and they had a list of all the names. So, they could look at the list and point out, "Okay, let's get rid of this guy and that guy on this street."

They were after the old party members, too. You know, sometimes you had to be a party member because of your work. Especially in the field of education, you had to be a member of the party to be able to have that job. You did not need to take an active part, but still, you had to be a member, and your name would be on those lists, too. You could have been at a low rank and stayed there forever. The party officials could ask you whether you would like to get to a higher rank or be more active, but you could apologize and say, "No, I really don't have the time." Say it in a nice way, and they would leave you alone.

I lived in Iraq until I left in 2006, so I was thirty years old then, and I never had any problem with the party. Once, when I was still a student in high school, a woman from the party came to our school and asked us, "Do you want to be a member of the party, to sign up for it?"

I said, "No."

The woman asked me why, and I explained, "At my age, I would not be able to contribute much because I have to focus on my studies, but maybe I will join some time later, in the future, after I graduate from college." I said that I would think about it. And she was okay with that. So, if you found a good excuse, they would leave you alone. And they came just once, and it was not just to me; they asked everybody, "Are you part of the party? Are your family members in the party?"

But you could politely just say "no," apologize, and no one would hurt you. Or, even better, if one of your family members was in the party already, the recruiter would know that you were not against them. My father was the headmaster of a school, so he had to be a party member because of his job. He was not an active member, but he had to be a party member. His position at work demanded it. Many of the students' parents were up in very high ranks of the Security Department of the government, so my dad had to be in the party to interact with them. Many of his students were the spoiled children of rich people, with parents often high up in the government.

As time passed, things in Iraq did not calm down nor get any better. We all three worked, so we were alright, although my sister did not get paid at work, and my salary was very low. My brother had a supermarket, and he was working all the time. Then, he opened another shop, a cell phone shop. He was the one who made the most money; he was our family "bank."

After we went back home from Syria in 2006, we were threatened again after a few months. My sister got married and left the country; she lives in Sweden now. She had to go to another country first to get her visa and then on to Sweden. So, I was left with my brother, just the two of us. There was a time when the transformer had exploded, and we did not have electricity for two weeks. Insurgents often did that so they could carry out their revenge in the dark.

One day, a neighbor friend called me on my phone. "The national guards are walking around in our street. Be careful." I told my brother about this warning, and we had another friend who used to drive a taxicab, and he took my brother to a friend's house to stay that night. I hurried home so I had time to hide all the documents and important papers before the guards came to our house. Somebody had to be at home to meet them, or they would break into the house and take everything. It was getting late, and without electricity, it was really scary to be there.

But I had some money and family gold and a lot of documents to put away, like the title to the house, ownership documents for my brother's two stores, our identity cards, passports, UNHCR papers, everything. I did not have time to bury everything properly, so I divided all papers up and hid them randomly, so if the guards found one thing, they might miss something else.

I put on pants with a lot of pockets so I could put money in them. If the guards asked me if I had any money, I could give some to them and still have some left in another pocket. I had a laptop in the house that had a lot of personal information on it, and I hid it under blankets. And I taped our most important documents on the bottom of the bed, with scotch tape. Then, the guards came. They knocked on the gate and came right in. There were twelve of them, in face masks with rifles, and they started questioning me and searching the house.

They asked, "Who lives in this house?"

I said, "My uncle and me with my brother."

"Where are they?"

"Our computer got broken, and they went to take it to the shop to fix it."

"Show me your family IDs!"

And I said, "My uncle took all our IDs with him when he went, so I don't have them in the house."

One of the guards saw CDs in the house and asked, "Are these CDs with pictures of people you killed?"

I said, "No, they are music CDs, some computer software, and computer games."

The guard looked at me, took the CDs, and smashed them all to pieces on the floor. They asked what my name was, and I told them my name. The thing is that from my name, they could not tell which part of Iraq or which ethnic group I belonged to. So, they were okay with that. Then, they asked how old my brother was, and I lied to them. "Oh, he is ten years old."

The guards took many of our papers and left that night, but as soon as they were out of the door, I started packing things up. I knew that the guards could return any day now, even the next day, because they had a way to check my story out. The guards took the papers, but since most of them were not educated, they probably could not read those documents right away, but I knew that they would take them to other people to read. So, I knew it was just a matter of time.

The following morning, I got up before sunrise and packed all I could. A friend had offered to take us to the border. We had to leave so fast that we hardly had time to get everything settled. My brother had tried to sell his business even before that night and had got a down payment for one, but the buyer refused to pay the rest of the money. He threatened us and told my brother to turn over the documents for the business anyway. The other shop got burned down.

Under such circumstances, we left the country for Syria in 2006. In Syria, we went to visit our friends who advised me, "Why don't you apply for the refugee program?"

I said, "We already applied, but we lost our documents."

The friends explained to me that I could go to the UNHCR office and ask them to pull up my case from their database. So, I went to that office again, and they pulled up my case. Then, in 2007, my friends advised me to go to the UNHCR and check on my case status again. I went, and the worker told me, "Your case has been transferred to the resettlement department."

I asked him, "What does that mean?"

He said, "You will get resettled to another country, somewhere."

I asked, "When?"

He said, "Wait for a phone call. It could be any time from now up to one year."

And four months later, we got a phone call, and they told us to come for an interview. We went, and after several interviews with UNHCR employees, we met with a person from the American delegation. And she said, "We looked at your case, and we are going to resettle you to the US. Do you agree or not?"

She gave us time to think, but we did not need to think too long; we said, "Yes." The US was our first choice, anyway. Actually, I checked about Sweden first because our sister was in Sweden. So, at first I asked that lady, "Could we ask to be resettled to Sweden?"

And she said: "No, Sweden really does not offer resettlement to anyone right now. And if you do not accept our offer, the UNHCR will close your case, and you will have no rights to apply again."

When I heard that, I said, "Oh, don't get me wrong, we are accepting. I was just checking." So, we were approved for resettlement to the US. It was back in 2007, and we waited until 2012 to come. It was really a long wait.

Six months passed, and they called us for another interview. It was the same person, and she said that this was the last interview for us. After that, they would transfer us to IOM. Then, two more months passed, and we went for an interview with IOM. And maybe one year later, we had another interview with IOM, and then, they seemed to have forgotten us. Nothing happened for a while. At the interview, they told us, "We are going to let you know when you can travel."

Since we both were adults, we had the option to travel separately, but we decided to come together. And thank God we decided on that because later, it turned out that my brother had a serious heart problem and he went through heart surgery, and I had to take care of him after that. But I kept calling the IOM office every month, and the clerk kept saying, "Your personal case has been approved, but since you are together with your brother, your case is still in process."

Finally, they called us for medical tests, and that was how they found out that my brother had a serious heart condition. In the past, he had felt that something was wrong; he got tired very easily, often felt fatigued, but nobody could tell us what was wrong. But now, the doctors discovered that my brother had an issue with his heart. The doctor advised him to get an operation right there in Syria because he was in a critical condition. The doctor said, "I know you may want to wait until you are in the US, but it could take too long a time for your case."

My brother's health was getting worse at that time, but at first, he refused to go for the surgery because he was afraid that we might miss the chance to travel. But finally, his health got so bad that he could not even leave the apartment. Then, I told him, "Forget about travel. Your health is more important."

So, my brother had the surgery in August of 2011, and I took care of him after that. He recovered well and is doing fine now. At that time, the situation in Syria was steadily getting worse. It had been going down since the end of 2010, and it was not easy to live there in those days. So, we were hoping to get to leave soon.

Our friends had told us about an IOM website where we could check the status of our case, and I used to check every day. Then one day, I signed into the website from work and looked at our "travel status," and it said "in progress." It meant that we were finally going! I remember that I was cheering, laughing, jumping up and down, and crying, all at the same time.

My coworkers got distraught and were asking, "What is it? What happened? What's going on?"

I told them, "It's okay, never mind, never mind. Everything is fine!"

Then, IOM called us. "You have your visa."

So, we were happy and started preparing for travel. I had packed all my suitcases, and I was waiting to go. I was so happy, but at the same time, the way I left Syria was horrible. It had become so dangerous in Syria that my brother and I decided to go to the airport on the evening before our travel day. Our flight was supposed to be at nine in the morning. It was not safe to be on the road in the early morning hours or during the night. So, my former manager offered me a ride to the airport, and I was really happy about it.

But we woke up at seven in the morning of the day before travel, and I looked out of the window. Oh, my! There were helicopters bombing neighborhoods nearby, and everything was on fire. Houses were burning everywhere around us. They were about to close all the roads in our area, and then nobody would be able to leave from our neighborhood. It was a security issue.

My manager called me. "What are you going to do?"

I asked him, "Could you send me the car now?"

He said, "But the roads to your area are blocked already."

I said, "I am going to walk up to the roadblocks to get out of here."

I knew that they would let me out because they could see that I was not a Syrian. The worker with the car called me and said, "I am waiting in this and that place. Can you come now?"

I asked him if he could come and help us with the luggage, and he did, and we said our goodbyes to the neighbors and walked all the way to the car. And, believe me, what I saw on the street was worse than anything I had ever seen in my country. I saw a helicopter as close as this tree here, and it was heading in our direction, bombing and bombing everything on its way. I could see it very clearly; it came so close to me. But we kept walking until we got to the car, got in, and the guy took us to the airport. We got there at 9:00 a.m., so we had to wait for twenty-four hours. But it was good that we were at the airport already. So, we stayed at the airport, and when the evening came, we slept there. But very early the next morning, around 4:30 a.m. or so, an IOM employee told us that our flight was cancelled. The Syrian government refused to let the plane from Jordan land at the airport. We stayed until noon, and I asked the IOM worker what to do, and he said, "I don't know."

A couple more people like us were waiting at the airport: another brother and sister from Iraq, and they told us, "It is our third time. We have been in this situation for over a year. We come to the airport, wait, then the flight gets cancelled, and we go back home."

They were Iraqi refugees, too. I asked them what to do, and they said, "Go home. And wait for a phone call." It was August 24, I think. And I was thinking, *Okay, we have paid the whole month of rent.* Then, I called my manager and asked if he could send the car for us again, and he asked, "Where are you? Still there at the airport?"

I said, "Yeah, the flight got cancelled."

My manager sent the car for us again, and we went back to our old apartment. I was so frustrated. I thought that I would never get out. They were still bombing my neighborhood, but I did not hear it, I was so upset. I was saying to myself, *Oh, no, I will end up here. I just lost my chance to get out!*

So, we stayed in our apartment that night, and around 2:30 a.m., an IOM employee called us. "If you can come to the airport now, we can put you on an 8:00 a.m. flight." It was a short notice, really, since we would have to head out to the airport right then. My brother asked him, "How can we get to the airport? It is the middle of the night!"

And he said, "Well, I don't know."

When we had gone back to the apartment, many of the Iraqi families had stayed at the airport because they had nowhere else to go, and the IOM took them to the closest hotel to stay overnight. They could just walk back to the airport. Now, we both were desperate, thinking, how could we get to the airport? It was the middle of the night. Thank goodness, we had not unpacked yet, just taken out some things we needed for sleep, so I quickly packed everything up again, and my brother went outside to look for transportation. The guards who were standing on the street asked him what he was doing, and my brother said: "I am an Iraqi, and I want to go back home to Iraq, and I need to get a taxi to get to the airport."

The guard asked, "Why are you leaving?"

IOM had advised us not to tell anyone that we were going to the US; it was for our own safety. So, my brother told the guards that we were going to Iraq. So, the guards helped us stop a taxi cab, and we jumped in that taxi cab, and off we went to the airport again! It was night, and the streets were all empty, but the taxi driver was shaking with fear, and we were scared, too. The situation in town was so bad that you had to be afraid of being stopped. And we did not know who could stop us—some rebels or gangs—and we did not know until the last minute how our trip would end. The taxi driver told us that he had been on his way home when the security guards had stopped him, and he was afraid to say, "No," to them, so he took us. He told us later, "I would never have stopped for you if not for these guards."

So, we got to the airport in time to make our flight. Everything was fine, but we had an incident at the airport with the security clerk. When we went for exit stamps, the clerk told us, "I am not going to let you leave until you pay me. You are Iraqi, and you are going to the US." It was the airport security control clerk at the Syrian airport, the one who puts an exit stamp in passports. Initially, my brother put four dollars in each passport for the clerk, but the man said, "No, no, dear, you will pay me one hundred dollars each."

I was ready to fight with the clerk, but my brother stopped me. "Be quiet. I will pay him just to get out of this hell."

So, we ended up paying him the money he asked for. Now, looking back at all that happened, I realize that we were really lucky to get out of Syria and be here. And for your information, neither one of us were involved in anything political—no party affiliations or religious groups.

The flight IOM got for us was from Damascus, Syria, to Amman, Jordan, and then on to Lebanon. From Lebanon, we went on to Dubai, then to Los Angeles, from Los Angeles to Dallas, and then finally to Abilene. Oh, my God! We left Syria on the twenty-fifth, and we got here on the thirtieth. The flight from Syria to Dubai took the whole day. We arrived in Dubai in the evening, and we stayed the whole night at the airport. And when we arrived in Los Angeles, we stayed in the hotel that IOM had got for us, and then we went on from Los Angeles to Dallas. Then, we flew to Abilene in that little plane. So, it really was a long journey.

It was a late evening, already dark, when we landed in Abilene. The IRC case worker took us to our apartment, and we had a shower and some food and went to bed. The next day, the case manager came, and after that we were left on our own because it was the Labor Day weekend and everything was closed.

Initially, Abilene seemed disappointing because in Iraq and Syria, I had lived in big cities with many people around us, and I was expecting the same here, to be in a bigger city. So, when we arrived here, it felt like we had landed in some remote place—no people on the streets, nothing. And we had struggled so much to get out of Syria and Iraq!

But now, I am quite used to Abilene. It is a small place, but safe and quiet, and we do not have to worry if we leave the house after dark. The heat does not bother me that much. The climate in Iraq is quite similar to what we have here.

The best thing that happened to me was that I started working in my profession. I got a job as an engineer. Now, it has been around two years since I have had that engineering job. I know that I need to refresh my professional knowledge, and I am researching my options right now. And I have no troubles here, no safety issues; I can really sleep peacefully here. I still feel afraid going out after dark, but I can manage it. I am an outgoing person and like to go out with friends, have a good time, but if it is after dark, I still feel a little scared. It is a feeling inside me that comes from years of insecurity in Iraq and Syria. And here, we feel like we have settled in, although we have not been in the US that long. Like, we lived in Syria for six years, but we always had that temporary feeling. We did not try to buy extra things for our apartment there because we never knew when we would be packing and leaving. But here, we are at home.

Overall, it is not easy to come to a different country and start things over. I think people have to invest more in learning the language and culture. How can you not join the community and speak the language? You cannot keep living in your own group, surrounded by your own culture. You have to venture outside and meet the real American community, and language is the key for that.

Summer 2014

From Nancy's personal photo album

Nick Kloster

Faces of Cuba: Storyteller Nancy Rojas Feria and her husband, Andres, (top) celebrate the first anniversary of their arrival in the US. Dallas, Texas, June 2010. They have lived in Abilene since 2009. They both appreciate life in a free country where they can work and have a decent living. Nancy (bottom) in 2017.

CHAPTER 12

A Story from Cuba

I AM WRITING ABOUT CUBA on the exact day that the American flag will be raised above its newly opened US Embassy. Secretary of State John Kerry will be participating in the official flag-raising ceremony that marks the big change in the relations between Cuba and the US after decades of embargo. I am not sure if the new policy will change anything for Cuban refugees and parolees. At present, the same laws are in effect—refugees arrive, and parolees cross the border.

I have asked several Cuban refugees and parolees what they think about the new developments, and they have responded with

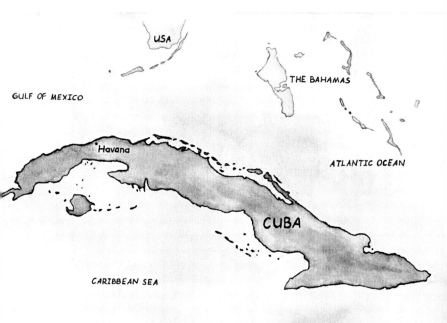

mixed emotions. Some say that the policy change will open Cuba to tourists from the US, and the Cuban government will not be able to keep everything under such tight control, which means the Cuban people will benefit. Others are more skeptical and say that "becoming friends with the Castro regime" negates everything they or their parents have been fighting for and will legitimize the current government. They are suspicious of any dealings with the repressive Castro government, afraid that the open relations will be advantageous only for the ruling elite. Time will tell.

As for the Cuban refugees resettled by the IRC in Abilene, our first ones came in the early summer of 2008, the same year as the Bhutanese-Nepali and the Iraqi refugee programs started. The first Cuban family arrived in June of 2008, and they had hardly settled into their apartment when they were ready to leave for Miami, Florida, which is undoubtedly the largest Cuban community in the US. It took a bit of convincing for them to stay in Abilene until their refugee assistance ended. Right after, they moved to Miami, Florida, as many other Cuban refugees do. The surprising thing was that they moved back to Abilene a short while later and seem to have settled here for life. Since 2008, between forty and fifty Cuban refugees have been resettled to Abilene, but only about a dozen have stayed here.

I had an opportunity to visit Cuba on a "People to People" program in 2010, and I was truly surprised that the seemingly distant "forbidden island" was physically so close to the US. We had a short forty-five-minute flight from Miami to Camaguey in Cuba. In the Camaguey airport, I felt I had taken a journey back to the past, and not simply "back to the fifties," as people often say about Cuba, but right back to my own "Soviet Union past." So much of Cuba's daily life reminded me of Soviet times: Spartan hotels with bare light-bulbs, the quiet but menacing presence of security guards around every government building, slogans and propaganda posters on every corner praising the accomplishments of the revolution, and special perks for the elites, including us tourists, who had American dollars in our pockets.

At the same time, Cuba was also different from my past, since it was "a most beautiful past"—an island surrounded by magical

Caribbean waters with palm trees gently swishing next to colorful, if crumbling, buildings. But for me, the best about Cuba was—and still is—the Cuban people: vibrant and energetic, despite the oppressive regime and poverty in Cuba.

Nancy: "One Day, Cuban People Will Be Free"

I have known Nancy and her husband, Andres, since the day they arrived in Abilene in 2009. They were not the first Cuban refugees to come, and when they arrived, we had a staff member who was a former Cuban refugee and could help them settle in and find a job. After the initial resettlement rush was over, I helped both Nancy and Andres file petitions for their adult children, who lived in Cuba. Nancy and Andres are in their fifties, and both have been married before. Their children are from previous marriages.

While we were working on the applications, Nancy told me about how she and Andres had been involved in the opposition movement in Cuba and how those activities eventually led to their coming to the US as refugees. Both of them talked longingly about their childhood places, and the names of those towns and villages in Cuba sounded like music to my ears: Camaguey, Oriente, Holguin, Cielo de Avila. I was already thinking about visiting Cuba as a tourist, and the way they described their homeland convinced me that I really had to go.

When I started thinking about people who might share their stories, I remembered Nancy and invited her to participate. She was happy to do so, although we had to work through an interpreter at times. Nancy was fine with recording parts of her story; other parts have also been documented in notes.

The translation from Spanish into English was provided by Manuela Rocio Toon.

I AM NANCY ROJAS FERIA, and I am from Cuba. I am not afraid to use my real name to tell my story—I want everybody to know that it is me.

I was born in a very poor family in Cuba. We were very poor. We lived in Holguin in the province of Oriente. My parents had three children: two sons and me, their only daughter. I was the youngest child in the family. My two brothers came to live in the US a long time ago, and they have both passed away by now. My father was a very strong communist; when he was young, he had fought for the Cuban revolution side by side with other rebels in the mountains of Sierra Maestra. My dad sacrificed a lot for the Cuban government, for the revolution, and received numerous medals for his loyalty and courage.

The paradox was that although I grew up with my mom and my communist dad, I joined the opposition movement. We were a group of dissidents, and we educated people about their human rights and the lack of freedoms in Cuba. We were against the Castro government. But my dad never reprimanded me for it; he did not treat me badly, nor did he ever say that I should not join the dissident movement. He loved me and valued me, and toward the end of his life, he realized that he had been wrong about the revolution and Castro and that he had sacrificed his life for nothing. It was so sad that he had to live all his life in extreme poverty after all he had done for the regime.

Imagine, my dad as an old revolutionary was given the right to own a motorbike. Fidel could have cars and a yacht and women, but my dad was allowed to have a bike. It was a little motorbike, "Karpaty," that ran on gas, and it was made in the Soviet Union. How do you like that? My dad could not even own a car! Fidel and all those government functionaries could buy everything they wanted, but the rest of the Cuban people had to live in utmost poverty.

So, as my dad was getting older, he came around and started thinking that what he had fought for was wrong. He would often say to me, "I fought together with Fidel in the mountains so that the Cuban people would be free, but we are not free. We don't have freedom of expression, we cannot do what we want, and we do not have rights to anything. I cannot even buy a car or go to a tourist beach."

You know, to go to the same beach where tourists go, we need American dollars, and Cuban people are not allowed to have American dollars. One can go to jail for just having American dollars.

So, my dad changed his mind when he saw what was really going on in Cuba, and he encouraged me to stay on my path. When he got really sick, he told me, "My daughter, I cannot help you with your struggle because I am too old and sick, but you are right. I fought for the revolution so I could see you all grow up with a beautiful ideal and have a better life than I had. But now, I see that I was wrong. We live in poverty. The government took away our Christmas, Three Kings' Day, and you may even have to change your date of birth if Fidel wishes it so. You have to do everything he says."

My father was very sick at the end. He had cancer and was dying. Since he was an old revolutionary, I went to the government to seek help, but they refused to do anything for my dad because I was a dissenter. So, they refused to help. But when my dad passed away, Fidel's functionaries came to my house and brought many wreaths, flowers—a lot of them. So, they acknowledged him, but only after he passed away. Only after he died! Can you imagine this? What kind of people would do that? So, when they came to where we were holding my dad's wake, I told them, "No."

I stood up to the group of communists. I said, "My father belongs to me now. I have not buried him yet, so leave him alone. I will not accept any wreaths or flags or any other tributes that you want to give him."

With these words, I sent them away, and they left. Back then, it was the tradition that the government would acknowledge the revolutionaries. "Why didn't I accept anything?" you may ask. And my answer is, "Because during his life, they did not help my father with anything. When I went pleading for help, they would not hear me. But after his death, they come to give him offerings! He did not need them anymore."

The functionaries came back when my dad was buried, and they put their decorations on his grave. I could not do anything about it. But while he was living, he had only me, his daughter. No one from the government helped him.

After my father died, I went to the US Embassy to talk with them about my situation. I wanted to leave Cuba and go to the US as a refugee. My dad's passing gave me an opportunity to go to the embassy and tell them everything. You know, many people go to the US Embassy and say that they want to leave, but not everyone is telling the truth. The embassy people listened to me and said, "Many people come to us, but they sometimes do not tell the truth. They just make things up because they are desperate to leave. That's why we check all the facts in our interviews and make sure that everything the people tell us is true."

I had three or four interviews over several years, and I had to tell them everything. I told them about my father's wake and what had happened. But I did not know at the time that somebody had videotaped my dad's wake, and somehow, that tape got to the embassy. The embassy people now could see for themselves how I had turned away Fidel's functionaries, so they knew that I was telling the truth. And it helped me make a case with them. But the whole process of refugee resettlement interviewing took about four years.

My older brother was the first one from our family who came to the US to live as a political refugee. He had been in the prisons of Cuba and in a labor camp called UMAP because he had refused to join the military service. He was just fifteen or sixteen when they put him in jail and then sent him to the labor camp. Those camps were terrible, more like concentration camps than anything else. I think I was around thirteen years old then, just a teenager, when they took him away. Even my parents could not do anything to stop it, and it broke my parents' hearts. You know, parents love their children equally, but they feel more attached to those who cannot take care of themselves, like my brother. I was always brave, so they did not need to support me much. My parents told me, "When you get to go to the US, you have to take care of your brother; he is sick and will need you."

My poor brother was kept in prison for sixteen years. They beat him, kept him half-starved, and he lost all his teeth. His health was destroyed in those camps and prisons. When he got out of the labor camp, he applied to come to the US as a refugee, to leave Cuba. There was a law in the US that everybody who had been in the UMAP labor camp would be approved for resettlement to the US, and my brother got approved. He came here when he was in his midthirties and lived in New Jersey all these years.

When I came to Abilene in 2009, one Cuban lady called me from New Jersey to say that my brother needed me, that he wanted to come here to Abilene and live with me. My brother had cancer and was very sick. Doctors had operated on him, removed his esophagus, and he needed care. Then, the Red Cross called one day to tell me they were planning to send my brother to me. They could send him only to Dallas because he was too sick to travel on the little plane to Abilene. So, I had to go and get him from Dallas. When that happened, I had lived in Abilene for just two months, and I did not know how I could bring my brother from Dallas to Abilene. I did not have a car or a driver's license, and I could not afford to go by taxicab. So, I was at home and thinking about how I could go and get him, but I did not know what to do. I was crying, and a friend came by and saw me, and she asked me why I was crying. I told her about my brother and that I did not know what to do. And she said, "Go take a shower, get dressed, and I will take you to the Dallas airport to get your brother."

So, she helped me to go for my brother. We went to the Dallas airport, and my brother arrived at 2:00 a.m. It had been twelve years since I saw him last. He had lived in the US for the last twelve years; when he left, our parents were still alive. When I saw him, I could recognize him, but he was like a different person; he was destroyed, very sick. We took him to my apartment and later made arrangements for hospice to help. At first, the apartment manager did not want to let me have my brother in our apartment, and then I asked Javier from the IRC to come with me to talk to her, so he could interpret. I said to the manager, "My brother came here to be with me to die because we have not seen each other for twelve years. He is very sick."

So, she let me have him in the apartment for a while. At that time, we did not know other Cubans here yet. We were new to town, and we lived in a different area. So, they did not get involved and did not do anything for us. But Javier helped us a lot and helped make arrangements for hospice care. Then, my brother was in hospice, and I could stay with him there.

He died about a month later here in Abilene, and before his death, he told me that he wanted to be cremated and have his ashes taken to Cuba. That was what my parents had always asked for, although they both had passed away by then. I did as my brother and my parents had wished, and my brother's ashes are now in Cuba. That was a very sad time for me. I was happy to be out of Cuba at last, but my brother was dying, and it was a time of grieving.

But let me tell you about our human rights movement in Cuba and how I started. I got seriously involved in 1971. Yes, it was January 29, 1971. We were collecting signatures from people who supported our human rights movement and wanted to have changes in Cuba, and I collected 11,000 signatures. People who signed up had to put their real names on the list and prove their identities with their identity cards. In Cuba, the document is called a *Carnet de Identidad*, somewhat like what we know here as our state IDs. So, if you signed up, your name would be known to the Cuban government and to the police. But people were not afraid. Imagine picking up all those signatures from people with their real names and ID numbers!

Then, we went to the government representatives, to Raul Castro's official representative, to Felipe Perez Roque.[13] But when we went to talk to the representatives, they treated us like pigs. They kicked us out. They did not beat us, no, but they talked to us as if we were some lower-class prostitutes, and it hurt us. But we were not prostitutes—no, it was not true. I had my husband and the others had theirs, so they treated us like that just to discredit us. If they could treat us as immoral women, then they could ignore us and our petition. It was a common practice in Cuba: mistreat everyone who opposes the government. But in Cuba, nuns from Spain and Chile visited my house. If I were a prostitute, nuns would have never visited my house. And all the women in our group were ordinary women; we all had husbands, homes, and children. We had families. We were organized women.

So, when we went there, they took the signatures we had collected, but they tried to do everything to discredit us and all those thousands of signatures. But we came out undefeated. We felt the power of the people who had signed up and who stood by us. People had signed the petition because they were tired of living without freedom and in poverty. They wanted changes.

It was my first husband, the father of my two children, who showed me how to protest. He was very smart, and although he worked with his hands, he was always thinking and following what was going on. When our kids started school, we saw how they were brainwashed to believe the lies our government was spreading. They were getting indoctrinated in Fidel's ideology. It was during the early 1970s. What parents were teaching did not count anymore. The children were taught that everyone had to be like Che and they had to worship the heroes of the revolution. You did not have to listen to your mom and dad. The schools changed your children's thinking; it was so easy to do. We could see it when our son started school.

My first husband was a very good father to our children. He always sat the kids down and would tell them, "Here in our house, you do not applaud Fidel, and you do not put up propaganda. You say 'no' to joining the communists and 'no' to the CDR." [*CDR is the Committee for the Defense of the Revolution.*] He never allowed the children to be part of any government-organized movements; the only thing they could participate in was their studies. My children's father was a very open-minded man; he was one of the people who helped me most. He told me I was on the right path. So, that's how I became a dissident.

Later on, we formed an organization called "The Democratic Alliance," and I allocated part of my yard for meetings. We were a group of about eighty people, and we were directly in contact with people from *Telemarti* and *Radiomarti*; those are information channels that broadcast from the US to Cuba. They started sending documents and equipment to us, including telephones, so we could be in touch, and they did it through the US Embassy. We would go there in a little car to get those things, and the police would always follow us. We had to disguise ourselves so the police would not recognize us, or we would end up in prison. A lot of people are still in prison. We used to call the embassy *chapa negra*. *Chapa negra* means "black license plate," and in Cuba, black license plates meant that your car belonged to official diplomatic business.

This started in about 1998 and 1999. We received books to guide our activities and to highlight the points we had to make when reporters came to interview us. *Telemarti* and *Radiomarti* people also explained what rights we would have when we came to the US. But to come here, we wanted to accomplish changes in Cuba first, and those have not happened yet. Although, we see some change, since Raul, not Fidel, is in power. He is more flexible, and he understands why we came to the US. But real change is not there yet.

When I got involved with the dissenters' movement, I told the government and the police openly that I wanted to go to the US to be free and have the right to free speech. I wanted to be free in a country where nobody could pick my friends for me or decide my destiny. In Cuba, my life was worth nothing. Although I was born in Cuba, I had no worth; people's lives were worth nothing.

As I said, it took about four years to go through the embassy interviews and get approved to come to the US. I left Cuba in 2009, yes, on July 3. On that day, I had to leave behind the greatest gift that we as mothers have: our children. My father had already passed away at that time, and my mother was not living anymore, so, I had only my two children. My family is really small. With a broken heart, I left my daughter and son behind. My body was in the US, but my thoughts and my heart remained with my children and my grandchild in Cuba. I will always have that connection while they still live there.

I came here with my second husband, Andres. We have known each other for twenty years. But before we arrived, the story of our organization was featured in a book that the US Embassy published. Embassy staff came to us, like Cecilia—I forget her last name—who took our photograph and recorded a video. Also, the story about me and my dad was in that book. I was the daughter of a devoted communist who changed his mind toward the end of his life. It is a very important book, and when you read it, you can see the real face of Cuba and its people. It speaks the truth.

But now, I live in the US, in Abilene. And I like Abilene, and I will never leave. I want to bring my family here to live. I have many friends in the Cuban community now, and not just Cubans. I have friends in many other communities, too. Remember how I did not have anyone when we first arrived and I needed help with my dying brother? Now, it is different. I have many good friends. For example, when I was in the hospital after an accident, Maria Elena and Blanca with her family came to visit. And people are nice here in Abilene.

Let me tell you one thing that happened to me here. I was leaving Rosa's Cafe at 1:00 a.m. after work. I didn't have a car then, just a bicycle. It was dark, and I was riding the bicycle without the flashing lights, and the police stopped me. The policeman put me and my bicycle in the police car and took me home. I admire this place because it is unbelievable that a police officer would drop you off at home and wait for you to go through your door to make sure you are safe.

At first, the policeman asked me for my documents, and then said, "Oh, Cuba! Yes, ma'am." He told me not to ride my bike after dark without lights. He could have given me a traffic ticket, but he did not because he saw that I was going home after work and that I did not have any other means of transportation. The police officer just said, "Don't drive without lights. It is dangerous." And the same police officer later took me to CityLink to sign up for evening transportation service. I signed an agreement that the evening bus would come for me from now on.

I love Cuba, and I will never fight against Cuba as a country. It is the place where I was born, where I have my children. Understand? But change has to come. It will come, and we will all be old by then, but the young—my grandchildren and great-grandchildren—will benefit. But now, my grandchild doesn't want to be in Cuba because Fidel is still alive and he controls everything, even though Raul is officially in charge.

I want freedom for the Cuban people, so we can do the same things in Cuba that people can do here. Like, if I want to take $10,000 to Cuba and open a gas station there, I want to be able to do it. But Cuban people are not allowed to do those things now. I don't want to lose my Cuban citizenship over it. Do you understand? How would it feel if you lost your citizenship in your own country, the country where you were born? It is not that I would go back to live in Cuba, but I want to keep my family ties and friendships. These are my people, the ones who understand what I did and why I joined the dissident movement, so I would like to visit them and to see change for the better.

But my flag is now the American flag. I am now in the United States, and in four years, this country has given me what I did not have in Cuba, even though I lived in Cuba for more than forty years. I have accomplished more here than I ever did in Cuba.

I have built a house for my son in Cuba that is worth about 90,000 or 100,000 Cuban pesos, and I did it legally. My daughter is qualified to come to the US as a professional. She is a nurse in Cuba, and I was told that she would be able to work as a nurse here as well. She just needs to learn English really well and pass the tests. These are just some of the good things that have happened since I came.

November 2014, February 2015 and May 2015

Refugees and the Resettlement Agency: Do We Have a Bond?

A FEW MONTHS AFTER I STARTED my job with the IRC, I went to a bookstore to find something about refugees and resettlement, the field I was entering. I was impressed with the number of books about refugees, mostly fiction based on "true stories" about the journey and hardships of an individual or a family from a war-torn homeland to safety in a host country. Another well-represented topic was refugee lives in the US and the cultural challenges they faced. But books about resettlement work itself were just not there.

I felt disappointed, since I thought that the daily interaction with newcomers from diverse cultures and all walks of life would have been a fascinating subject. Even now, some ten years later, when I looked again for such books, I came away empty-handed. A few good movies turned up, like *The Good Lie*, which features an employment counselor working with a group of Sudanese refugees, but no books. I noticed that even those books that detailed the refugees' first steps in the US almost never acknowledged the existence of resettlement agencies and their staff. Instead, things "just happened" to refugees, although I could tell from my own experience that there had to have been a case worker or employment counselor behind the scenes. I still wonder why they were missing from the pages of these publications.

A typical book starts with refugees arriving in the US, usually at the airport of their new hometown. What happens next? They just "start living" in their new apartment, which, by some miracle, has furniture, household supplies, toiletries, and a fridge full of groceries. The electricity and water have been turned on. In real life, a case worker has done all the work to make the apartment ready and then gone to the airport to meet the new arrivals and take them to their new dwelling. Even though meeting the refugees at the airport might seem like "no big deal," in fact, flights often arrive after regular office hours—even late at night—and just as often are delayed or rescheduled. The case worker has to be at the airport for the newly arrived, rain or shine.

As one of the storytellers recalls, "Our plane was delayed. When we finally arrived in Austin, Texas, it was late at night. We saw two ladies waiting for us at the airport; of course, we did not know them, but we saw the agency sign and knew they were waiting for us. Then, the ladies took us to our apartment, where beds had been made for us, and showed us how everything worked there...After they left, we opened the fridge, and it was full of food. My dad told us, 'I guess it is ours; let's eat.' We all realized that we were hungry after the long day. Some of the food was strange, but then we found some bread and butter and ate it. After supper, we went to sleep."

In the books I found, the newcomers also "just happen" to start working a few weeks after arrival. How did this happen? More than likely, that "invisible" agency staff member helped. Then, more time passes, and all of a sudden, a missing spouse or children arrive, and everyone is happy to be reunited again. Is this another miracle? Or has an agency employee helped file an immigration petition? These are just a few examples of things that resettlement agency staff does "behind the scenes."

I have not had an opportunity to ask authors why they "forgot" to mention resettlement staff. Perhaps telling about agency employees doing their job was not as exciting a topic as recounting the daily struggles of the refugees themselves. Or, the author was simply unaware that there are organizations that help refugees after their arrival. In any event, this omission prompted me to reflect on our agency's relationship with refugees more closely and also to ask refugee storytellers to share their thoughts about their resettlement agency and its staff.

How did we as resettlement staff feel about refugees? Did we develop a special bond, friendship, trust, respect? During the first program months, we spent quite a lot of time with individual refugees, as we talked, went job searching together, or dreamed up the best plan for a refugee's future. Did we think of "our refugee clients" in a way that was different, let's say, from a bank teller and her bank clients or a grocery store cashier and his customers?

I spent my working hours doing things for and with refugees and caring and worrying about them. They were more than just "clients." Some days, I brought these worries home: before my own bedtime, I wondered if Mon Maya was alright and how Japhet's or Sally's first day at work went, or if Bouake found the right bus to take him home after work. I reassured myself that the newly arrived Clarence remembered his home address and that Sandy did know how to set her alarm clock to wake up in time for work. I believe that the majority of my coworkers felt the same way, or we would not be in resettlement work. I remember a former coworker saying, "I feel responsible for all of them, and I cannot sleep at night unless I know that I have done everything [that I was supposed to do]. That gives me peace of mind."

Resettlement work has always been known for its dynamic nature, and my average work day at the IRC was always fast-paced, often unpredictable, and involved a lot of responsibility. A case worker could not just call in sick and not meet an arriving family at the airport or employment specialist fail to find a job for a new arrival before the financial assistance program ran out. All the new refugees were going through cultural shock, and they often did not have a clear understanding of what to expect from the agency and from us as their case workers.

Quite a few tried to push for special treatment. One Congolese man wanted a better job right away because the manager in his current one did not give him enough hours. How would he pay his rent? A woman complained that her job was too far from home and the long bus ride made her nauseous. Several Turkish refugees had set their minds on working in construction and pleaded with me to find them an opportunity. A Liberian refugee had been in Abilene for more than three months already, but his wife was still in Ivory Coast, waiting to come. Why didn't the agency do anything about it? One family accused me of pocketing their financial assistance money because the checks they received seemed too small. They had come from a country where corruption and stealing was a daily occurrence. My life as a staff member was not always very easy. I had to learn to push back those clients who demanded too much, but do it gently not to hurt their feelings. At the same time, I had to live up to refugee expectations.

Also, town residents and other organizations often viewed the IRC and its staff as those who ultimately were responsible for all refugees, not just the new arrivals or the ones still going through the resettlement program.

One of my former coworkers recalls, "I noticed that in the eyes of our town, we at the agency were the ones who were responsible for refugees forever. They often did not understand what we could and could not do as case workers. Like, one doctor wanted me to stay in the delivery room all night with a refugee woman who was giving birth so that I would be at hand for him as an interpreter. And I said, 'No, really, I am not going in there, and I cannot stay all night. I am not her husband or her mother; I am a case worker and will help with interpreting, but within reason. That's as far as I can go.' But being around that young woman who was giving birth changed something in me. In the past, I used to think that I did not want any children, that it was not for me, but after witnessing how the baby was born, I told myself, 'It was not as bad as I had feared—I can do it, too.' And now, I have two children."

As resettlement staff, we helped refugees change their lives as they changed ours.

Another practice that made me wonder about the relationship between us as agency staff and the refugees we served was all the "resettlement jargon" we used in the office. It was everywhere—case notes, reports, agency emails, and other communications—and seemed to turn "real people" into the "resettlement statistics" and "measurable numbers" that were needed for grant reports. The verbs in passive voice were most often used, thus depriving refugees of any opportunity to be active "agents" who take responsibility for their own cases—at least on paper. It seemed to me that at the moment human beings got "registered" and "assigned refugee status," they became subject to "higher powers" that made decisions for them and initiated actions on their behalf: refugees were *interviewed, approved, assigned, assured, prepared, notified, invited, resettled,* and *received*. Then, they were *met* at the airport and *taken to* their new homes, *enrolled* in assistance programs, *placed* in jobs, *referred* for medical screenings, *signed up* for ESL classes, *vaccinated*, *visited* at home, *oriented*, and yes—I almost forgot—their children were *enrolled* in school. It seemed like certain "higher powers" took possession of refugees and were whisking them around, while the refugees themselves said not a word.

Even so, I believe that it was just the language of resettlement agencies, while I know from my own experience that it was not how we thought and felt about refugees during our daily interactions. We saw them as individuals, with distinctive personalities, goals, and aspirations, even when some of them chose to learn from their own mistakes rather than follow the advice of case workers. In any event, we got to know the refugees who resettled in Abilene well. We cared about them and kept up with the developments in their lives, even after they had completed the refugee program. Living in a small town definitely made these relationships more personal than they would have been in a big city.

In refugee stories, two agencies and their staff appear most frequently: the overseas organizations that had helped refugees throughout the resettlement approval process and the US agencies that helped them adjust to the new life in the US. While staff in the overseas agencies often played the role of "magic helpers," staff in the US resettlement agencies took on a somewhat different and more realistic role. Since I knew from my own experience what case workers did to help refugees after they had arrived in the US, I was curious about how the storytellers remembered those days and how they evaluated working with the agency five or more years after the fact.

Almost all of the storytellers mentioned that most of all they valued the "advice" and "teaching" provided by the agency staff. Contrary to my expectation, the storytellers took "the things done for them" for granted as part of the job description of resettlement staff, but the advice they received about jobs and career planning and the "teaching" through various "cultural orientations" and workshops were appreciated most and had stayed with them the longest. Also, help with "finding a good job" seemed to be highly valued and appreciated. With one or two exceptions, nobody mentioned that they were especially grateful to the case worker who had met them at the airport or thought much of the fact that an apartment had been arranged for them. This help was acknowledged only as part of what was expected.

On the other hand, a storyteller from Congo DR expressed what many others did as well when she said that the IRC staff had treated her and her family "very well" and "with respect" and that they had taught them "the right things." A woman from Liberia appreciated the fact that "you [the agency] helped us understand how the system works here." Several mentioned how they had appreciated staff efforts to find a job and then to provide advice about how to keep a job or how to advance. A Rwandese storyteller reflected, "You helped me find a new job when I lost the first one. And I put your name down as a reference when I applied for the hospital job, remember?" A storyteller from Congo-Brazzaville reminded me, "Remember, you took me to several places to apply, and then I got a job offer in production, and you advised me to take it. And see, I am still there after eleven years!"

Teaching about life and social norms in the US helped refugees become independent—able to live in the US like "everybody else." It transcended the mundane daily tips and focused on general life principles and American ideals and values. Ellie from Rwanda summed it up quite nicely: "Americans are very independent, and they do what they have set up their minds to do. And you at the IRC trained us in that spirit of independence. It was not easy at first because we did not know enough about this country when we came."

Refugees unanimously agreed that in the beginning, life in the US had been challenging, mostly because they did not speak English and "did not know how everything worked." Time passed, and most now feel that they are in charge of their own lives.

Another important role of the resettlement agency in newly arrived refugees' lives—mentioned more than once—was the feeling of security in an unknown environment and country. A Burundian storyteller acknowledged that when she and her family had just arrived, it was important to know that the IRC was there and that they could rely on it. "The agency took care of everything, and we were like kids who did not have to worry about food on the table when they come home from school." The "feeling of security" encompassed not only financial or physical safety, but also the assurance the IRC was there and ready to help with problem-solving when needed. As a Rwandese storyteller put it, "You know how it is in Africa—when you have a problem, you go to your family to get help solving. Here, we went to the IRC when we had a problem, like we would go to our family. We got advice from you, and even when the IRC could not help, you could tell us where to go. As one of the first refugees here, it was very important for me."

Even after the initial resettlement program was over, refugees continued to feel loyalty to the IRC, no matter what. Otherwise, why would they come back to the agency just to visit and talk? Sometimes refugees would come with a need and bring up a problem in their community that had to be "fixed." Somebody had been scammed out of all of his savings when led to believe he was a "million-dollar lottery winner." That was a problem that needed to be fixed. At other times, people came to share their successes and joys. A former refugee family had just opened an ethnic store or a restaurant, and that was something to celebrate. Another refugee family had bought a new house and wanted to tell us about it. A young couple was getting married, and we were all invited to the wedding. Another family's daughter was about to graduate, and we received an invitation to her graduation party. Refugees often came in to say, "You—the agency—is like our mother, so we came to let you know…" or, "We came to tell you…" or, in a more demanding way, "You *are* our mother; you *have to* help us."

Somebody had surgery and sought compassion and a kind word, so he turned up on our doorstep on crutches. We had to acknowledge that, just like anyone in the family would, and sent him a "get well" goodies basket. Like it or not, this attribution of an identity as "mother," "parent," or "family" was—and still is—there in the refugee community, and as such, it obliges agency staff to act or react in appropriate ways. Do we as staff members want to attend every refugee community wedding or graduation party? It's an individual choice, but in all honesty, probably not. Many refugees truly try to make sure we stay informed about their successes. I used to hear quite often, "You are our agency; we have to tell you…" When accidentally meeting former refugee clients in town, we always stop and catch up on the latest news: "How are you doing these days?" "What are you up to?" or, "Oh, I heard your sister is getting married soon."

I am not sure how far we can go with the "mother" or "family" comparison, but I sometimes do think of the refugees we helped resettle as college students who have graduated and moved on in life. Some do well, others not that well. Just as we all remember our college years and professors, refugees remember their first days after arriving in the United States and "their case workers" at the agency who resettled them. When time puts distance between "back then" and "now," they also look back and think about how much agency staff helped them—maybe not so much with doing things for them, but with being there for them when they needed answers and with teaching them how to do things for themselves. Just like college professors remember and care for their graduates, we remember the refugees we resettled and want to find out how they are doing after their "graduation" from the refugee program.

Many refugees do the same thing that college graduates would do: they stop by to have a short chat about their latest projects and accomplishments, their children's graduations or weddings, their promotions, their new status as US citizens or as homeowners. They are always welcome at the agency.

Notes

1Why did the Congolese gentleman speak Russian, you may ask? I found out that during the seventies and eighties, Congo-Brazzaville had been friends with the Soviet Union, and many high school students had studied Russian as the second foreign language in school. As for me, we had to study Russian since it was compulsory under the Soviet regime. So, we both found good use of the Russian language right here in Abilene, Texas.

2I will limit my description of "refugees" as interpreted in the US refugee resettlement program. Situation in Europe is different.

3USA for UNHCR: The UN Refugee Agency. "What is a Refugee?" www.unrefugees.org/what-is-a-refugee.

4USA for UNHCR: The UN Refugee Agency. "Figures at a Glance." www.unhcr.org/en-us/figures-at-a-glance.html.

5Stephanie Hanson, "CFR: Violence in Eastern Congo Could Lead to War," *Newsweek* Online. www.newsweek.com /cfr-violence-eastern-congo-could-lead-war-84823.

6US Department of State. "The Reception and Placement Program." www.state.gov/j/prm/ra/receptionplacement/index.htm.

7International Rescue Committee. "Yemenis Suffer from the Largest Humanitarian Crisis in the World." Press release, March 20, 2017. www.rescue.org/press-release /yemenis-suffer-largest-humanitarian-crisis-world.

8The actual resettlement process is much more complex than I have described above, but I've provided a short overview of who refugees are and how they eventually find themselves in a country like the US.

9I do not mean to compare refugees to children, maybe just Abilene to a village in the sense that many residents seem to share the communal spirit that motivates them to take interest in others; they will help you if you are in need: if your car breaks down, somebody will stop very soon and offer you help; police officers will take you home if they find you walking or riding a bicycle late at night.

10Heb. 13:2.

11United Human Rights Council. "Genocide in Rwanda." www.unitedhumanrights.org/genocide/genocide_in_rwanda.

12In November 2015, UNHCR reported that Bhutanese refugee resettlement has surpassed 100,000. See www.unhcr.org/564dded46.html.

13Felipe Perez Rogue was the Minister of Foreign Affairs of Cuba from 1999 to 2009. https://en.wikipedia.org/wiki/Felipe_Perez_Roque.

Index